1987

[signature]

Brig Gen

USA Ret.

THE
STRANGLING OF PERSIA

Mr. W. MORGAN SHUSTER, LATE TREASURER-GENERAL OF PERSIA.

THE
STRANGLING OF PERSIA

STORY OF THE EUROPEAN DIPLOMACY
AND ORIENTAL INTRIGUE THAT RE-
SULTED IN THE DENATIONALIZATION
OF TWELVE MILLION MOHAMMEDANS

A PERSONAL NARRATIVE

BY

W. MORGAN SHUSTER
EX-TREASURER-GENERAL OF PERSIA

ILLUSTRATED WITH PHOTOGRAPHS AND MAP

Mage Publishers
Washington, D.C.
1987

Library of Congress Cataloging-In-Publication Data

Schuster, W. Morgan (William Morgan) 1877-1960.
The strangling of Persia.

Reprint. Originally published: New York : Century,
1912.
Includes index.
1. Iran–Politics and government–1909-1945.
2. American Financial Mission (1911-1912 : Iran)
3. Schuster, W. Morgan (William Morgan) 1877-1960–
Journies–Iran. I Title.
DS315.S5 1987   955'.05   86-31244
ISBN 0-934211-06-X

TO THE PERSIAN PEOPLE

In the endeavor to repay in some slight measure the debt of gratitude imposed on me through their confidence in my purposes toward them and by their unwavering belief, under difficult and forbidding circumstances, in my desire to serve them for the regeneration of their nation, this book is dedicated by the author.

Publisher's Note
1987 Edition

ما بدین در نه پی حشمت و جاه آمده ایم   از بد حادثه اینجا به پنا ه آمده ایم

Not in pursuit of pomp and pageant, to this door we have come:
For shelter from ill fortune, here we have come.

Hafez

In 1911, the newly democratic government of Persia appointed an American, W. Morgan Schuster, to help organize the finances of a nation recently freed from an age-old autocracy.

But only one year later, Schuster was ejected from the country, a victim of British and Russian diplomatic intrigue.

The Strangling of Persia is W. Morgan Schuster's first-hand account of these events. It offers keen insight into the timeless methods powerful nations use to achieve their own ends—at the expense of traditional societies struggling to live and govern themselves.

Today, more than 75 years after its original publication, **The Strangling of Persia** remains a powerful indictment of short-sighted diplomacy that crushed a fragile but promising democracy.

At a time when Iran's destiny is in the hands of every Iranian—and indeed every conscious citizen of the world—we reprint this book for insight and inspiration to those who dream of a free Iran in a free world one day.

CONTENTS

CONTENTS

LIST OF ILLUSTRATIONS

LIST OF ILLUSTRATIONS

LIST OF ILLUSTRATIONS

FOREWORD

THE interest shown by the public in the recent happenings in Persia, and a desire to place on record, while the memory is still green, a detailed account of the remarkable series of events which resulted in the writer's expulsion from the post of Treasurer-general of Persia in January of this year, are responsible for this book.

The facts are taken from the most authoritative sources available, supplemented by a private diary kept by the writer during the entire period of his sojourn in Persia. To this story have been added only such historical references and explanations as seemed necessary to give a clear understanding of recent events, and such comments as the writer felt justified in making.

I was deeply disappointed at being forcibly deprived of the opportunity to finish my intensely interesting task in that ancient land; but such rancor or bitterness as I may have felt at the time of my departure has certainly disappeared, and the cordial reception given me on the occasion of my visit to London, last February, and subsequently by the press and my countrymen in America, has so amply repaid me for any inconvenience or annoyances that I suffered during the last two months of my service at Teheran, that no sting whatever remains.

Only the pen of a Macaulay or the brush of a Verestchagin could adequately portray the rapidly shifting scenes attending the downfall of this ancient nation,— scenes in which two powerful and presumably enlightened Christian countries played fast and loose with truth, honor, decency and law, one, at least, hesitating not even at the most barbarous cruelties to accomplish its political designs and to put Persia beyond hope of self-regeneration.

In the belief that the real interests of humanity and the betterment of international relations demand that the truth be told in cases of this kind, I have written down the facts with a bluntness which perhaps, under other circumstances, would be subject to criticism.

The Constitutionalists of Modern Persia will not have lived, struggled, and in many instances, died entirely in vain, if the destruction of Persian sovereignty shall have sharpened somewhat the civilized world's realization of the spirit of international brigandage which marked the *welt-politik* of the year 1911.

W. MORGAN SHUSTER.

Washington, D. C., April 30, 1912.

INTRODUCTION

THERE are several peculiar features about writing any detailed account of the recent political events in Persia which make necessary some slight explanation.

The first point is that Persian political affairs, fraught as they are with misfortune and misery for millions of innocent people, are conducted very much as a well-staged drama — I have heard some critics say, as an *opéra bouffe*. The reader will find the same old characters weaving in and out of the story, at one time wearing the make-up of a Royalist Minister, at another the garb of a popular patriot. Cabinets are formed and dissolved with unreal rapidity. Men high in the councils of the nation sink in a day into perfect obscurity,— only to emerge again as the ceaseless whirl of intrigue drags them into public favor. All these men belong to what may be described as the professional governing class in Persia, and there is very distinctly such a class. Indeed it is only in recent years that the idea has been even admissible that a man of mediocre parentage, or without a title, could fill any official position. Thus the fortunes and hopes of millions of voiceless subjects are largely dependent upon the line of action which some professional cabinet officer, or governor, or self-styled general may decide to adopt at a given time. Couple with this the fact that the principal object of holding office has always been, with slight exception, to enrich oneself and one's friends, and the strange actions of Persian personages become somewhat clearer.

A proper understanding of the character, motives and type of some of these men, whose personal actions and motives have played such a large part in Persia's recent political happenings, is essential to the correct reading of her history.

Another feature which is very puzzling to the uninitiated is the — to foreigners — absurdly complicated system of names and titles. Ordinary Persians have merely names, yet I have known but few who did not possess some form of title, and the failure to know or recognize a man's title is not easily over-looked.

Imagine a gentleman in American political life deciding that he would adopt and wear the title of "Marshal of the Mar-shals," or "Unique One of the Kingdom," or "Fortune of the State." Having duly taken such a title, and obtained some form of parchment certifying to his ownership, he drops his real name and is thereafter known by his high-sounding title. It is rather difficult for foreigners to remember these appellations, espe-cially as a great many of them end with one of the four words *Mulk* (kingdom), *Dawla* (state), *Saltana* (sovereignty), or *Sultan* (sovereign).

The present Regent was formerly known only by his title of *Nasiru'l-Mulk* (The Helper of the Kingdom), but since he has become Regent he is also referred to by another title, that of *Naibu's-Saltana,* or "Assistant of the Sovereignty."

Still another difficulty is in spelling with Roman characters these names and titles. Half a dozen people are apt to write a Persian name in six different ways. Thus, one of the prominent Persian cabinet officers during the past year writes his own title in English as *Vossough-ed-Dovleh;* others write it *Vossuk-e-Dowleh;* while Professor E. G. Browne, of Cambridge Uni-versity, and a most distinguished Persian scholar, transcribes this title as *Wuthuqu'd-Dawla.*

To avoid confusion the writer has deemed it best to follow, so far as possible, the method of spelling these names and titles which has been adopted by Professor Browne in his various writ-ings on Persian history.

Most readers are more familiar with ancient Persian history than with modern events in that strange land. The purpose of this book is not historical in any but a very limited sense, and the following brief résumé of the Persian *Risorgimento,* or revolutionary movement, which resulted in what may be termed the establishment of a constitutional monarchy on August 5, 1906, during the reign of Muzaffaru'd-Din Shah, is given only that the more recent political events which are narrated herein, and in which the writer had some part, may be better understood.

During the past generation the most striking evidence of the power and desire of the Persian people to have even a small voice in their public affairs was the remarkable prohibition on the use of tobacco proclaimed by the Islamic clergy and immediately obeyed by the people when, in 1891, the famous Tobacco Concession was actually put into force. The previous year Nasiru'd-Din Shah Qajar had granted to a British corporation in London a monopolistic concession for the entire handling, buying and selling of all tobacco raised in Persia. The corporation was capitalized at £650,000, and was expected to make an annual profit of about £500,000. One quarter of the profits was to go to the Persian government, which meant to the Shah and his ministers and. court.

Even the long-suffering Persians had grown tired of this wholesale selling of their rights and industries, and in December, 1891, as a result of a religious decree, all the tobacco-shops closed their doors, the people destroyed or put away their water-pipes, and in a marvelously short time the use of tobacco practically ceased. This agitation did not stop until the Shah had been forced to rescind the Concession, after agreeing to pay the British corporation an indemnity of £500,000, which was borrowed by the Persian Government at 6%, thus arbitrarily fastening upon the people an annual interest charge of £30,000, for whch they received no tangible return.

Nasiru'd-Din Shah, who had ascended the throne on September 20, 1848, was shot on May 1, 1896, after nearly fifty years of power. His assassin was a fanatic named Mirza Muhammad Riza, of the city of Kirman, and the motive, though never clearly established, was not unconnected with the general belief that the rights of Persia were being rapidly sold out to foreigners.

The Crown Prince, *Muzaffaru'd-Din Shah Qajar,* was made Shah on June 8, 1896, and reigned until January 4, 1907, when he died. Some six months before his death the Persian people, whose discontent with the tyranny of their rulers had been constantly increasing, commenced an open agitation for the granting of a constitution, and in July, 1906, by a measure which was as remarkable as it was successful, they brought about this result.

Some 16,000 people of Teheran, from all walks in life, after being exhorted by the *Mullahs* or priests, took refuge or sanctuary — *bast* it is called in Persia — in the vast compound of the British Legation, and in the mosques and other sacred places. The crowds gathered there in the utmost good order; they established their commissariat and sanitary arrangements, and by these purely passive measures succeeded in compelling the Shah to dismiss an obnoxious minister, the Aynu'd-Dawla, and to grant them a code of laws or constitution. After various attempts to break up this peculiar form of resistance, the Shah and his government were compelled to yield, partly through the strange humiliation which the adoption of this course by the people conveys to the minds of the Persian governing class against whom it may be directed, and partly through fear of further and more active measures of opposition. On August 5, 1906, the so-called constitution was granted and the people resumed their homes and ordinary avocations.

Thus, by an almost bloodless revolution, the centuries-old absolutism of the Persian monarchs had been legally modified by constitutional forms, imperfect in many respects as they were, and, what was even more important, the people had learned something of their real power and were more determined than ever to save their nation from the straight road to disintegration and decay along which it had been for generations skilfully piloted by its hereditary rulers.

The principal modification in the Shah's absolute power obtained by this revolutionary action was the right of the people to have a *Medjlis,* or national elective assembly, which should

NASIRU'D-DIN SHAH (with overcoat) AND A GROUP OF HIS MINISTERS AND ATTENDANTS.

have a voice in the selection of ministers and in the framing of laws. After many negotiations and even a second *bast,* commenced in the British Legation grounds early in September, 1906, the actual elections took place during the first days of October, and on the 7th of that month, without awaiting the arrival of the deputies from the provinces, the first Medjlis was opened at Teheran, and a speech from the throne was read.

At the death of Muzaffaru'd-Din Shah, on January 4, 1907, he was succeeded by the Crown Prince, Muhammad Ali Mirza, who had been at Tabriz, governing the rich and important province of Azarbayjan. This infamous individual arrived at Teheran on December 17, 1906, the Shah being very ill, and was crowned on January 19, 1907, having previously pledged himself to observe the constitution and rights granted by his father.

Muhammad Ali Shah Qajar was perhaps the most perverted, cowardly, and vice-sodden monster that had disgraced the throne of Persia in many generations. He hated and despised his subjects from the beginning of his career, and from having a notorious scoundrel for his Russian tutor, he easily became the avowed tool and satrap of the Russian Government and its agent in Persia for stamping out the rights of the people.

The reign of Muhammad Ali Shah started out most inauspiciously. He began by ignoring the Medjlis and mutual suspicions and open dissensions became the rule. The Medjlis proposed to exercise some of its hard-won authority, while the Shah with his favorites, thoroughly reactionary ministers and court party, was equally determined to wield all that old arbitrary and cruelly oppressive power for which the House of Qajar has been notorious. He intrigued with Russian emissaries against his own people, and actually contracted with Russia and England for a secret loan of £400,000, to be squandered by himself, though the arrangement was shortly afterwards discovered and balked by the mullahs and the Medjlis.

The deputies of the Medjlis were becoming more and more convinced that the Shah and his party regarded them as enemies to his plans, and they determined to assert their strength to bring about the reforms which were most urgently needed. They particularly desired to prevent any further loans from Russia and England, as they had come to regard the rapidly increasing foreign indebtedness of the Persian nation as a source of danger to her independence and safety. They sought therefore to limit the Shah's expenditures for his court and civil list, to diminish the rampant fraud and corruption in the system of farming out the taxes to the Shah's favorites, and to put an end to the malign influence of a certain Mons. Naus, a Belgian who, with a number of his countrymen, had been employed for some years to organize the Persian Customs, and who had succeeded in acquiring a large fortune and in establishing himself as a political and financial power of the most baleful description. The Medjlis also planned to establish a national bank, to be capitalized with money raised from internal subscriptions, in order that their dependence on foreign financial assistance might be lessened.

On February 10, 1907, the Shah was compelled to dismiss Mons. Naus, and this one achievement vastly increased the prestige of the Medjlis with the people.

The Shah now decided to invite the famous Aminu's-Sultan (also known as Atabak-i-Azam) to return to Persia and resume the post of Prime Minister. This grandee, the Atabak, is perhaps the strongest figure in recent Persian history. Of unusually broad European education, widely traveled, but thoroughly despotic and corrupt, he had been condemned by the mullahs for his dishonest participation in the two Russian loans to Persia of 1899–1900 and 1902, and had been forced into exile in 1903. When his consent to return became known, the Russian Government lost no time in resuming warm relations with him, and he was conveyed across the Caspian to the Persian port of Enzeli in a Russian gunboat, with the highest official honors. When he landed, the people of Resht, the capital of the province, compelled him to swear fidelity to the Constitution before permitting him to continue on his journey to Teheran.

On reaching Teheran, the 26th of April, the Atabak found a state of disorder and chaos in every department of the government. The treasury was in its normally void condition and there were uprisings and disturbances throughout the entire Empire. The Medjlis knew more or less what should be done, but the Shah was determined that they should do nothing unless to carry out his own plans. The people of Isfahan had already revolted against the rule of the Shah's uncle, the Zillu's-Sultan; the city of Tabriz was in a ferment, and in June that Persian "madcap," Prince Salaru'd-Dawla, brother to the Shah, openly revolted in the district of Hamadan and proclaimed his intention to seize the throne at Teheran. After a three days' fight with the Shah's forces at Nihawand, he was defeated and captured in June, 1907.

Matters went from bad to worse, and during the month of August, Russia, which had never been content with the establishment of a constitutional régime in Persia, began to threaten the Medjlis with intervention. Troubles with Turkey also arose, and an army of 6,000 Turkish troops crossed the northwestern Turco-Persian frontier, and after occupying a number of Persian towns, actually threatened the city of Urmiah.

All this time the Atabak had been working to bring about another Russian loan, though he was afraid to contract the same without the approval of the Medjlis. By the end of August he had almost succeeded in winning over to his project a majority of the deputies when, on August 31, he was shot and killed, as he was coming out of the Assembly building, by a young man named Abbas Aqa, of Tabriz, who immediately committed suicide. This youth was a member of one of the numerous *anjumans* or secret political societies which had sprung up in great numbers, and his undoubted motive was the, to him, patriotic idea of saving the constitutional government from ruin and betrayal at the hands of the clever and intriguing prime minister, whom he considered a traitor.

The assassination of the great Atabak was taken as positive

evidence of the existence of a large body of men who had sworn to uphold the Constitution and to remove all those who opposed its representatives, even at the cost of torture and a felon's death.

A period of great confusion followed, during which the Shah and Medjlis were unable to agree on a cabinet, until towards the end of October, 1907, Nasiru'l-Mulk (now the Regent of Persia) succeeded in doing so. Most of the members of this cabinet were believed to be favorable to the Constitution. They remained in the office until December, when they resigned.

On August 31, 1907, the so-called Anglo-Russian Convention had been signed at St. Petersburg between England and Russia. On September 4 it was made public at Teheran, and despite its carefully worded assurances of respect for the integrity and independence of Persia, this famous document produced a most painful impression on the Persian people.

The importance to subsequent history of this much-discussed agreement is such that the parts most vitally affecting Persia may well be inserted here:

CONVENTION.

[1] His Majesty the King of the United Kingdom of Great Britain and Ireland and the British Dominions beyond the Seas, Emperor of India, and His Majesty the Emperor of All the Russias, animated by the sincere desire to settle by mutual agreement different questions *concerning the interests of their States on the Continent of Asia,* have determined to conclude Agreements destined to prevent all cause of misunderstanding *between Great Britain and Russia* in regard to the questions referred to, and have nominated for this purpose their respective plenipotentiaries, to-wit:

His Majesty the King of the United Kingdom of Great Britain and Ireland and of the British Dominions beyond the Seas, Emperor of India, the Right Honorable Sir Arthur Nicolson, His Majesty's Ambassador Extraordinary and Plenipotentiary to His Majesty the Emperor of All the Russias;

His Majesty the Emperor of All the Russias, the Master of his Court Alexander Iswolsky, Minister for Foreign Affairs;

Who, having communicated to each other their full powers, found in good and due form, have agreed on the following: —

[1] The italics are the author's.

MUSHIRU'D DAWLA.
Minister of Justice during the time the American finance officials were in Teheran.

AYNU'D-DAWLA, ONE OF THE PERSIAN GRANDEES OF THE OLD REGIME.
He commanded part of the Royalist forces at the siege of Tabriz in 1908-09.   Prime Minister from January 24, 1904, to August, 1906.

ARRANGEMENT CONCERNING PERSIA.

*The Governments of Great Britain and Russia having mutually engaged
to respect the integrity and independence of Persia,* and *sincerely* desiring
the preservation of order throughout that country and its peaceful development, as well as the permanent establishment of equal advantages for the
trade and industry of all other nations;

Considering that each of them has, for geographical and economic reasons,
a special interest in the maintenance of peace and order in certain provinces
of Persia adjoining, or in the neighborhood of, the Russian frontier on the
one hand, and the frontiers of Afghanistan and Baluchistan on the other
hand; and being desirous of avoiding all cause of conflict *between their
respective interests* in the above-mentioned **Provinces of Persia;**

Have agreed on the following terms: —

I.

Great Britain engages not to seek for herself, and not to support in favor
of British subjects, or in favor of the subjects of third Powers, any Concessions of a political or commercial nature — such as Concessions for railways, banks, telegraphs, roads, transport, insurance, &c.— beyond a line
starting from Kasr-i-Shirin, passing Isfahan, Yezd, Kakhk, and ending at
a point on the Persian frontier at the intersection of the Russian and
Afghan frontiers, and not to oppose, directly or indirectly, demands for
similar Concessions in this region which are supported by the Russian
Government. It is understood that the above-mentioned places are included
in the region in which Great Britain engages not to seek the Concessions
referred to.

II.

Russia, on her part, engages not to seek for herself, and not to support
in favor of Russian subjects, or in favor of the subjects of third Powers,
any Concessions of a political or commercial nature — such as Concessions
for railways, banks, telegraphs, roads, transport, insurance, &c.— beyond
a line going from the Afghan frontier by way of Gazik, Birjand, Kerman,
and ending at Bunder Abbas, and not to oppose, directly or indirectly, demands for similar Concessions in this region which are supported by the
British Government. It is understood that the above-mentioned places are
included in the region in which Russia engages not to seek the Concessions
referred to.

III.

Russia, on her part, engages not to oppose, without previous arrangement
with Great Britain, the grant of any Concessions whatever to British sub-

jects in the regions of Persia situated between the lines mentioned in Articles I and II.

Great Britain undertakes a similar engagement as regards the grant of Concessions to Russian subjects in the same regions of Persia.

All Concessions existing at present in the regions indicated in Articles I and II are maintained.

IV.

It is understood that the revenues of all the Persian customs, with the exception of those of Farsistan and of the Persian Gulf, revenues guaranteeing the amortization and the interest of the loans concluded by the Government of the Shah with the "Banque d'Escompte et des Prets de Perse" up to the date of the signature of the present Arrangement, shall be devoted to the same purpose as in the past.

It is equally understood that the revenues of the Persian customs of Farsistan and of the Persian Gulf, as well as those of the fisheries on the Persian shore of the Caspian Sea and those of the Posts and Telegraphs, shall be devoted, as in the past, to the service of the loans concluded by the Government of the Shah with the Imperial Bank of Persia up to the date of the signature of the present Arrangement.

V.

In the event of irregularities occurring in the amortization or the payment of the interest of the Persian loans concluded with the "Banque d'Escompte et des Prets de Perse" and with the Imperial Bank of Persia up to the date of the signature of the present Arrangement, and in the event of the necessity arising for Russia to establish control over the sources of revenue guaranteeing the regular service of the loans concluded with the first-named bank, and situated in the region mentioned in Article II of the present Arrangement, or for Great Britain to establish control over the sources of revenue guaranteeing the regular service of the loans concluded with the second-named bank, and situated in the region mentioned in Article I of the present Arrangement, the British and Russian Governments undertake to enter beforehand into a friendly exchange of ideas with a view to determine, in agreement with each other, the measures of control in question and to avoid all interference which would not be in conformity with the principles governing the present Arrangement.

The other clauses of the Convention refer to Afghanistan and Tibet.

This Convention was made purely between Russia and England, and ostensibly to arrange questions concerning their respective " interests "— all self-created — in Persia, and other countries, as between themselves. To it Persia was not a party, either directly or in any manner. In fact, the Medjlis was in total ignorance of the conclusion of the Convention until its unheralded publication in Teheran on September 4.

The Persian people decidedly resented having their country " partitioned " over-night, even by imaginary geographical lines drawn by self-styled friendly governments which proclaimed so unequivocally their " mutual engagement to respect the integrity and independence of Persia " and their " sincere desire for the preservation of order throughout that country, and its peaceful development."

The populace at Teheran grew very excited, and there were demonstrations and the usual ferment in the *bazaars*. On the following day the British Minister at Teheran, Sir Cecil Spring-Rice, made an official communication to the Persian Government, explaining the true intent and meaning of the obnoxious Convention in the following language:

TRANSLATION OF THE OFFICIAL COMMUNICATION CONCERNING THE NATURE AND OBJECTS OF THE ANGLO-RUSSIAN CONVENTION, TRANSMITTED IN PERSIAN BY THE BRITISH MINISTER IN TEHERAN TO THE PERSIAN MINISTER FOR FOREIGN AFFAIRS ON THE 4TH SEPTEMBER, 1907:

[1] Information has reached me that the report is rife in Persia that the result of the Agreement concluded between England and Russia will be the intervention of these two Powers in Persia, and the partition of Persia between them. Your Excellency is aware that the negotiations between England and Russia are of a wholly different character, since the Mushiru'l-Mulk recently visited both St. Petersburg and London, and discussed the matter with the Ministers for Foreign Affairs of both Powers, who explicitly declared to him the objects aimed at by their respective Governments in Persia, which assurances he has no doubt duly reported.

Sir Edward Grey has informed me of the substance of his conversations with the Mushiru'l-Mulk, and also of the substance of M. Iswolsky's declarations, officially communicated to the British Government.

Sir Edward Grey informs me that he has explained to the Mushiru'l-

[1] The italics are the author's.

Mulk, *that he and M. Iswolsky are completely in accord on two fundamental points.*

Firstly, neither of the two Powers will interfere in the affairs of Persia unless injury is inflicted on the persons or property of their subjects.

Secondly, negotiations arising out of the Anglo-Russian Agreement *must not violate the integrity and independence of Persia.*

Sir Edward Grey also observes that hitherto antagonism has existed between England and Russia, each of whom has endeavored to prevent the continuance of the other in Persia, and had this antagonism been prolonged in the present uncertain state of Persia, one or both of these two Powers might have been tempted to interfere in the internal affairs of Persia, so as not to allow the other to profit by the existing state of things, or to profit by it to the detriment of others. The object of the present negotiations between England and Russia is to prevent such difficulties from arising between them and these negotiations are in truth in no wise directed against Persia, as M. Iswolsky has clearly explained to the Mushiru'l-Mulk, saying, " *Neither of the two Powers seeks anything from Persia, so that Persia can concentrate all her energies on the settlement of her internal affairs.*" Both Ministers are entirely in accord as to the policy of non-intervention in Persia, and *have left no possible ground for doubt in the matter.* M. Iswolsky's words, which include the intentions of England, are as follows: —" Russia's general principle will be to refrain from any kind of intervention in the internal affairs of other countries so long as nothing injurious to her interests is done; and it is quite impossible that she should deviate from this principle in this present case."

As to the reported partition of Persia between Russia and England, concerning which it is asserted that the two Powers above mentioned wish to define spheres of influence for themselves, Sir Edward Grey and M. Iswolsky have explicitly declared that these reports have no foundation. What the two Powers desire is to come to an agreement which will prevent future difficulties and disputes from arising, by guaranteeing that neither Power will aim at acquiring influence in those parts of Persia which are adjacent to the frontier of the other. This Agreement is injurious neither to the interests of Persia nor to those of any other foreign nation, *since it binds only England and Russia* not to embark on any course of action in Persia calculated to injure the interests of the other, and so in the future *to deliver Persia from those demands which in the past have proved so injurious to the progress of her political aspirations.* This is what M. Iswolsky says: —

" This Agreement between the two European Powers which have the greatest interests in Persia, based as it is on a guarantee of her independence and integrity, can only serve to further and promote Persian interests, *for henceforth Persia aided and assisted by these two powerful neighboring States, can employ all her powers in internal reforms.*"

MUHAMMAD ALI SHAH MOUNTED ON HIS FAVORITE HORSE.

AMINU'S-SULTAN, "ATABAK."
The famous Reactionary Prime Minister recalled to power by
Muhammad Ali Shah. He was the most intelligent and
forceful personage in recent Persian history.

From the above statements you will see how baseless and unfounded are these rumors which have lately prevailed in Persia concerning the political ambitions of England and Russia in this country. The object of the two Powers in making this Agreement is not in any way to attack, *but rather to assure for ever the independence of Persia.* Not only do they not wish to have at hand any excuse for intervention, but their object in these friendly negotiations was *not to allow one another to intervene on the pretext of safeguarding their interests.* The two Powers hope that in the future Persia will be for ever delivered from the fear of foreign intervention, *and will thus be perfectly free to manage her own affairs in her own way,* whereby advantage will accrue both to herself and to the whole world.

The British Blue-Book up to December, 1911, did not contain this important state paper, but it has since been ascertained through questions put to the British Secretary of State for Foreign Affairs, on the floor of the House of Commons, that the above communication was in fact made to the Persian Government on September 5, 1907, by the British Minister at Teheran.

The disordered condition of Persia had continued unabated and in November the Teheran press attacked the Shah in articles whose bitterness, scorn and lightly-veiled threats almost surpass belief. On November 4 the Shah had visited the Medjlis in state and for the fourth time solemnly sworn on the Koran to be faithful to the Constitution.

It was apparent that, early in December, Muhammad Ali Shah had made up his mind to destroy the Medjlis. For this purpose he had two forces, the so-called "Cossack Brigade," a body of from 1200 to 1800 Persians, commanded by Russian army officers detailed by the Russian Government for that purpose, but paid from the Persian treasury, and an undisciplined organization made up of his own servitors, grooms, and muleteers, augmented by the discontented rabble of the capital. The Persian army had fallen into such abandon and disrepute that nobody paid much attention to it as a serious factor in affairs.

On December 15 the Shah sent for the members of Nasiru'l-Mulk's cabinet, which had just resigned, and forcibly detained them, including the Prime Minister himself.[1] Meanwhile, the Shah's hired ruffians started a disturbance in the "Gun-Square," in the central part of Teheran, and began an agitation against the Medjlis. No adequate steps were taken, however, to occupy the *Baharistan* — the building where the deputies held their sessions — so that, on the following day, the Medjlis sat as usual, while all the approaches and entrances were guarded by armed volunteers from all classes of the people who had responded immediately and spontaneously to the threat against their constitutional representatives. Neither the Shah's rabble nor the Persian Cossacks dared to attack the Medjlis under these circumstances, and as a result a truce was declared, the Shah agreeing to exile and dismiss certain of his court favorites and ministers, to punish the *lutis* (roughs) who had been disturbing public order and plundering the inhabitants of Teheran, to bring the Cossack Brigade and other royal troops under the Ministry of War, and again to send to the Medjlis a solemn, sealed oath to obey the Constitution. In the meantime the people throughout the provinces, on hearing of the threatened destruction of the Medjlis, immediately telegraphed offers of support to the deputies and people, and actually despatched several armed contingents towards the capital.

On December 20, 1907, after order had been restored, a new cabinet was proposed by the Shah, with Nizamu's-Saltana as Prime Minister. The Medjlis continued in its conciliatory attitude towards the Shah, but fresh incidents continued to arise.

Towards the end of February, 1908, an attempt to assassinate the Shah was made while he was driving in Teheran. He was seated in a carriage, being driven behind the royal automobile in which he was believed to be. A bomb was thrown at the top of the automobile and exploded, slightly injuring the chauffeur, a Frenchman named Varnet. Muhammad Ali Shah himself escaped with nothing worse than a severe scare. The Shah of

[1] Nasiru'l-Mulk was released through the intervention of the British Legation. He was a classmate of Sir Edward Grey and a friend of many prominent British statesmen.

course suspected the Constitutionalists of this attempt on his life, and his relations with the Medjlis became very strained.

Towards the end of May, 1908, each party had formulated certain demands upon the other, and it was agreed that both the Royalists and the Constitutionalists should act simultaneously in complying with them. On June 1, therefore, the Shah reluctantly dismissed a number of his reactionary courtiers, the one most hated by the people, Amir Bahadur Jang, taking refuge in the Russian Legation.

On the following day began the open intervention of the Russian and British Legations which so directly contributed to the overthrow of the Medjlis and the bombardment of the Baharistan by the Cossack Brigade just three weeks later.

In effect, the Russian Minister, Mons. de Hartwig, and the British Chargé d'Affaires, Mr. Marling, called on the Persian Minister of Foreign Affairs and threatened the Government with Russian intervention if the opposition to the Shah's plans and wishes did not cease. The Russian Minister took the lead and framed the threats and demands, and the British representative merely announced his Government's approval of the Russian Minister's words.

How this threat by Russia and England to interfere forcibly with Persia's purely internal affairs was reconciled with the declarations of the Anglo-Russian Convention, and with Sir Cecil Spring-Rice's *communiqué* to the Persian Government, does not appear. It was, of course, a flagrant breach of the promises therein made.

This ominous message from the two Legations was immediately communicated to the Medjlis, where it had the effect evidently intended by the diplomatic representatives. The Medjlis was constantly in the greatest fear of foreign intervention, and its members, after having practically forced a treacherous and perjured ruler to live up to the law, were compelled to let their struggles go for naught at the behest of two legations whose sole desire seemed to be to keep matters in the country *in statu quo,* apparently that they might " fish in troubled waters."

On the next day, June 3, 1908, the Shah's nerves drove him to leave the city and take up his residence in the *Bagh-i-Shah* (Garden of the King), just outside the walls. In order to protect himself from any possible interference while making this short journey through the streets, the Shah created a panic in the city by letting loose some 2000 guards and 300 Cossacks with artillery, and under cover of this was escorted by Colonel Liakhoff, commander of the Cossack Brigade, to the Bagh-i-Shah.

The next day a large crowd of people, believing that the Shah was meditating another attack on the Medjlis, demanded that his deposition should be proclaimed.

On June 5 the Shah caused to be arrested a number of Constitutionalists, whom he had invited to confer with him at the Bagh-i-Shah, but one of them escaped and immediately reported the occurrence to the Medjlis. This affair caused intense excitement in the capital.

Between June 6 and June 23, the Shah continued his open and threatening preparations against the Constitutionalists. He collected troops, arms and munitions at the Bagh-i-Shah, seized the telegraph offices, thereby cutting off communication between the Medjlis and the provinces, appointed well-known reactionaries to government posts held by Constitutionalists, made a number of prisoners, declared martial law in the city, and placed the Russian Colonel, Liakhoff, in supreme command. He then sent Cossacks with an ultimatum to the Medjlis, threatening bombardment of a mosque if the people there did not disperse, demanded the expulsion of a number of pro-Constitution editors and orators, and finally deceived the Medjlis and the people by agreeing, on June 22, to submit all questions in dispute to a mixed committee of *Royalists* and *Nationalists*.

Before sunrise on June 23, over 1000 Cossacks and other troops surrounded the Medjlis buildings and occupied the adjoining streets. The deputies and others who rushed to the scene were allowed to enter but not to come out. An hour later, Colonel Liakhoff, with six other Russian officers, arrived and disposed the troops and six cannon so as to command the

RUSSIAN AND PERSIAN OFFICERS OF THE NOTORIOUS "COSSACK BRIGADE."
This has been one of the chief instruments of Russian influence and oppression in Persia.

locality. Colonel Liakhoff then mounted a horse and rode off, whereupon the troops and guns, under the command of the remaining Russian officers, opened fire on the Medjlis buildings, killing at the first volley a number of Nationalist volunteers who were there.

The 100 or more armed Nationalists who were present now returned the fire, putting three of the Cossack guns out of action. Cossack reinforcements arrived, and despite the odds against them, the volunteer defenders of the Medjlis kept up a stout resistance for seven or eight hours until the buildings were badly damaged by the shells and shrapnel, and the inmates were either killed, captured or put to flight.

Many well-known Nationalists were arrested and strangled or imprisoned, and some who were being sought succeeded in making their escape. Colonel Liakhoff and his troops bombarded and looted for several days the homes of persons disliked by the Shah. The records of the Medjlis even were destroyed. Colonel Liakhoff remained the virtual dictator of Teheran. Although he was a Russian officer, wearing a Russian uniform and receiving pay from his Government, the Russian Cabinet, in the face of the British and European criticism of the part he had played, promptly disclaimed either responsibility for or knowledge of his acts, claiming that he was entirely under the orders of the Shah. There has been considerable evidence brought forward, however, tending to show that in planning and executing the destruction of the Medjlis and Constitution, Liakhoff was actually carrying out the designs of the so-called " forward party," a reactionary clique who surrounded the Czar at St. Petersburg, and of whom Mons. de Hartwig, Russian Minister at Teheran, was such a striking example.

Meanwhile, riots had broken out in the provinces, principally at Resht, Kirman, Isfahan and Tabriz — from which latter place the deposition of the Shah was announced, and from which a force of 300 horsemen was despatched to Teheran to defend the Constitution.

The prospects at this time for the restoration of constitutional government were decidedly poor, and it is little wonder that the Persian people in Teheran felt that their last hope had gone.

At Tabriz, the next important city in Persia after the capital, street fighting broke out between the Nationalists and the Royalists on the very day that Colonel Liakhoff was bombarding the Medjlis at Teheran. The inhabitants of Tabriz had learned to know and dislike Muhammad Ali Shah during the time that he was Crown Prince and Governor of that province.

For ten months after the destruction of the Medjlis at Teheran the Constitutionalists at Tabriz kept up the unequal struggle against, first, the Royalists, whom they practically expelled, and then against famine when the roads were closed and the blockade of the city was complete. In October, 1908, it began to be rumored that Russia intended sending troops to intervene at Tabriz, on the ground that the Russian Consul considered that there was serious and imminent danger to Europeans. During this period the Russian Consul-General, Mons. Pokhitonoff, was discovered to be intriguing with the Royalists to supply them with arms and ammunition. The Nationalist forces were careful to respect foreign lives and property, and there is ample testimony from Europeans to the effect that a remarkable degree of order was maintained under the local constitutional government.

On October 11 a force composed of 400 Persian Cossacks, with four guns, and commanded by Russian officers of the Cossack Brigade, left Teheran for Tabriz, to overthrow the Nationalists. In Tabriz, however, by October 12 the Nationalists were in undisputed possession of the city.

In the latter part of November, despite the arrival of the Cossacks and guns to reinforce the besiegers of the city, the Tabriz Nationalists continued to win victories. Thus time was given to the Nationalists in other provincial centers to formulate their plans, and during the next four months they succeded in gaining control also of Resht, Isfahan, Lar, and later at Shiraz, Hamadan, Meshed, Astarabad, Bandar-i-Abbas and Bushir.

On January 5, 1909, two chiefs of the Bakhtiyari tribesmen, the Samsamu's-Saltana and the Zarghamu's-Saltana, with 1000 of their men, were in possession of the city of Isfahan, and the so-called Royal troops were dispersed. The Bakhtiyaris had decided to side with the Nationalists.

At Resht, in the north, the Nationalist movement was aided by that remarkable personage, the Sipahdar-i-Azam, who, a few months before, had been in command of the Shah's forces besieging Tabriz.

During the month of January the inhabitants of Tabriz were in severe straits. Many were dying from hunger or barely subsisting on grass. The city was surrounded by the savage tribesmen of Rahim Kahn and by the troops of the Shah, who had been kept at the task only by promises of unrestricted rapine and loot, if they succeeded in taking the place.

In their attempted sorties to open one of the roads and obtain provisions for the city, the Nationalists were joined by two foreigners, Mr. W. A. Moore, a Britisher, who had come out to Persia representing several English newspapers, and Mr. H. C. Baskerville, an American, who was a teacher in the Boys' School conducted in Tabriz by the American Presbyterian Mission. In a sally made on April 21 Baskerville was killed.

When the food situation at Tabriz became desperate, suggestions were made that all foreigners should leave, and the commander of the Shah's troops was instructed to give them safe-conduct. Nearly all the foreigners, however, were unwilling to abandon their interests, and on April 20 Russia decided to send troops into the city, to facilitate the entry of provisions, to protect the foreign consuls and subjects, and to assist any who might wish to leave the town.

On April 29 a Russian force composed of four squadrons of Cossacks, three battalions of infantry, two batteries of artillery, and a company of sappers, arrived outside Tabriz and entered the city on the following day. The Russian Government gave the most explicit assurances that the troops would remain only so long as might be necessary to guarantee the security

of the lives and property of foreign consulates and their subjects and that they would abstain from taking part in the
political conflict.

As was to be expected under such circumstances, friction
and more serious difficulties occurred between the 4,000 Russian troops in and about Tabriz and the native inhabitants; and
the promised withdrawal of the Russians, although order was
completely restored, has never taken place. During March
the Nationalists of Resht had occupied a portion of the road
leading from the Caspian Sea to Kasvin and Teheran. Their
progress was slow, as they were awaiting the concurrent advance of the Bakhtiyari forces from Isfahan and the south.

As a result of a strong note presented to the Shah by the
Russian and British Legations on April 22, the Shah, on May
10, again solemnly promised to restore and observe the Constitution, but the Nationalist leaders and the people had by this
time lost all confidence in his pledges.

The combined advance on the capital by the two Nationalist
armies therefore continued. The troops from Isfahan were
commanded by the Bakhtiyari chieftain, the Samsamu's-Saltana,
who was joined about May 7 by his more active brother, the
Sardar-i-Asad, who had returned fom Europe by way of the
Persian Gulf. Against this force the Shah had despatched
some Royalist soldiers.

By this time the Nationalist force from Resht had taken possession of Kasvin, some 90 miles to the north of Teheran. They
were commanded by the Sipahdar-i-Azam, although the mov-
ing spirit of this expedition is said to have been an Armenian
named Ephraim Kahn. Kasvin was taken on May 5, and
on May 6 a force of Persian Cossacks with two Maxim guns,
commanded by the Russian Captain Zapolski, was despatched
from Teheran, to guard the pass and bridge at Karaj, about
30 miles northwest of the capital. The Nationalist force was
less than 600 men.

At this juncture the Russian Legation again intervened by

MUHAMMAD ALI SHAH (now ex-Shah) AND HIS SUITE.
At the Bagh-i-Shah near Teheran.

sending a threatening communication to the Sipahdar, demanding, in effect, the cessation of his march on Teheran.

On June 16 the Bakhtiyari forces, composed of about 800 men, actually started for Teheran, and shortly thereafter they were in communication with the Nationalists at Kasvin. Both the British and Russian Legations exhausted every effort to deter the Bakhtiyari leaders from their purpose, but without success. On June 23 the advance guard of this force had reached Qum, eighty miles to the south of Teheran.

In spite of repeated threats from the Legations the Sardar-i-Asad announced that he had certain demands to make on the Shah, and the advance continued. Still endeavoring to frighten the Nationalist forces, the Russian Government began to assemble an expeditionary army at Baku to be sent into Northern Persia.

At this time the Shah's troops were reported to be some 5000 at Saltanatabad and 1350 soldiers of the Cossack Brigade, of whom 800 under Colonel Liakhoff were at Teheran, 350 to the north of the capital, and 200 to the south, awaiting the approach of the Bakhtiyaris. On July 3, the force at Karaj fell back to Shahabad, only 16 miles from Teheran, and on the next day a skirmish between this body and the advancing Nationalists took place. The Persian Cossacks, under Captain Zapolski, with two Russian non-commissioned officers and three guns, lost one Persian officer, three men killed and two wounded. The Nationalists lost twelve.

Meanwhile, Russia was despatching her troops from Baku and by July 8 some 2000 of them were on Persian soil. On July 11 they had reached Kasvin. The Legation had also warned the Nationalists that any further advance by them towards the capital would be followed by foreign intervention.

Further endeavors to frighten or persuade the Nationalist leaders were made, but without effect.

On July 10 an engagement took place between troops of the Cossack Brigade and the Bakhtiyaris at Badamak, fifteen miles to the west of Teheran, but the result was indecisive. Skirmishing continued for the next two days, and on July 13 the two Nationalist forces, to the utter surprise of the Cossack Brigade and Royalist troops, slipped through their lines and quietly entered Teheran at 6:30 in the morning. The skill of the manœuver was undoubtedly due to Ephraim Khan, the Armenian leader who has been mentioned heretofore.

There was street fighting in Teheran during the entire day. The people received the Nationalist forces with the greatest enthusiasm, and July 13 was regarded as the day of their salvation. On the next day the Cossack Brigade, under Colonel Liakhoff, was still besieged in its barracks and square in the center of the city, and the Russian Colonel wrote to the Sipahdar, as head of the Nationalist forces, proposing terms for the surrender of the Brigade. The Nationalist troops behaved themselves throughout with the utmost discretion and gallantry. On July 15 they were in full possession of the capital, although the Cossack Brigade still held the central square.

On July 16 at 8:30 A. M. the Shah, with a large body of his soldiers and attendants, took refuge in the Russian Legation in Zargundeh, some miles outside the city, and thus abdicated his throne. He had previously obtained the consent of the Legation to his doing this. Both Russian and British flags were hoisted over the Russian Minister's home as soon as it was occupied by the Shah. In the meantime Colonel Liakhoff had practically surrendered to the Nationalist leaders, and had formally accepted service under the new Government, agreeing to act under the direct orders of the Minister of War.

Late this same evening an extraordinary meeting took place at the Baharistan grounds, and the Shah was formally deposed. His son, Sultan Ahmad Mirza, aged twelve, was proclaimed his successor, and Azudu'l-Mulk, the venerable head of the Qajar family, was declared Regent.

Thus, on July 16, 1909, the apparently lost cause of constitutionalism in Persia had been suddenly revived, and by a display of courage, patriotism and skill by the soldiers of the

Mr. H. C. BASKERVILLE, THE AMERICAN TEACHER IN TABRIZ.
He was killed leading a sortie of Persian defenders of Tabriz on April 21, 1909.

Mr. W. A. MOORE.
The young Englishman, who with Baskerville, led the sortie from Tabriz against the troops of Muhammad Ali Shah.

people, their hopes for a representative government had been restored, almost over-night.

Prolonged negotiations followed between the National Council, or Emergency Committee, of the restored Constitutional Government and the British and Russian Legations, as to the terms upon which Muhammad Ali, ex-Shah, should leave Persia, give up the Crown jewels, pay off the debts and mortgages on his private estates — lest these latter should fall into the hands of the Russians — and, lastly, as to his pension. On September 7 an agreement was reached, and a protocol embodying the various stipulations was signed by the representatives of the British and Russian Governments and by the other parties. The ex-Shah's pension was fixed at about $80,000 per annum. On September 9 he left the Russian Legation, accompanied by his family and retinue, and started towards the Caspian Sea, to journey to Odessa. He sailed from the Persian coast on October 1, and was conveyed from Baku to Odessa in a special train furnished by the Russian Government.

On July 18 the young Shah had been acclaimed by the Regent at Saltanatabad and on July 20 he entered the capital, which was illuminated in his honor. Shortly thereafter the new constitutional régime was formally recognized by England and Russia.

The National Council proceeded to nominate a cabinet, and Ephraim Khan was placed in charge of the policing of the city.

The free press which had sprung into being during the existence of the first Medjlis now appeared again. During the following October the elections for deputies to the Medjlis had taken place throughout the country, and on the 28th of that month some sixty-four, three more than the number required for a quorum, were gathered in Teheran.

On November 15, 1909, the solemn opening of the new Medjlis took place. All classes of the people were represented. The Sipahdar was made Prime Minister and Minister of War, and it was he who read out the speech from the Throne.

During all this time large bodies of Russian troops were

quartered at Tabriz, Kasvin, Resht, and at various other points in Northern Persia, and their presence was the source of increasing distrust on the part of the Nationalists, who harbored well-founded suspicions as to Russia's ultimate designs.

Despite the frightful odds and conditions by which they were confronted, the new Medjlis and Cabinet set bravely to work to restore order, to police the country, to gather revenue, and to provide for the security of lives and property. The entire nation was, of course, in a terrible state of disorder, the worst feature of all being the financial chaos and heavy foreign indebtedness under which Persia labored.

A French gentleman, Mons. Bizot, was employed to assist the new Government in its financial work, but during the two years which he remained in Teheran he accomplished no actual reforms, and conditions went from bad to worse. Unfortunately for Persia, the patriotism which impelled numbers of her brave Nationalists to fight to depose the ex-Shah, and to exercise an admirable self-restraint in the hour of victory, did not suffice to keep many of them from profiting personally through the chaotic state of the public treasury, and through the entire absence of any check on fraud and corruption in the financial administrations, so that with an empty treasury, a large foreign debt, a rapidly growing deficit and but the ruins of absolutism on which to build, it is little wonder that the members of the Medjlis decided that some new plan must be tried if the nation and its newly established Government were to escape speedy and humiliating disintegration.

Despite the brilliant success of the Persian Nationalists in forcing the deposition and exile from the country of the late Shah after his repeated violations of his promises and oaths to faithfully observe the Constitution and the rights of his people, the prospects of Persia being able to evolve from the complicated situation confronting her a reasonably stable and orderly government were far from encouraging. Such a government must both command the respect and support of the majority of the Persians and remove all reasonable pretext for a further intervention in her internal affairs by the so-called friendly powers claiming to have special interests in her as a nation. The general administration of the Government under the former Shahs — and above all the conduct of the financial departments — had become so absolutely disorganized and broken down that Persia had neither credit abroad nor with her own people, and the utmost courage and patriotism were necessary on the part of her intelligent classes, if she was to extricate herself from the abyss of administrative chaos and ruin into which she had fallen. The internal difficulties alone made the task an almost hopeless one; but to these were to be added the open hostility of Russia and the scarcely less injurious timidity of England so far as thwarting Russia's evident designs upon the success of the Constitutional Government in Persia was concerned. The new Constitutional Government was therefore confronted at the outset with a most extraordinary and peculiar relationship towards certain foreign powers, which relationship had been forced upon her regardless of her rights as a sovereign nation.

The poor of the provinces were compelled, under one régime after another, to pay taxes, not a cent of which was ever used for their benefit, and to be ever the prey of brigands without and of the brigands within — the so-called Government officials whom fate had placed above them. The people themselves were, to a very large extent, too ignorant to realize the duties which devolved upon them as subjects of a constitutional monarchy, or to feel the responsibility which rests always upon those who would maintain a free and democratic form of government. But the most pressing danger of all was that before they could ever hope to acquire education sufficient to enable them to grasp those things, their country would have probably disappeared from the map as an independent and sovereign nation. A most heavy responsibility, therefore, rested upon the more intelligent and enlightened Persians who, during the eighteen months which followed the deposition of the ex-Shah, had succeeded to power and places of influence in the new régime. And it is not strange that true to the traditions of their past, these men at first regarded their newly acquired positions quite as much as a means to self-advancement as a sacred trust to be administered for those who looked to them to uphold and protect their interests.

As has been said, a large number of Russian troops had been sent into Northern Persia, although both the Russian and the British Governments had stated that they would be withdrawn as soon as they were no longer needed, " for the protection of foreign rights and property from the possibility of danger."

Due partially to the presence of these troops, and partially to the class of local disorders which always follow in the train of political upheavals such as Persia had been witnessing during the preceding four years, the new Constitutional régime was hampered by fresh and increasing difficulties. In September, 1909, the famous brigand, Rahim Khan, had attacked the town of Ardabil, in Northern Persia, and his action had been promptly seized upon by the Russian Government as an excuse to send still more troops into the country and to postpone the promised withdrawal of the troops which were already stationed at Kazvin. The Persian Government was compelled to spend considerable sums in the equipment of forces sent against him, but on January 24, 1910, he had been so surrounded by the troops under the command of Ephraim Khan, that his only method of escape was across the Russian frontier. The Russian Government, in plain defiance of Article XIV of the Treaty of Turkmanchay, permitted him to cross into Russian territory, where he was safe from pursuit and where he remained until January, 1911, when he again returned to Tabriz, to become a further source of expense and difficulty to the Constitutional régime.

In May, 1910, a certain Persian Prince, Darab Mirza, who had been naturalized as a Russian subject and held a commission in a Russian Cossack regiment which formed part of the forces quartered at Kazvin, started a movement to overthrow the Constitutional Government. Despite the protests of the Persians, who desired to deal with the incipient insurrection themselves, Russian troops intervened and pretended to arrest him. He was in their company returning to Kazvin when the Russian soldiers encountered a Persian force which had been sent out to capture him, and fired upon them, killing the Persian officer who was in command of the troops. Although the Russian authorities denied all complicity in this attempt to provoke civil war, it was proved that a certain Russian Colonel at Kazvin had supplied a number of Darab Nirza's accomplices with letters of protection signed and sealed by the Colonel himself, declaring the bearers to be under the protection of the Emperor of Russia and threatening severe punishment for any Persian who might interfere with them or their followers.

In February, 1911, Russian troops massacred some 60 villagers, including women and children, at Varmuni, near the town of Astara, in Persia.

In the meantime, the Persian Government, starting in December, 1909, had been seeking to obtain a loan of about $2,-500,000 from the Russian and British Governments, but the conditions which the two powers endeavored to impose upon the granting of this assistance were so dangerous to, and even destructive of, Persia's independence, that the Medjlis was compelled to reject them. Shortly thereafter Persia entered into negotiations with a private banking house in London for a loan and it was upon the point of being concluded on terms mutually satisfactory, when, in October, 1910, the negotiations were brought to an end through the action of the British Government, working in harmony with Russia, whereby Persia was prevented from realizing money on the Crown jewels which she was ready to pledge for the loan. All this time Russia had been openly endeavoring to extort a number of valuable concessions from the Persian Medjlis as the price of withdrawing her troops from Northern Persia. The general attitude of the two powers towards Persia was marked with increasing unfriendliness and hostility. The so-called " forward party " in the Russian Government was increasing in power and influence at St. Petersburg, and the appointment of such a man as Mons. Pokhitanoff, who had distinguished himself by his cold-blooded intrigues and bitter hostility to the Constitutional Government while he was Russian Consul at Tabriz, to be the Russian Consul-general at Teheran, was a fair sample of the course which Russia had marked out for herself toward the Persian people. On October 16, 1910, the British Government delivered its now famous " ultimatum " to Persia, complaining of the condition of the southern roads and trade routes, and practically demanding that a number of officers of the British-Indian Army should be placed in charge of the policing of these roads under the general supervision of the British Government, the expense of the work to be paid out of the Persian Customs revenues. This action provoked the greatest alarm and protest in both Persia and Turkey, and an appeal was telegraphed by certain Muhammadan elements to the German Emperor, requesting him to display his friendliness toward the people of Islam. The only effect of this attempt to involve Germany in Persia's political affairs appears to have been to hasten the Potsdam Agreement which was reached on November 5, 1910, and came as a great surprise to both the French and British Governments. This entente between Russia and Germany,[1] both because of the nature of the disclosed terms of the agreement and because of what has since been generally reputed to be an even more definite and remarkable secret understanding, enabled Russia to adopt a harsh and drastic attitude toward the Persian nation without fear of interference or adequate protest by her partner to the Anglo-Russian Convention of 1907, on which all actions of Britain and Russia towards the Persian people were supposed to be based.

On October 29, 1910, the then Persian Minister of Foreign Affairs, Husayn Kuli Khan, had informed the British and Russian Legations that the Persian Government, having discovered treasonable correspondence between the ex-Shah and

[1] For detailed discussion of this Agreement see Chapter X.

some of the chiefs of the Turcoman tribes on the northeast Persian frontier, proposed, in accordance with the terms of the Protocol of August 25, 1909, to stop the payment of the next instalment of his pension until further investigation could be made. The two Legations not only refused to pay attention to this just demand, but subjected the Persian Minister of Foreign Affairs to the vulgar insult of sending Legation servants in uniform to follow him about the streets of the capital and to stand outside the door of his private house until the money was forthcoming. According to diplomatic usage this action was an unprecedented and unjustifiable outrage and insult. A month later the Russian Minister demanded an apology from this same Persian Minister for an alleged insult to the Russian Consular Agent at the town of Kashan. This Russian agent was, in fact, a Persian of evil reputation to whose appointment the Persian Government had most strongly objected. After undergoing the humiliation of tendering this apology it became so evident to Husayn Kuli Khan that the Powers were bent upon getting rid of him, that he felt compelled to resign, which he did a month later.

In the meantime, the ex-Shah had left Odessa and started on a tour through Europe, ostensibly for his health, but in reality to lay plans for the attempt to overthrow the Constitutional Government, which culminated in his landing upon Persian soil with an armed force in July of the following year. On February 1, in the city of Isfahan, a certain ex-official of police wounded the Constitutional Governor, killed his cousin, and then took refuge in the Russian Consulate there. Five days later the Persian Minister of Finance, Saniu'd-Dawla, was shot and killed in the streets of Teheran by two Georgians, who also succeeded in wounding four of the Persian police before they were captured. The Russian Consular authorities promptly refused to allow these men to be tried by the Persian Government, and took them out of the country under Russian protection, claiming that they would be suitably punished. On

February 8 the new Regent, Nasiru'l-Mulk, who had been elected after the death, on September 22, 1910, of the first Regent, Azadu'l-Mulk, reached Teheran, and the Russian garrison at Kazvin, with the exception of some eighty Cossacks who remained, was withdrawn a month after his arrival, it is said, as a compliment to him.

This brings us down to the arrival in Persia of the American finance administrators. And perhaps, at this point, a few words as to the physical characteristics of this strange country where there is so much politics may not be inappropriate.

Persia is an elevated plateau surrounded and intersected by mountains. In the North, along the Caspian Sea, there is abundant rainfall, and all kinds of fruits and vegetables, and rice, are produced. Silk worms are grown in great numbers. In Teheran whenever a question is asked as to the origin of the better articles of food, the answer is almost invariably that they are " from Mazandaran," a province on the Caspian.

In the Province of Azarbayjan the trees and fruits there, grapes, melons, peaches, pears, plums, etc., are not to be surpassed. The central part of Persia is a large salt desert.

The mountains are generally treeless and rocky. Their snows act as storage reservoirs, and thousands of streams pour down all summer, furnishing water for the plains, large areas of which, for want of any or proper irrigation arrangements, go to waste.

The soil responds promptly to irrigation, and the potential agricultural wealth of the country is unlimited. From what is known of the mines of turquoise, gold, copper, and coal, mineral wealth is also an important item. Up to the present not a railroad has been allowed to enter Persia, lest some strategic advantage should be obtained or lost by Russia, Great Britain or Turkey.

At present, camels, mules and donkeys spend weeks on the roads, transporting Persian goods to the ports of Bushir, Bandar-i-Abbas and Mohammerah on the Persian Gulf, and to

MUHAMMAD ALI SHAH AND HIS SUITE.

Ahwaz, near the Gulf, on the Karun River (upon which ply the steamers of the Lynch Transportation Company), or to Enzeli and other ports on the Caspian, and Trebizond on the Black Sea, in Turkey, or out through Kirmanshah to Bagdad and the Tigris River. Little merchandise goes out to the eastward, as the British Protectorates of Afghanistan and Baluchistan block that way. Of interior commerce there is no lack, particularly the business of transporting grain and other foods from the fertile or irrigated portions of the country to other sections. Teheran, not being in a grain section, is thus supplied from a distance, although its neighborhood when watered, as at Shah-Abdu'l-Azim, just to the south of the city, produces splendid wheat.

Wood and coal are carried by pack animals. Coal is brought from the mines some thirty miles to Teheran. It is of good quality and somewhat resembles the bituminous coal of West Virginia.

Of the great trade routes, one crosses the country from north to south, that is, from the Caspian at Enzeli, via Teheran, Qum, Kashan, Isfahan, Shiraz, to Bushir. Mails and merchandise from India, and at times from Europe, come all the way from Bushir to Teheran over this route. Another route, known sometimes as the Lynch-Bakhtiyari road, connects at Isfahan with this one, and goes to Ahwaz, in the southwest corner of Persia, near the only oil territory which has been developed. Goods come also from Europe through the Suez Canal and the Red Sea around to Bushir and Ahwaz.

A long trail connects Teheran with Trebizond, passing through Kasvin and Tabriz. By her transit tariff Russia drives the merchants of other nationalities to detours via Trebizond or the Persian Gulf — long tedious routes, when they might take a short cut by rail through Batum, on the Black Sea, and Baku, the Russian oil city, on the Caspian. This tariff, supplemented by the most vexatious Batum Custom service, has been very effective.

Other somewhat less important routes go northeast from Teheran to Meshed and various ports on the eastern shore of the
Caspian. One road goes from Isfahan to Yezd, Kirman, Sei-
stan and Bandar-i-Abbas, in the southeastern section of Persia.
Kirman is the principal rug-making district of Persia.

The long route through the Bakhtiyari district to Ahwaz is
closed by the snows on the mountains in mid-winter. The route
from Bushir to Shiraz, Isfahan and Teheran is sometimes in-
fested with robbers, but to a much less extent, it is believed,
than the British traders, with their headquarters in India, are
willing to have merchants of other nationalities believe, since
the British naturally desire to monopolize this trade.

There are several telegraph lines in Persia, chiefly British,
running to Europe, Turkey, India, and connecting all of the
chief Persian cities and towns. Telephone lines are established
from Enzeli to Teheran and to Hamadan, but only for the use
of the road company on the Russian-built road. There is an
interior parcels'-post system, and a mediocre postal service.

The population of Persia has been singularly misrepre-
sented; an old so-called census of sixty years ago seems to be
the basis of the low figures given in some books and generally
accepted by outsiders. Certain it is that no census has been
taken since then, but Europeans who are familiar with the
situation estimate the total population at from 13,000,000 to
15,000,000. Teheran has increased in the past forty years
from 100,000 to some 350,000 inhabitants.

The climate is very agreeable. The weather is usually clear,
and dry and bracing,— if anything, a little too stimulating, especially at Teheran, which has an altitude of 4000 feet.

Such inconveniences as may be inferred from an absence of
railroads and such faults as may be expected in human nature
tyrannized over and corrupted by an aristocracy of selfish landowners are to be found, but Persia, when one becomes accustomed to it, is an attractive and comfortable place in which
to live. Every house of any size is the center of a beautiful
garden of flowers, fruits and fountains. The servants are

AYVAN, ONE OF THE TWO ASSASSINS OF THE PERSIAN MINISTER OF FINANCE, SANIU'D-DAWLA, WHO WAS SHOT IN FEBRUARY, 1911.

SANIU'D-DAWLA, THE MINISTER OF FINANCE.

He was assassinated in February, 1911, on account of his hostility to Russia. The assassins, Georgians, were claimed by Russia.

neither good nor bad. The people are kind and hospitable and capable of rapid development in Western ways. Thousands have traveled or been educated abroad. French is very generally spoken, and an increasing amount of English, especially among the younger Persians.

THE STRANGLING OF PERSIA

" Time with whose passage certain pains abate
But sharpens those of Persia's unjust fate."

THE
STRANGLING OF PERSIA

CHAPTER I

PERSIA DECIDES TO OBTAIN FINANCIAL ADMINISTRATORS FROM AMERICA. THE AMERICANS ARRIVE AT TEHERAN.

D URING the months of November and December, 1910, the idea had been discussed among the deputies of the Medjlis of securing finance administrators from the United States in the hope that officials who were free from any European influence would be able to accomplish some practical results in the reorganization of the archaic and chaotic treasury of Persia.

As a result of a growing sentiment in favor of taking this step, the Persian Cabinet, 'through its Minister of Foreign Affairs, Husayn Kuli Khan, sent, on December 25, 1910, the following instructions to the Persian Legation in Washington:

Persian Legation,
    Washington.
    Request immediately Secretary of State put you in communication with Imperial American financial people and arrange preliminary employment for three years subject to ratification by parliament of disinterested American expert as Treasurer-general to reorganize and conduct collection and disbursement revenue assisted by one expert accountant and one inspector to superintend actual collection in provinces secondly one director to organize and conduct direct taxation assisted by one expert inspector similar to above.
    American Minister informs us Secretary of State ready and willing, avoid

3

other methods of proceeding and irresponsible persons who may offer advice and services.

Give exact copy to Secretary of State and do whatever he may suggest. Wire reports briefly No. 9876.

HUSAYN KULI.

As a result of the friendly negotiations entered into between the Persian diplomatic representative at Washington and the American State Department, the writer was tendered by the Persian Government a contract to serve as Treasurer-general of the Persian Empire for a period of three years, to organize and conduct the collection and disbursements of the revenues of Persia. Four American assistants were likewise engaged to serve under the Treasurer-general in this important work.

I had never even dreamed of going to Persia before my appointment, but the eloquence of the Persian Charge d'Affaires at Washington, Mirza Ali Kuli Khan, removed my early doubts and I finally decided to do what I could to help a people who had certainly given evidence of an abiding faith in our institutions and business methods. One of the first things I did was to read Professor Browne's book on the Persian Revolution, and his high opinion of, and desire to secure justice for, the nascent constitutional movement in Persia, strengthened my own determination to proceed.

Before we started, I had a clear understanding with the American State Department as to its relationship to the affair, and I realized perfectly that I was not going to Persia in any manner as the representative of the American Government.

I asked the Department for a written statement of its position in the matter, and can best describe it by setting out here the official reply which I received:—

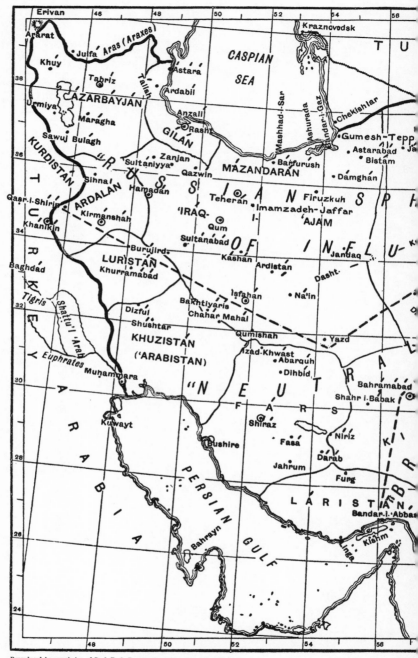

MAP SHOWING THE THREE "SPHERES" (RUSSIAN, BRITISH AND ?)

(It will be noticed that all the principal towns of Persia except Dizfúl, Shúshtar, Shíráz and Kirmán, as ? consists mostly of desert, and cor?

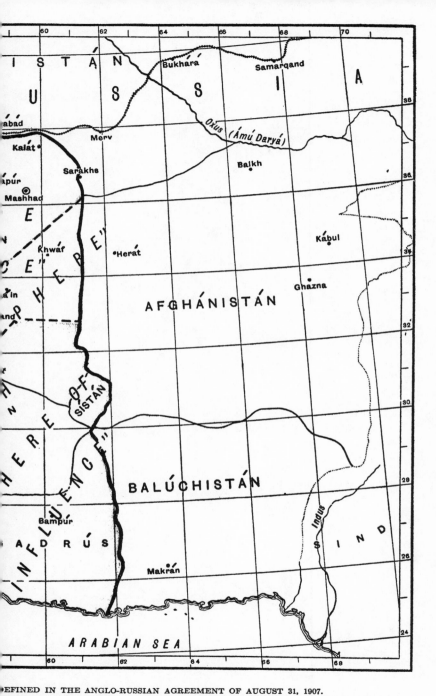

DEFINED IN THE ANGLO-RUSSIAN AGREEMENT OF AUGUST 31, 1907.

t fertile and populous part of the country, are included in the "Russian Sphere." The "British Sphere"
town of importance, *viz.* Kirmán.)

February 24, 1911.

Mr. W. Morgan Shuster,
Union Trust Building,
Washington, D. C.

Sir: The Department is in receipt of your letter of the 14th instant, in reference to the employment by the Persian Government of five American financial advisers, and making inquiry as to the facts which led to your selection for the office of Treasurer-general of the Persian Government.

In reply you are informed that in December last the Persian Chargé d'Affaires in this city, acting in accordance with instructions from his Government, requested the assistance of this Department in placing the Legation in communication with American financial experts, with a view to the ultimate employment by the Persian Government of five American financial assistants. In compliance with this request the Department submitted a list of names, including your own, of persons with whom it was suggested that the Persian Charge d'Affaires might appropriately communicate in reference to this matter. The Department is happy to note from your letter and from a communication from the Persian Legation dated the 17th instant that you have been selected for the position of Treasurer-general under the Persian Ministry of Finance.

I am, sir,
Your obedient servant,
For Mr. Knox:
(Signed) HUNTINGTON WILSON,
Assistant Secretary of State.

I have been informed on good authority that when Russia first found that the idea of securing finance administrators from America was making headway among the deputies of the Medjlis, she gave the matter her official attention at Teheran. An early attempt was made by Russian emissaries to employ certain persuasive and notorious members of the Parliament to defeat the project. Failing, however, to change the purpose of the great majority of the deputies, the story runs that Russia next approached the American State Department, which at that time was in complete ignorance of the idea of the Persian Government, and delicately intimated that it would be unwise or unkind to send American financial experts to Persia. The

State Department replied, with entire candor, that it knew nothing of the affair, and that the question would be dealt with when it arose.

When, shortly afterwards, the Persian Government did request that the American State Department should lend its assistance to secure the services of five American financial experts, the British Government was asked whether the objections previously expressed by Russia to Americans going to Persia for this task were shared by England. The British reply was that such *had been* the view of their Government, but that the objections no longer existed. The Russian Government was then obliged either to object openly to the employment of American citizens as such, or to use smooth diplomatic language and allow the matter to proceed.

On February 2, 1911, the Medjlis approved the terms of our contracts by a large majority and amid great enthusiasm.

We went to Persia, therefore, in good faith, and in the natural belief that the two powers having (to use their own language) " special interests " there offered no objection to the fair and honest accomplishment of our task.

On April 8, 1911, I sailed from New York with a party of Americans consisting of Mr. Charles I. McCaskey of New York; Mr. Ralph W. Hills of Washington, D. C.; and Mr. Bruce G. Dickey of Pine Island, Minnesota, to take up the work of reorganizing the finances of the Persian Government. Mr. McCaskey, Mr. Hills and myself were accompanied by our families, making with children and servants a party of sixteen.

I had agreed to serve the Persian Government for three years as Treasurer-general, having entire control of the financial operations and fiscal affairs of that country. Mr. McCaskey [1]

---

[1] Mr. Charles I. McCaskey, who was engaged as Inspector of Provincial Revenues in Persia, was born on August 7, 1877, at Fort Snelling, Minnesota. His parents are Major-General and Mrs. William S. McCaskey, United States Army retired. Mr. McCaskey went to the Philippines with his

MR. F. S. CAIRNS, DIRECTOR OF TAXATION AND MR. SHUSTER'S PRINCIPAL ASSISTANT IN PERSIA.

MR. CHARLES I. McCASKEY, INSPECTOR OF PROVINCIAL REVENUE AND SECOND ASSISTANT TO THE TREASURER-GENERAL.

had accepted the post of Inspector of Provincial Revenues, Mr. Hills that of Accountant, and Mr. Dickey[1] that of Inspector of Taxation, all for the term of three years, under my supervision. Mr. F. S. Cairns,[2] then Collector of Customs at Iloilo in the Philippine Islands, had been appointed Director of Taxation, and was to follow us to Teheran as soon as possible. He was to be the Treasurer-general's principal assistant. The men engaged for this work had enjoyed a number of years' experience at somewhat similar tasks, and were thoroughly acquainted with organization problems and revenue work in undeveloped countries.

We traveled via Paris and Vienna, reaching Constantinople

father in March, 1899, and after being in the field and in action with his father's regiment, he returned to Manila, and on April 15, 1899, entered the Customs Service as an Inspector, remaining in this service from that date until the summer of 1907, having been promoted to the position of Deputy Surveyor of Customs at Manila. In the spring of 1905, Mr. McCaskey returned to the United States on a leave of absence, and on arriving at San Francisco, was married to Miss Selden Fant, of Holly Springs, Mississippi. He has three children.

Early in 1907, on account of the illness of his wife, he was obliged to resign and return to the United States, where he was appointed an Inspector of Customs at the Port of New York. On September 7, 1909, he was promoted to Acting Deputy Surveyor of Customs, which position he held until he went to Persia.

[1] Mr. Bruce G. Dickey, who went to Teheran as Inspector of Taxation, was born at Pine Island, Minnesota, on April 25, 1881, and resided there until the year 1899, at which time he went to the Philippine Islands and entered the Customs Service at Manila as Inspector of Immigration. He was subsequently promoted to the positions of Appraiser of Merchandise and Chief of the Passenger and Baggage Division of the Manila Custom House. Later, he was made Assistant Cashier of the Custom House at Manila, which position he resigned in 1908 to return to this country. He is unmarried.

[2] Mr. F. S. Cairns was at the time of his appointment as Director of Taxation the Collector of Customs for the Port of Iloilo, in the Philippine Islands. Prior to 1898, he had been a Special Agent for the United States Treasury Department for several years.

After the first American occupation of Cuba starting January 1, 1899, he became Chief of the Special Agents of the Cuban Customs Service, in which position he served until 1901, when he was appointed Surveyor of Customs for the Philippine Islands. He served in this position with great credit until 1910, when he was appointed to the Collectorship at Iloilo, the second largest port in the Philippines.

on April 25. Thence we went by sea to Batum, Russia, where we arrived May 3, taking the train next day for Baku. We sailed from Baku at 4 o'clock in the afternoon of May 6, on the Russian steamer *Bariatinski,* a little side-wheeler, and crossing that part of the Caspian Sea during the night, we arrived the next morning at the Persian port of Enzeli, about 9 o'clock. Once on land, and the Customs formalities over, we went by launch and sail-boat, and then by carriage, to the town of Resht, which is the capital of the Persian province of Ghilan. Here we were entertained for two days by the Acting Governor of the Province while arrangements were being made for the transportation of our party and our baggage to Teheran, which lies some 220 miles to the south. This journey was made in unwieldy postchaises of antique type and dilapidated appearance drawn by four scrawny and diminutive ponies which were changed at the stations every ten or twelve miles along the road. Our party occupied four carriages, and left Resht on May 9, at 8:30 in the morning, having sent the heavy baggage on in advance in two large, springless wagons. We were advised to take the trip rather slowly on account of the women and children in the party, and after a number of interesting adventures along the road we reached the last station before arriving at Teheran on May 12, about 2 o'clock in the afternoon. Here we found our trunks awaiting us, although they were in a decidedly damaged condition due to three days and nights of alternate rain and dust and the jolting of the springless wagons. If we had not been warned at the last moment before despatching them at Resht to have them sewed up in native felt, they would probably have been useless by the time we saw them again. About four miles outside of the Kazvin gate of the city of Teheran we were met by the American Minister, Mr. Charles W. Russell, and his family and by a number of American missionaries and Persians.

We took city carriages and were driven at once to Atabak Park, a very beautiful residence and grounds on a palatial scale, which had been prepared for us. The building was formerly the summer palace of the great reactionary Prime Minister of that name. He was also known as Aminu's-Sultan, and was assassinated on August 31, 1907. This palace and grounds, covering about eight acres in the portion of Teheran occupied by the legations and European residences, had passed into the hands of a very patriotic and wealthy Parsee merchant named Arbad Jemshid. He had very generously placed this residence at the disposal of the Government for our entertainment while in Teheran. The building itself was of white stone, two stories high, containing about thirty rooms, a number of which were extremely spacious, and it was filled with a most remarkable collection of curious bric-a-brac and strange furniture from all corners of the world, including a number of very fine and rare Persian rugs. The grounds were laid out in an immense park with several artificial lakes and water-courses, and the entire place was surrounded by a high and very thick baked mud wall, which is typical of the larger private residences in Teheran.

I well recall the impression produced upon us by our arrival in the early evening at the gates of this park. For three days and nights we had been traveling through dust and rain, in the alternate cold of the Elburz mountains and the heat of the plains, sleeping in uncomfortable road-houses and eating such food as we could take with us from place to place or find upon the journey. We were sunburned, covered with dust, dirty and tired; and to be conducted through a beautiful drive-way in the cool of the evening, under trees sparkling with lanterns, up to the magnificent entrance of the palace where a crowd of strikingly uniformed servants and guards awaited us on that beautiful May night of our arrival, was a change which made Teheran almost a fairy land. After dinner we spent several hours on the balcony listening to the songs of the Persian nightingales in the trees around the house.

Before we could unpack a trunk, callers of all kinds began to pour in upon us, and for two months the stream, from early morning till late at night, never seemed to diminish.

To see and talk with one tenth of the people who sought an interview consumed a great amount of time, but we were able to acquire by this means a great fund of valuable information and we were told that these people were all important personages who would be mortally offended if they were not given the opportunity to explain their views on the situation and point out the steps which they deemed necessary to reorganize the Government.

At Enzeli we had been met by a Persian gentleman named Hormuz Khan, who had been sent there by the Government to receive us and act as our courier and guide on the road to the capital. Hormuz Khan presented us his card on which he described himself as an " American Student "; he spoke English fairly well, and was most anxious that we should receive a favorable impression of his native land. His conversation and his songs on the way along the road and at the stopping-places did much to relieve the monotony of the journey. If we appeared fatigued by many hours of travel over a dusty and arid plain, he would point out a mountain somewhere in the distance and call our attention to the beauties of nature, thus strewn before the weary wayfarer. Although a good Muhammadan, he was a firm believer in the efficacy of an occasional cup of cognac upon trips of this kind, and never failed to remind some one of the party when he considered that a sufficient time had elapsed since the last one. On our arrival at Teheran, Hormuz Khan felt that his personal services to our party had been such that he should immediately be rewarded with the post of Assistant Treasurer-general, or Chief Tax Collector, and it was through

MR. AND MRS. SHUSTER IN ATABAK PARK.

his disappointment at my inability to confer this trifling favor upon him within the first few days after our arrival, that an estrangement took place which gradually led us into different paths.

The day after our arrival at Teheran was spent in conference with Minister Russell and with a number of other callers, among them the then Minister of Finance, Mumtazu'd-Dawla, a very intelligent man who had formerly been a President of the Medjlis. He spoke French fluently, as do all educated Persians, and was most cordial in his offers of assistance and his assurance of entire coöperation and support in our efforts to build up the financial administration of his country. We began to discover about this time that there was a large number of very intelligent Persians apparently permanently attached to our household in various capacities which we were unable to figure out. They all spoke either English or French, and some remained for weeks on duty, always ready to interpret, if necessary, or to assist in any other way, merely in the hope of being found useful by those to whom they looked to aid their country and their people.

On May 16, by previous arrangement between the Minister of Finance and the Minister of Foreign Affairs, Muhtashamu's-Saltana, we called upon the latter at the Foreign Office, accompanied by Minister Russell, and indulged for the first time in the necessary official ceremony of taking tea. In driving through the streets of the city and walking through the grounds of the Government buildings, called the *Darbar,* we were made aware of the fact that we were objects of very unusual curiosity. Looking back to that time, I am still unable to imagine what the name " American " conveyed, or what any American could have previously done, to have excited the interest of the Persian people to the extent which we apparently did. Later that afternoon we were taken over to the official reception palace of His Highness, the Regent, Nasiru'l-Mulk, to whom we were formally presented. I found the Regent to be a most kindly and intelligent-looking man with a perfect command of the English language. Nasiru'l-Mulk is an Oxford graduate, and was a classmate of Sir Edward Grey, the present Secretary of State for Foreign Affairs of England. We talked with him for ten or fifteen minutes, and he especially invited me to call upon him without ceremony at any time and to discuss my work with him in the freest manner.

That evening I made the acquaintance of a man who was destined to become the best and truest friend that the Americans in Persia found during their stay in that country. Arbab Kaikhosro is a Parsee gentleman who had been educated abroad and, having returned to Persia, had thrown in his lot with the Nationalist movement and been elected one of the deputies from Teheran to the second Medjlis. He represented the Parsee community of the city, and was a merchant and property-owner. He was a man of the most pleasing personality, with a good command of English, and later proved himself to be of both inflexible integrity and unfailing courage under the most trying and difficult circumstances. He promised me in our very first interview that he would give us every assistance in his power, and from that moment until the day that we left Persia, he never ceased, day or night, to work for our success in his country and to defend the American finance officials against intrigues and attacks from every source.

On the next day we went with Minister Russell to call on a very remarkable official, His Highness, Sipahdar-i-Azam, who at that time was Prime Minister holding the portfolio of War. The Minister of Finance, Mumtazu'd-Dawla, and the Vice Minister of War, Amir Azam, were present at this interview. Those who have read the introductory chapter of this story will recall that the Sipahdar, or " greatest of the marshals," as his title means in Persian, took a very prominent part in the second

A GATHERING IN THE DEMOCRATIC CLUB AT TEHERAN.
The American Minister, Mr. Charles W. Russell, is in the middle.

Nationalist uprising which resulted in the capture of Teheran by the combined Nationalist forces and the deposition of the Shah in July, 1909. Until shortly before that time the Sipahdar had been commonly regarded as a supporter of the Shah and as a reactionary grandee of the most pronounced type. He possessed vast landed estates in two or three of the provinces of Persia, owned hundreds of villages, and was generally reputed to be the richest man in the Empire. A tall, thin, weazened figure, of about 60 years of age, with small black eyes, grizzled hair and mustache, and a very nervous manner, he gave one the impression of being rather more an arch intriguer than the leader of a victorious army. He was one of the few prominent Persian officials who could talk neither English nor French, and his Vice-minister, a fat and oily giant, who spoke French quite well, served as our interpreter. I mention this distinguished personage with such care because of the part which he will play in the subsequent incidents of our stay in Persia.

The next four days were spent in exchanging visits with members of the Persian Cabinet and prominent deputies of the Medjlis. At the request of the leading Persian newspaper editors of Teheran, I gave them an interview in which I outlined the general plan of the work which the Americans hoped to accomplish. We had from that time on the undivided support of the Persian press, not only at Teheran, but throughout the entire country wherever a paper was printed. One of the evidences of the Persians' inexperience in political affairs is their laughable sensitiveness to any form of newspaper criticism. From the Regent down, every Persian Government official lived in daily terror of being held up by the newspapers to public condemnation or ridicule. Despite the freedom of speech provided for in the constitutional decrees, it was a frequent occurrence for the Minister of the Interior to suppress one or more papers in Teheran for casting even some very general

aspersion on the Government's actions or motives.   The doughty
editors, however, always managed to resume after a few days or
weeks.   The principal papers in Teheran at this time were the
Esteklal, the organ of the so-called Moderate Party in the
Medjlis, and the *Irani-Noh,* the organ of the Democrats.
The latter was perhaps the best and most fearlessly edited journal in Persia, and it did yeoman service for the American
finance officials from the day of their arrival in Teheran.

On May 22 the *chef de cérémonie* of the Ministry of Foreign Affairs, conducted us to the temporary offices in the *Darbar,*
or government center, which had been provided for us.   Here
the Vice-minister of Finance and the different chiefs of the offices were presented to us and a great quantity of tea and cigarettes was consumed.   Also much time.   Each chief was
desirous of having a series of private interviews running over
several days in order that he might properly explain the organization of his office, his own thorough grasp of the needs of the
situation, and the failure of the Government to provide him or
his employees with sufficient pecuniary lubricant to grease the
wheels of his department.

The Minister of Finance, Mumtazu'd-Dawla, was aiding us
in every possible way, and we had just reached a tentative basis
for commencing work when, on May 23, eleven days after our
arrival, there was a Cabinet " crisis " and he resigned.   It seems
that the Prime Minister and Minister of War, Sipahdar, felt
that the Finance Minister was not signing checks and warrants
with the freedom and abandon which the Premier had a right
to expect.

I was somewhat disturbed by this Cabinet change right at the
outset of our work, but later grew to take such things more phil-
osophically.

Among the various officials of the Finance Department whom
we met was a Mr. Lecoffre, a British subject, of French éxtrac-

tion, who had been in Persia for a number of years. He was a great deal more of a Frenchman than anything else, and he occupied the post of *Controleur*. After all the other officials had left our office, Mr. Lecoffre sat down, looked me in the eye, and said: " I am glad, Mr. Shuster, that you have come, because *between us* we shall be able to straighten the miserable finances of these people." I thanked him for the encouraging thought.

On May 25, Mr. Hills and his family, who had been compelled to remain behind in Constantinople on account of the serious illness of their infant daughter, arrived at Teheran. Unfortunately another of his children fell ill just after their arrival and he was compelled to give up his post and return to America. They left Teheran on June 2, to the great regret of our entire party.

On our arrival at Atabak Park we had found fifteen or twenty very efficient Persian servants, who had been placed there by some Persian gentlemen who were entertaining us for a day or so until we could get our bearings. When we took over the *ménage* two days later we naturally retained these domestics, who had all been highly recommended to us. It was not until several weeks afterwards that the rumor began to reach me that the Americans were believed to be *Bahais*,[1] and that we had come to Teheran, not to reform the finances, but to proselytize. Finally the Minister of Finance very gravely called my attention to the matter, and suggested that I should discharge our servants as " they were all *Bahais*." This was news to me. I had never thought to put our personal servants to a religious test as to their orthodoxy, especially as it is against civil service principles in America. I told the Finance Minister that the

---

[1] The *Bahais, Bahaists* or *Babis,* are a religious sect among the Persians who are greatly disliked by the Muhammadans. Up to quite modern times they were cruelly persecuted by orthodox Moslems. They are now tolerated, and include many of the most enlightened and patriotic Persians.

Americans were *not* Bahais, but that I did not propose to have
the Persian Government or people pass on the religious faith
of ourselves, or our servants, or the color of our neckties, and
that if the Government had not something more important than
that to think about, it should find something.   That was the
last I heard officially, but the tale was spread broadcast by certain
elements who were antagonistic to our work, and we were car-
tooned in some of the local newspapers.   Finding that we were
attending to our own business, the public soon forgot the matter.

About this time I received an insight into the so-called " intrigues " which were going on in connection with our arrival
and contemplated duties.   Nearly every one with whom I
talked brought out, at some point in the conversation, the word
" intrigues."   " The Cabinet is making *intrigues* against you."
" The Belgian Customs officials are *intriguing* against the
Americans."   " This is a terrible place, Mr. Shuster, for
intrigues."   " Persia is the land of *blague* and *intrigues*."   In
sheer self-defense I was compelled to tell every one that Americans thrived on intrigues and rather liked to see them going on.

The first tangible one which we met, however, was engineered
by a Mons. Mornard, a Belgian Customs official, who held the
post of Administrator-general of the Customs Department of
Persia.   This gentleman had been a Customs employee in his
own country of very inferior grade, and had gone to Persia as
an assistant to his notorious countryman, Mons. Naus, who had
been employed by Muzaffaru'd Din Shah to organize and establish the Persian Customs Department, a thing which he did with
such startling success that he quickly became extremely influential and wealthy, and was highly regarded by the Russian
Government.   One of the first acts of the original Persian
Medjlis was, on February 10, 1907, to compel the Shah to dismiss Mons. Naus, who by that time occupied a number of high
positions.   He is now reported to be enjoying his handsome

chateaux and estates in Belgium. It was this gentleman who negotiated several highly important fiscal affairs for the Persian Government, such as the present Persian Customs Tariff and two of the Russian loans, which are now such a burden on the Persian people. Of the Customs tariff, more later.

Mons. Mornard had become one of Mons. Naus' principal assistants and protégés, and when Mons. Naus was driven out by the Medjlis, Mons. Mornard was left to fill one of his numerous posts,— that of Chief of Customs.

With Mons. Mornard at the time of our arrival were some twenty-five or thirty of his countrymen in charge of all the custom-houses in Persia. We were informed that Mons. Mornard, with the active support of the Belgian and Russian legations, had tried hard to obtain for himself the post of Treasurer-general, .but the Medjlis apparently wanted a complete change. Finding themselves blocked in this attempt, the Belgian Customs officials sought another plan to nullify as far as possible the effect of the employment of the Americans.

Very shortly before our arrival, the negotiations had been completed for a loan to the Persian Government of £1,250,000 sterling by the Imperial Bank of Persia, a British corporation. All the terms had been agreed upon, and about two weeks before our arrival at Teheran, the resolution of the Medjlis approving the contract had actually been passed. A portion of the deputies had favored the idea of awaiting our advice before taking the final step, but the Cabinet was extremely anxious· to see the affair concluded, and the vote was taken.

Mons. Mornard, in connivance with certain well-known Russian agents in and out of the Medjlis and Persian Cabinet had prepared, just before our arrival, a draft of a law placing the entire control of the expenditures of the money derived from this loan in the hands of a " commission " composed of fifteen members, of which he was to be the head and center. Thus the

American Treasurer-general, who had come to take charge of the Persian finances, would have found himself in the delightful dilemma of either serving as a *subordinate* to Mons. Mornard on this "commission," which was to supervise the Government expenditures, or of staying away and seeing the only available funds of the Government controlled by other hands. The project for this law was already before the Medjlis when the matter was first brought to my attention. I immediately drafted and presented to the Persian Cabinet a brief report on the then existing situation in the Ministry of Finance, and asked whether they desired " to add another room in the house of chaos." With this report was transmitted a simple project of law placing the control of the refunding operations and expenditures growing out of the £1,250,000 loan contract in the hands of the Treasurer-general, where it belonged.

The Cabinet promptly approved this and it was sent to the Medjlis and on May 30 it was duly made into law. Thus the first attempt by foreign elements to tie our hands before we could even get started had failed, and the deputies of the Medjlis expressed their delight that we had discovered the situation to them.

During this time I had an experience which it seems worth while to recount as showing what trifling matters are regarded as important with an oriental people. As I had received literally hundreds of visits from Persians and foreigners since our arrival — according to the hospitable custom in that country — I was somewhat surprised to receive a call from a young man who explained that he was the Secretary of His Excellency the Sardar-i-Asad, who, it will be remembered, was one of the Bakhtiyari chieftains, or " Khans," who took a prominent part in the overthrow of the late Shah in 1909. The young man said that His Excellency had been awaiting my visit to him, as he was anxious to know me. I told him that I was nearly al-

MONS. NAUS (in center), THE NOTORIOUS BELGIAN EX-MINISTER OF THE PERSIAN CUSTOMS.

This picture was taken at a fancy dress ball at which Mons. Naus appeared as a "mullah" or Muhammadan priest. The affair greatly offended the Persians and hastened his expulsion by the Medjlis.

ways at home at the Atabak Park after five in the afternoon,
and that I would be delighted to see His Excellency. He departed and on the next day sent me a note saying that the Sardar-i-Asad would await me at six that evening at his residence
in Bakhtiyari street. The day following the Secretary again
called to inquire why I had disappointed His Excellency, " who
was a very powerful man and of great pride." I told him that
in my country we did not allow those minor considerations to
outweigh the ordinary social customs and rules of hospitality,
and that I would be glad to receive his distinguished chief.
That evening the Sardar-i-Asad called and we had a friendly
talk. I returned his call the next day. I afterwards learned
that His Excellency at the instigation of his clansmen, had
tried to make the American Treasurer-general call on him as
special mark of distinction and prestige, in order that he might
lower the prestige of his great rival, the Prime Minister, Sipahdar. Had I gone, I should have made a sworn enemy of the
latter.

A week after our arrival in Teheran one of my Persian visitors took occasion to inquire politely when I would find time
to call at the Russian Legation; a little later an emissary came
apparently on a similar errand from the British Legation. I
replied that I would not have my household furniture or be settled, after such a long journey, for at least a month. From this
time on scarcely a day passed that I did not receive a direct or
indirect intimation that the foreign legations were awaiting my
call. After two weeks the affair became truly laughable, and
when I was able to inquire what was the custom in such matters
when Persian officials arrived at the capital, and learned that
the newcomers into official circles always received the first call,
it became almost interesting. It seems absurd as a statement,
but the question of whether or when I would call on the foreign
legations (meaning thereby the British and Russian Legations)

actually became the all-absorbing topic, not only in European social circles, but in Persian officialdom.

I had been told the sad history of Mons. Bizot, the eminent French " finance-doctor," who had arrived at Teheran some two years before us, and finding that the Russian, British and other foreign diplomats were most charming and hospitable men, ever ready to advise him as to his work, had been so thoroughly entranced by their good fellowship and the numerous social festivities given at the different legations in his honor, that he completely forgot the trifling fact that he had gone to Persia to reform the finances of that country, and not merely to drink tea, play bridge and ride out for his health.   If he ever awoke to a sense that he ought to take hold of his duties, he doubtless found that the Medjlis, whether rightly or not, had already classified him with his Belgian predecessors, and that so far as doing anything with Persian support and coöperation was concerned, he might as well start back to *la belle France*.   At all events, Mons. Bizot displayed a masterly inactivity in making any financial reforms during his two years at Teheran, and at the end of that time he bequeathed to the patient and trusting Persian Government a thirty-page typewritten report, edited in beautiful French, and expressing Bizot's opinion as to *what somebody should do* to reorganize Persia's fiscal system.   He returned to his Government post at Paris greatly improved in health, but the Persian finances continued to stumble and stagger as before.

Finally the Regent, in one of our talks, asked me whether I was going to call on the Russian and British Ministers.   Having no desire to debate these delicate subjects I replied, in truly oriental fashion, that I was very busy getting my house in order and preparing a basic financial law for submission to the cabinet and the Medjlis.   Finally, at one of the sessions of the Cabinet, to which I was often invited, the Minister of Foreign Affairs, a most oleaginous personage, Mutashamu's-Saltana by name, brought solemnly before his colleagues the fact that the foreign ministers at Teheran did not know why I had not called on them and were anxious about it. Said he: " The Belgian, French and other employees in the Persian service have always considered it an honor to call at the legations. The diplomats cannot understand why the Americans do not follow the same rule."

I said: " Your Excellency, there are a number of points to this very delicate and complicated question, but before going any further I should like to inquire whether I am not an official of the Persian Government; if I am, should I not observe the rules of etiquette laid down by that Government? "

After some discussion, the entire Cabinet agreed and decided that I was under no obligation to pay first calls; quite the contrary, and they seemed rather to like the idea of a foreigner considering himself to be a genuine part of their Government, instead of merely condescending to accept their money.

As I look back now, the case seems even more amusing. The Russian and British Ministers knew that I was intending to present to the Medjlis a financial law for enactment; Russian agents and protégés had openly threatened to kill that law, or at least to emasculate it; they had found that the great majority of the deputies, after some three weeks' intercourse with us, had a surprising degree of confidence in our plans and our desire to help their country, and they, the diplomats, were confronted by the dismal prospect of a foreigner, a mere outsider, actually walking in and assuming his duties without first doing public homage to them.

One little call, or even a bent card, and the music would have begun to play, the dinner invitations to rain in, with return calls to follow, and we would have been socially certified as fit for the rarefied atmosphere of Eastern diplomatic circles,— and, merely *en passant,* my finance law would never have passed the

Medjlis and we might have spent the rest of our time in Persia playing tennis and bridge.

During this little by-play the Persian people were not entirely idle. They rubbed their eyes a few times and then commenced to have a new sensation. *" Inshallah,* have we a *faranghi* among us who takes not his orders from the foreign legations. Let us help him."

In the real East rumor wears seven-league boots, and on the 13th day of June, just one month after our arrival at Teheran, the deputies by a practically unanimous vote, passed a law giving to a foreigner full and complete powers in the handling of their finances, and we were ready to commence work in earnest.

As it seems now, I think that we would have called on the foreign diplomats,— certainly as soon as the pressing matter of establishing and defining by legislation our official status and positions had been arranged,— but these diplomatic gentlemen, by their own loud outcries and running around in circles, from the very day after our arrival, had so attracted the attention of every one and so sharpened this point of the whole affair, that for me to have yielded at that time would have lost for us, with the already suspicious and oft-deceived Persian people, the last chance of gaining their confidence and obtaining the legislative authority necessary to give to our efforts any hope of success. Thus before we could arrange a chair to sit on at home, there had been thrust upon us a mild diplomatic intrigue in full swing. If we had succumbed to it, by that trifling action we would have lost any real coöperation of the Persians, and by refusing to walk into the prearranged trap, we have been charged with the high-crime of lack of tact.

At this point the reader may laugh without offending the writer in the least; he feels that way himself, but this little story is told because it shows the real spirit pervading certain

quarters in Teheran which shortly set on foot the countless intrigues and chicaneries which during the succeeding months of
our stay in Persia were employed to distort the truth, to falsify
the record, and to discredit publicly a few men who refused to
become the mere tools of alien political interests.

On June 1 the Sipahdar gave a garden fête at his beautiful
and spacious park in Teheran. It was understood that one
of its purposes was to bring the Americans into contact with the
diplomatic society of the capital. I remember very well driving with my wife through the dusty streets towards the Sipahdar's that rather hot afternoon. On the way, as we neared the
British Legation gate, the distinguished-looking Minister and
his wife drove out, escorted by Indian *sawars* with their lances,
and preceded us up the roads. It was the first time that I had
seen Sir George Barclay. Once in the garden, the air was cool
and fresh. Dozens of beautiful fountains played on all sides.
We approached the reception tent by a winding road, bordered
with trees and flowers, while the Royal band played martial airs
in the background.

Arrived at the entrance to the tent, after greeting our host
and his receiving party, we were ushered into the midst of a
gloomy and forbidding circle of European ladies and gentlemen
who, posed in attitudes of studied indifference, stared stonily
at the intruders. Though the tent was closed on three sides
and not a breath of air was stirring, I could detect a distinct
atmosphere of frost. We stood in the very center, my wife and
I, with Mr. and Mrs. McCaskey, who had come with us, and,
recognizing the situation, I whispered to the others to give their
best representation of four people conversing in a desert. The
trouble was partly with the Sipahdar and his *chef de cérémonie,*
Mutashamu's-Saltana, Minister of Foreign Affairs. These
worthies had been willing to bring " hostile foreign elements "
into the same enclosure, but as for deciding *which* one should

be presented to the *other* — *Inshallah!* no; that would be going too far.

There we stood, gazing in awe and admiration at the various archaic types of top-hats worn by the gallant secretaries of the legations,— most of them of rare vintage (the hats), and many sizes too large. Why the young Englishmen wore top-hats which were prevented from engulfing their entire countenances only by their ears puzzled me for sometime afterwards. I subsequently learned that the supply of these social weapons is limited in Teheran and, as they are hard to transport over the Elburz mountains, they are treated by the junior diplomats as official heirlooms. From which I take it that megalocephalia was prevalent among their predecessors in office.

After ten minutes of standing around, during which we gave no cry of distress, the ice thawed somewhat and the guests began to mingle. Some friends of ours arrived and Mr. McCaskey informed me that Sir George Barclay (whom he had met) was desirous of making my acquaintance — as I was his. After meeting Sir George and while chatting with him as to the financial situation of Persia and the prospect of doing any work, I noticed a very distinguished gentleman whose uneasy expression suggested to my mind a diplomat of high rank. He gazed long and hard at Sir George, and finally catching his eye, nodded very distinctly. Said Sir George: "My dear Mr. Treasurer-general, have you met Poklewski, the Russian Minister,— a splendid fellow, you know." I expressed regret that I had not been favored. "I think he may be passing this way soon. I will introduce you," added Sir George. As I soon learned, the uneasy gentleman standing not eight feet away, was Mons. Poklewski. At this precise moment it occurred to him to stroll by us, swinging his cane and gazing at the concourse. As he passed, Sir George touched him on the arm, and by this accident Mons. Poklewski and I met, without further disturbing the diplomatic balance of the world. The French Minister was likewise present in the tent, but either missed his cue or changed his mind, and I never had the pleasure of his acquaintance during my stay in Teheran.

Sir George Barclay and Mons. Poklewski-Koziell were on this occasion, as ever afterwards when I talked with them, most pleasant and polished gentlemen. But their official tasks in Persia seemed to weigh heavily upon them, and their duties, I fear, were not infrequently distasteful.

One must at times separate a gentleman and a diplomat from his official acts performed under orders from his home government; otherwise great confusion and injustice would occur. Some governments have a little way of telling those who represent them abroad and especially in the Orient, to get such and such a thing done, and done it must be. Nor would those high Government officials at home care often to hear the painful details of the successful execution of many such orders which are given.

One of the first financial questions submitted to me for an opinion was that of the continuance of the salt-tax which had been established about a year. The people were complaining very bitterly about it, and I found on investigation that there was a tax of 64 krans (about $5.70) per 600 pounds on Persian salt mined within the country, whereas the Customs tax on foreign salt imported was only $.09 for the same quantity. As no internal tax could be imposed, under the Customs stipulations, on imported articles, the salt-producers of Persia and the people living in the interior districts were most unjustly treated. In addition, the Persian Government had received in the course of a year from this purely revenue-producing measure the insignificant net sum of 42,000 tumans (about $37,000), although the gross taxes collected from the people were nearly 209,000 tumans,— the expenses of collection absorbing all the difference. I immediately recommended the abolition of this unproductive and uneconomic law and the Medjlis approved the proposal.

This comparatively trifling affair did much to strengthen the prestige of the Constitutional Government with the people in the provinces, who had really been suffering from a measure which benefited no one but the tax-collectors who fattened on its proceeds.

CHAPTER II

THE POLITICAL AND FINANCIAL SITUATION IN PERSIA AS WE
FOUND IT. POWERS OF THE REGENT, THE CABINET AND THE
MEDJLIS. FORM OF GOVERNMENT AND SOURCES OF REVENUE.
THE PUBLIC DEBT. THE VARIOUS FOREIGN LOANS.

FROM the day that we reached Teheran we were constantly
warned that we would never be allowed to do any real
work in behalf of Persia; that other foreign advisers and officials who had come to Teheran and attempted to bring about
practical reforms had early been compelled either to leave the
country or to " go over to the other side," and that we had
better make our peace with those in power. " The other side "
and " those in power " we soon found to mean the clique of reactionary Persian officials, principally hold-overs from the
despotic past régimes, and comprising men of great wealth,
power and influence, who, as a rule, had received a European
education and training. They had reached the conclusion that
it was far safer and easier to become the tools, agents and protégés of the Russian Government, for instance, and have its
powerful influence exerted in their favor, than to side with their
own people who were struggling heroically, but with all the
faults of inexperience and ignorance of the technique of representative government weighing heavily against their efforts.

It early became the jest of the diplomatic corps at Teheran
that the Americans would not remain in Persia three months;
the wife of one distinguished foreign minister said that a month
would see them on the road back to Enzeli; and the idea that
any serious attempt would be made to straighten out Persian
financial affairs only called forth laughter.

On our way to Persia we had spent five days at Constantinople, where there is a large colony of Persians. The Turkish
capital is always in close touch with Teheran, and there we
met many Persians who had but recently come from their own
country. Some were in political exile, like the famous Constitutionalist deputy from Tabriz, Taqi-zada, who called on me
and talked for an hour of the troubles in Persia. Others whom
we met had taken prominent parts in the Nationalist movement, among them being merchants, priests, foreign-office officials and diplomats. Here I received my first insight into the
conditions prevailing in Persia and I confess that the prospects
were not particularly encouraging.

I was given friendly warning of many things, ranging from
foreign intrigues to personal injury, but among all the diverse
advice vouchsafed there was a clear agreement of opinion to the
effect that the Persian Medjlis, or National Parliament, represented the actual progressive movement of the people of Iran,
and that it was, both by law and by reputation, the symbol of
Persian nationalism and liberty. " Gain the confidence and
good will of the deputies of the Medjlis," said our friendly
callers, " and half of your work will already be done. Fail to
obtain its coöperation, and you may as well give up your efforts
to accomplish any real results."

It was not so very long afterwards that we all saw how true
this statement was. Ignorance of the fact, or wilful neglect
of its portent, was the rock upon which preceding foreign advisers and administrators in Persia had invariably split. No
one of them had ever experienced any difficulty in gaining the
confidence of the innermost diplomatic circles in Teheran — the
method of doing so was plain and even inviting — but the very
evident intimacy thus established by them with the representatives of certain foreign powers, which the Persian people believed were hostile to their aspirations, sealed the fate of any

such foreign adviser or administrator so far as winning the confidence and support of the Medjlis or of the Nationalist party was concerned.

The diplomatic corps at Teheran was composed at this time of the Russian, British, German, American, Italian, Austro-Hungarian and Dutch Ministers, and the Turkish Ambassador. With the exception of the first two and the Turkish Ambassador, three who had political rôles to play, these distinguished representatives had no greater task than to keep a number of their citizens and subjects on the salary and pension rolls of the bankrupt Persian Government. Most of these pensioners bore splendid titles, it being rare to find less than a colonel, while one Italian officer who was supposed to be in some manner dimly connected with the Persian War Office rejoiced in the self-created rank of full general.

This work is not put forth as a study of Persian geography, nor as a chronicle of social life in the oriental center of civilization, but it would be cruel to leave this subject without paying a tribute to the real authors of the fascinating and continuous round of gossip, scandal and small talk which so thoroughly enlivens existence in the European colony at Teheran. Imagine, if you will, a fast decaying government amid whose tottering ruins a heterogeneous collection of Belgian customs officers, Italian gendarmes, German artillery sergeants, French savants, doctors, professors and councilors of state, Austrian military instructors, English bank clerks, Turkish and Armenian courtiers, and last, but not least, a goodly sprinkling of Russian Cossack officers, tutors and drill instructors all go through their daily task of giving the Imperial Persian Government a strong shove toward bankruptcy, with a sly side push in the direction of their own particular political or personal interests. In this pleasant diversion the gentlemen and even the ladies of the foreign legations were somewhat peacefully engaged, when several unfortunate Americans landed on Persian soil with the truly extraordinary idea that they were to be employed under the orders of the Persian Government. Later, lest the gaiety of the scene should diminish, some ten or more Swedish officers were added to the list of those whom the *raiyat* of the provinces paid their tithe to maintain.

For several weeks before the financial law of June 13 was voted by the Medjlis, we had been seeking to obtain some accurate information as to Persia's financial condition.

The Customs service under Mons. Mornard had its own books and records, but there was no way of our getting reports from them at that time. Certainly none were volunteered. In the other departments of the Ministry of Finance there was nothing in the way of permanent or coherent records or statistics. The desks and chairs themselves were as eloquent of facts as the suave but uncommunicative Persian gentlemen who then presided over the financial destinies of their native land.

I might say that the Persian finances were tangled — very tangled — had there been any to tangle. There were no Persian finances in any ordinary sense of the word. The so-called Ministry of Finance, presided over by a succession of frequently changing Persian gentlemen whose sole claims to financial genius lay in their having run through their own money and thus become in need of pecuniary recuperation, was in reality an unorganized collection of under-officials who had charge of various bureaus or offices through which the internal taxes, called, generically, *maliat,* were supposed to be collected for the benefit of the Persian Government. There were no such things as civil service, or examinations or tests for fitness or integrity. The places were doled out by the different Ministers of Finance to those having sufficient family or political influence to obtain them. No official could be sure of

PRINCE SALARU'D-DAWLA.

The brother of Muhammad Ali and twice pretender to the throne.   He entered Persia and captured
Hamadan during the summer of 1911 with several thousand Kurdish tribesmen
from the Turkish frontier

retaining his post even over night, and the general atmosphere of the department might be summed up in the time-honored adage, *carpe diem.* There had never been any attempt made at centralizing the revenues in order that the Government might know just what it should receive from its various taxes and what it did not receive; nor was there any attempt to control the expenditure of such funds as did, in some mysterious manner, percolate into the coffers of the so-called treasury at Teheran. One of the first inquiries that I made was for the budget — the national budget — from which I hoped to gain some idea of the total gross revenues or receipts of the Government from all sources and of the amounts which were supposed to be allotted to the different ministries and departments for their maintenance and upkeep. I soon learned that no budget existed, although Mr. Lecoffre, of whom mention has been made heretofore, had spent nearly two years in working, under impossible conditions, to produce something which might be designated as a budget. This gentleman possessed more information as to the supposed source of revenue and the supposed expenditures of the different ministries and departments of the Government than could be accumulated from all the other so-called official records and accounts put together. From the day that he started upon the task of ascertaining where the money came from and how it was alleged to be spent he had been looked upon with suspicion by every minister of finance and tax-collector who had come into power, to say nothing of the low esteem in which he was held by the gentry of the Persian War Department, who claimed the time-honored privilege of disposing of about one-half of the total nominal revenues in exchange for conducting the commissariat, arsenals, general staff, medical corps, infantry, cavalry, and artillery divisions of the Persian regular army — a mythical corps worthy to take rank with the gnomes who disturbed the slumbers of Rip Van Winkle or with that most elusive of human conceptions, the Golden Fleece. During the eight months which I spent in Teheran — of which four were filled with active military preparations by the Government to defeat the filibustering expedition of the ex-Shah and his eccentric brother, the Prince Salaru'd-Dawla, I never encountered the Persian regular army in appreciable quantities except upon the requisitions for their pay presented at the end of each month or in the form of bills for large orders of uniforms and other equipment which it was the privilege of the War Office to submit to the Treasurer-general for liquidation.

Persia is divided into a number of provinces or districts, each having its capital city. The principal ones of these are Azarbayjan (capital, Tabriz); Mazandaran (capital, Sari); Ghilan (capital, Resht); Khorasan (capital, Meshed), all in the North, and Isfahan (capital, Isfahan), and Fars (capital, Shiraz), in the South. At each of these cities and towns, and at a great many other towns which were the centers of smaller districts and providences, there was supposed to be a financial agent of the Central Government whose duty it was to collect during the year the different taxes from the people and to remit them, minus the expenses incident to the collections and including his own compensation, to the Minister of Finance. Of the exact details of this system more will be said in another chapter. It is enough to state at this time that the Minister of Finance found it much easier to draw warrants or checks addressed to these different financial agents or tax-collectors and thus to smilingly honor the requisitions made upon him by his colleagues of the Ministries of War, Justice, Public Instruction, Interior, and Foreign Affairs, than ever to have any dealings upon the basis of vulgar cash. The question of whether any funds could ever be obtained upon these paper-writings, so copiously dispensed by every minister of finance, was entirely aside from the issue, and as each finance minister naturally strove to make a reputation for himself as a successful fiscal administrator, as well as to gratify the legitimate demands of his colleagues and of the public by punctually meeting in full all Government obligations of every description, it so happened that in the course of years an immense flock of these little paper birds had flown forth from the central treasury to settle in the pockets of more or less unsuspecting creditors of the Government, petty tradesmen, minor public employees and ignorant pensioners, to the amount of so many millions of dollars that no sane person would ever dream of attempting either to calculate the sum or to redeem the obligations. In speaking, therefore, of the public debt of Persia, no account is taken of this floating and intangible mass of quasi-obligations, constituting, as they do, a problem which only the all-curing hand of time can definitely settle.

On June 13, after the basic financial law which I had recommended to the Medjlis had been adopted, I asked His Excellency, Muawinu'd-Dwala, who had by that time become Minister of Finance, to please turn over to me, as Treasurer-general, in accordance with the terms of the new law, the bank balances and cash belonging to the public treasury. His Excellency smiled back at me in the most friendly manner and agreed that such was the proper course. Said he: " Monsieur Shuster, I am ready at once to transfer these important matters to you. Our current account is kept with the Imperial Bank of Persia. I believe that at present it consists of a deficit or overdraft of 440,000 tumans (about $400,000). Here is an order upon the bank instructing them to place the account to the credit of the new Treasurer-general." I thanked His Excellency, and upon that same day commenced my duties as Treasurer-general of the Persian Empire under the favoring auspices of this deficit and a cloud of urgent demands by

3

His Excellency's colleagues of the Cabinet for the payment of pressing obligations, all necessary, so I was informed, to keep the Persian Government from immediate disintegration, and totaling up to the modest sum of $700,000.

There was one department of the Ministry of Finance which came nearer to dealing with actual money than any others. This was the Imperial Mint, located several miles outside of the city, where, with rather antiquated and worn-out machinery, the Persian silver krans (worth about nine cents each in United States money) were coined from silver bars imported under contract by the Imperial Bank of Persia, which needed silver money in large quantities for its current business. I had sometime previously sent Mr. Dickey, one of my two American assistants, to inspect this plant and to prepare to take over its administration, which he had done.

I therefore found myself seated in the office which had been arranged for our occupation, looking across my desk at my other assistant, Mr. McCaskey, and trying to realize that I was in charge of the " entire finances, both collections and disbursements, of the Persian Empire."

A letter was sent to each one of the five banks doing business in Teheran, informing them that from that date no checks, drafts, warrants, orders of payment, or Government obligations of any kind, were valid or payable unless they bore the signature of the Treasurer-general. The banks were likewise informed that all balances or accounts standing to the credit of any government department or government official were to be turned in to the credit of the Treasurer-general, to be disposed of on his order. One result of this apparently heretofore unknown procedure was to gather in a list of comparatively small but very interesting accounts and balances, of the existence of which we should probably never otherwise have known. Among them was an account standing to the

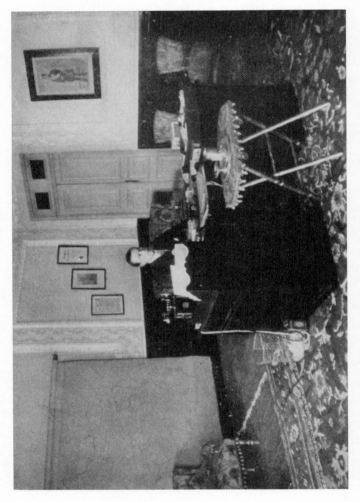

MR. SHUSTER IN HIS PRIVATE OFFICE IN ATABAK PALACE.

credit of Mons. Mornard, the Belgian Administrator of Customs, known as the " F. R. C. account," which was grossly irregular.

Of Persia's political situation at this time, it is not necessary to speak here at length. The Government was perhaps correctly described as a constitutional monarchy, although the monarchial features were limited to the existence of a Shah on the throne, represented, during his minority, by a Regent, and surrounded wherever he went by a large and expensive coterie of parasitic gentlemen who styled themselves members of His Majesty's Court. The real functions of government were vested in the Medjlis or National Parliament, composed of some eighty deputies, who were elected, according to the population, from the various provinces and districts of the Empire. To this body was submitted, from time to time, for approval, a cabinet of seven members, nominated under the direction of the Regent; but, as the Medjlis, according to the Persian constitutional decrees, had exclusive legislative power and, in addition, could instantly depose any cabinet by a vote of lack of confidence at any time, the real power lay in the representatives more or less chosen by the direct vote of the Persian people.

The two foreign powers which, to use their own words, had " special interests " in Persia, were Russia and Great Britain. As will be remembered, these two governments had signed a convention in the year 1907 in which they purported to define the geographical spheres of their respective interests, Russia in the north, and England in the southeastern corner, of the Persian Empire. Nominally, at least, the Persian Constitutional Government was that of a sovereign nation to which the diplomatic representatives of foreign European governments were duly accredited, as well as one from the United States, and this sovereignty had been expressly recognized and proclaimed by the voluntary action of the Russian and British nations in signing the Anglo-Russian Convention of 1907.

The Persian foreign debt consisted of several loans which had been made to the different shahs by the Russian Government and which had been consolidated through the *Banque d'Escompte de Perse,* a branch at Teheran of the Russian State Bank. There was also the so-called Indian Government loan made in the time of the former shahs by the British Government from the funds of the Indian Empire; and, lastly, there was the so-called Imperial Bank loan of 1911, which was ratified and approved just before our arrival at Teheran. Of the details of these loans more will be said in another chapter. In addition to this, there was a large and unknown amount of foreign claims against the Persian Government, most of which were unliquidated, but aggregating several millions of dollars.

This, then, was the general situation of the Persian Government on June 13, 1911, when I assumed charge of the financial affairs of that country.

CHAPTER III

IT seemed perfectly obvious to us that no headway at all
could be made toward straightening out Persia's financial
affairs unless full powers to deal with the chaotic situation
were conferred by proper authority upon those to be charged
with the task. It would have been entirely useless to attempt
to accomplish any definite results by acting in an advisory
capacity to the different ministers and other Cabinet officials
who, up to that time, had been occupying themselves with the
collection and disbursement of the revenues. These gentlemen
were neither equipped by experience, and training, nor suited
by character and disposition, to undertake the somewhat thank-
less task of stamping out the corruption and venality which
marked the administration of Persian finances, both at Teheran
and throughout the provinces.

If anything was to be done, therefore, it must be accomplished through the independent initiative of foreign
finance administrators free from the necessity of receiving
either the support or the approval of the Persian official who
might, from time to time, be occupying the post of Minister
of Finance, or from the control of the rapidly changing groups
who might constitute the Persian Cabinet.

My purpose in drafting the law of June 13, 1911, was to
establish a central organization to be known as the office of

the Treasurer-general of Persia, which should be responsible for and have charge of the collection and of the disbursement of all revenues and Government receipts, from whatever source derived — an office which should make and authorize all payments, for whatever purpose, in behalf of the central Government of Persia. Up to that time, collections of money had been made not only by the officials of the Ministry of Finance, but by certain departments of the Ministry of Posts and Telegraphs, of the Ministry of Justice, of the Ministry of the Interior, of the Ministry of Public Instruction, and by the Passport Bureau of the Ministry of Foreign Affairs. In like manner, these different government departments had been expending, without supervision or control, such funds as they were able to collect. There was no one office or department in which these various lines crossed; hence it was manifestly impossible for the Government to know, however desirous it might be, what the public revenues were, whence they came, or whither they went. If we had waited to perfect an organization before assuming this heavy responsibility, it is probable that some change would have occurred in the spirit or temper of those in authority, subject as they were to the constant intrigues and even threats of reactionary agents hostile to any improvement; and even the attempt to modernize the Persian fiscal system would have never been made. As it was, despite the handicaps under which those charged with the new law labored, and despite the abnormal conditions of war and disorder into which Persia was plunged but a few weeks after this law was passed, during the eight months of our work in Teheran a large proportion of the taxes stated to be due were collected both at the capital and throughout the provinces, the extraordinary expenses incident to the attempt of Muhammad Ali Mirza to regain the throne were promptly met, the salaries of the diplomatic representatives of Persia abroad were sent

HAJJI AGHA.

One of the few reactionary deputies of the Medjlis.
He took part in the plot to destroy the
Constitutional Government.

ALAU'D-DAWLA.

A powerful reactionary grandee. He was suspected of plotting in favor of the return of
Muhammad Ali and was shot in the streets
of Teheran on December 1, 1911.

MUMTAZU'D-DAWLA.

Minister of Finance, who assisted Mr. Shuster on
his arrival in Teheran. He was formerly the
President of the Medjlis.

MUTASHAMU'S-SALTANA.

Minister of Foreign Affairs, when the American
finance officials arrived at Teheran.

them for the first time in several years, all foreign obligations and the current salaries of the different ministries were promptly paid, and a complete and accurate record of every receipt and expenditure was kept in the central office of the Treasurer-general.

What there was about this plan or its proposed execution to excite the hostility of any foreign power, no matter what its legitimate interests might be in connection with Persia, it is difficult to imagine. Certainly, so far as the rights or interests of foreign creditors, whether governments or individuals, were concerned, the only change in the old order of things was by way of affording additional guarantees and safeguards for those payments. Yet the very day that this law was passed, although it had been discussed publicly in the Medjlis in several previous sessions, the Russian Legation openly declared war upon it and the *Russian Minister* announced that the Belgian Customs employees should not be subjected to the control or supervision of the American Treasurer-general, and even went so far as to threaten to have Russian troops seize the customs-houses in the north and put Russian officials in charge. During the next two weeks the Russian, French, German, Italian and Austro-Hungarian Legations at Teheran rained protests upon the Persian Foreign Office, many of them couched in the most undiplomatic, impolite and insulting language, in a brazen attempt to bulldoze the Persian Government into giving up its rights to act as it saw fit in this purely local and internal affair. The British and Dutch Legations, and Turkish Embassy, and, of course, the American Legation, kept clear.

In the course of this remarkable campaign, Count Quadt, then German Minister at Teheran, saw fit to send a written communication to the Persian Government, protesting against the infringement of German interests which he alleged would result from the checks in payment to certain German subjects in Teheran being signed by the Treasurer-general of Persia instead of by Mons. Mornard, the Administrator-general of Customs, as had previously been the case. On examination I found that these German "interests" consisted of two subsidies of 6,000 tumans ($5,400) paid annually to two German subjects who were in charge of the so-called German School and German Hospital, which has been established in Teheran on the subsidy demanded and obtained by one of the richest and most powerful nations of Europe from the impoverished Persian Government. Count Quadt, in his official communication, referred to the Treasurer-general of Persia, with delicate sarcasm, as "a certain Mr. Shuster." The Italian Chargé-d'Affaires, whose principal interest in Persia appears to have been to keep an aged and distinguished subject of his country on the pay-roll of the Persian Government as a military instructor with the title of general — although this gentleman was incapacitated from doing anything more active than passing his time in an arm chair — not to be outdone by his German diplomatic colleague, referred, in his protest addressed to the Persian Government, to the "so-called Treasurer-general."

Thus encouraged by Russia, Mons. Mornard let it be known that he did not propose to obey the law of the Government whose paid official he was, nor to recognize the American Treasurer-general. That he had good reason for taking this stand was made plain shortly afterwards, when, in fear of having his lucrative contract canceled by the Medjlis, as I had been compelled to threaten to recommend, he reluctantly turned over his balances, among which we found certain items which could only be explained on the ground of gross irregularity.

This harassing campaign kept up until the middle of July, when the Belgian Customs officials decided to agree to obey the law, and Mons. Mornard so informed me. It was not, however, until having drawn a number of checks on the Cus-

toms revenues in favor of various foreign employees in the
Persian service, it was found, on presenting them at the banks,
that they would not be honored, that he decided to take this
step.

Having once received the promise of the different banks that
they would respect the law of the Government and would not
honor checks signed by any one but the Treasurer-general, we
could afford to await patiently the time when the different
foreign employees, who had a natural desire to receive their
salaries, decided to desert their doughty diplomatic representatives and incur their displeasure in cashing checks signed by
an American.

In the meantime the new Treasury had been having some
difficulties with the Cabinet. The Prime Minister, Sipahdar,
had been very active in supporting my recommendations for the
new financial law, and he had on more than one occasion assured me of his entire support and coöperation in stamping out
abuses in the Government service. He was even kind enough
to admit that while he was a natural military genius, there
might be some things which he did not know about the organization of the War Department — as to which he would gladly
have my advice. Inasmuch as that branch of the Government
was the roosting-place for the most brilliant galaxy of uniformed loafers, masquerading as generals, commissaries, and
chiefs of staffs, of petty grafters, amiable cutthroats and all-
round scoundrels which it has ever been my fortune to encounter,
the Sipahdar's generous admission greatly increased my opinion
of him. He was particularly anxious to know when I was
going to be able to raise some ready cash at the Bank, and he
explained that it was only by his great personal influence and
prestige with the people of Persia, that he was able to keep the
governmental fabric from dropping apart until a little pecuniary
assistance could be furnished for the gallant men of the regular

army.   On June 4 (before the finance law was actually passed
by the Medjlis) I had arranged with Mr. A. O. Wood, the
chief manager of the Imperial Bank of Persia, for a temporary
advance of 250,000 tumans, to be secured on the new loan.   At
seven o'clock that same evening the Sipahdar's carriage drove
into Atabak Park, and I was requested to drive to the private
residence of His Excellency, who awaited me there with the
Minister of Finance.

I arrived at his beautiful park just about dusk, and was conducted between long lines of soldiers and military gentlemen
of varying rank, back through the grounds to a small out-
residence, on the flat tile roof of which handsome rugs, tables
and chairs had been arranged.   Here I found the Minister of
Finance nervously pacing up and down.   Lamps were lighted,
the inevitable tea and cigarettes served, and we sat down to
await His Excellency's arrival.

The evening was a very clear and beautiful one, and from
the roof we could look out over the walls of the city towards
the snow-covered mountains some twelve miles away.   Nestling
in their lower folds and at their feet were the summer quarters
of the different Legations, — Zargundeh, Gulhak and Tedjrich,
and the villages and summer palaces belonging to the grandees
of Teheran.

Of a sudden there were hoarse commands, the grounding
of arms, much " salaaming " by the double row of servants
standing in front of the house, — a quick, nervous step on
the stairs, and the great Sipahdar had arrived.

A casual military salute, an air of great preoccupation, and
he was seated.   Before we could begin any conversation a venerable priest of Islam presented himself, and approaching the
Sipahdar appeared to ask some favor.   As he lingered a moment, the Prime Minister called a near-by officer, gave him
a sharp order, and the priest retired.

NASIRU'L-MULK, REGENT OF PERSIA

In front of the Parliament building shortly after his arrival in Teheran in February, 1911 to assume the Regency. The figures in the front row from left to right are: Samsamu's-Saltana, the Regent, Sipahdar-i-Azam, Mutashamu's-Saltana, Amir Azam, Sardar-i-Asad and Sardar-i-Jang.

The solemn-visaged Minister of Finance shook his head slowly, and spoke to me in French:

"You see, Mons. Shuster, what a dominating man His Excellency is, and how great is his power. Did you notice that he refused the supplication of a "mullah" and that the prisoner in whose behalf the appeal was made is to be hanged to-morrow morning?"

Once free to devote a few moments of his valuable time to us, the Sipahdar referred lightly to the financial needs of the War Department. Speaking in Persian (for he knew very little French), he had the Minister of Finance interpret to me and explain the dangerous crisis which confronted us. "If the *poul* [money] is not forthcoming," declared the Premier, "even our own lives will not be safe!"

This was the first, but not the last time that I was able to distinguish the ever-recurring word *poul* in conversations in Persian.

I made bold to describe to His Excellency the same dangerous financial crisis which we of the Treasury were endeavoring to live through; then asked him what sum was absolutely the minimum with which the raging troops could be temporarily held in check.

The Premier pulled a slip of paper from his pocket and handed it to the Minister of Finance to read to me. As he did so, his feelings apparently overcame him and he stepped down-stairs for a few moments. The Finance Minister gravely read the items and the total. The trifling sum of 406,000 tumans was a *sine qua non*. Of this, nearly half was not for the unpaid troops, but for stores, uniforms, artillery horses, and incidentals.

I made no comment. The Premier returned with a busy but anxious look. I thought I saw the eye-signals cross; perhaps I was mistaken.

Said the Minister of Finance : " His Excellency requests your answer as to this important matter."

I threw up my right hand in a despairing gesture: *"C'est impossible, Excellence."*

The Sipahdar jumped as if he had been shot. Volley after volley of eloquent persuasion and martial imprecation seemed to pour from his lips. The amiable Finance Minister grew pale and advised me that I was making a mistake. I tried to ascertain from His Excellency, in the French language, whether he knew any successful method of extracting blood from a stone. He had nothing to suggest, except that the funds should be forthcoming.

Three hours later we compromised on 100,000 tumans, and in the light of subsequent experience and knowledge even that payment has troubled my conscience at times.

As I passed out, I could almost hear the whisper of His Excellency the Premier to His Excellency the Minister of Finance : " The *faranghi* fights hard, but, *inshallah,* we will get him next time."

Eleven days passed, during each one of which I had the honor of at least one call from His Excellency, Amir Azam, Vice-minister of War, who outdid Verestchagin in painting the horrors of mutiny, rapine and bloodshed which would shortly result from the unwillingness of the Treasurer-general to produce the modest sums demanded by that great patriot, the Premier, Sipahdar. Nothing but a heart of flint coupled with an empty coffer could have resisted his pathetic appeals.

On June 15, just two days after the finance law giving the Treasurer-general absolute control of the Government's moneys was passed, His Excellency Sipahdar arose in the Medjlis and voiced his displeasure with the fact that an arbitrary restraint was being put upon him in the performance of his onerous duties as Premier and Minister of War. As he looked into the unsympathetic faces of the deputies, who all knew of his valiant efforts to secure cash for the War Office, his anger rose and he strode proudly from the chamber. Stepping into his carriage, which with its mounted escort, awaited him at the gate, he remarked to his coachman, " *Buru faranghistan !* " the meaning of which is, " Drive me to Europe." The Premier's carriage passed swiftly out the city gate and started up the two hundred and twenty mile road to Enzeli on the Caspian Sea. At this same time the rumor spread that a brother of the ex-Shah, Prince Salaru'd-Dawla, had captured the city of Tabriz, in Northwestern Persia, promising the people that if they would seat him on the throne, he would abolish all taxes except those necessary to supply his personal expenses. The public mind was therefore divided as to whether the infuriated Premier would join the ex-Shah's brother or pass over the Caspian to Russia and Europe.

For a week preceding this event the Regent, Nasiru'l-Mulk, had been strongly intimating his desire to leave Persia, alleging that the Medjlis had passed a new court budget, greatly reducing the allowances for that purpose, without consulting him. His Highness sent for me on June 8 to come to his private residence, and for three hours discussed his troubles and anxieties, which were, beyond doubt, very real. I told His Highness that his departure from the country at that time, or even the rumor of it, would not only greatly embarrass the new financial work, but would throw the Government into disorder generally.

He promised to give up the idea, but after talking the situation over with some of the deputies, we deemed it wise to take the matter up with Sir George Barclay, the British Minister, with the suggestion that Sir Edward Grey, the British Secretary of State for Foreign Affairs, should send a personal cable message to the Regent, who knew and highly regarded Sir Edward, urging him to remain in Teheran. This was done, but in the meantime His Highness had apparently abandoned his intention of going.

During this period I had almost daily talks with His Highness, who seemed greatly worried by the situation in Persia and extremely pessimistic as to the ability of the people to hold the Government together. There was constant friction between the Cabinet and the Medjlis, and intense animosity between the different political parties or groups themselves.

The sudden departure of the Sipahdar had added to the confusion and uncertainty. The other Cabinet ministers were holding frequent telegraphic conversations with him at Resht, where he arrived by the 18th. His anger had apparently cooled somewhat by that time, and though he still asserted his desire to go to Europe for his health, the other ministers were of the opinion that he should either come back to the capital or resign.

In the meantime I had been attending the sessions of the Cabinet, in an endeavor to get the ministers to realize the seriousness of the situation and cease demanding impossible sums of money. The loudest in his complaints and dire predictions of impending disaster was His Excellency Amir Azam, now rejoicing in the title and dignity of Acting Minister of War. The Amir Azam was a man whose general reputation would warrant a long sentence in any workhouse. I had an agent look into some of the financial transactions of the War Office and particularly the private bank balances of the Acting Minister. When, therefore, in a council of the ministers of June 19, at which I was present, he proclaimed that a general rising of the " Army of Teheran " would take place the following day, if a mere 42,000 tumans was not at once forthcoming for their pay and rations, I politely asked him what disposition had been made of the similar sum which I

AMIR AZAM (IN LEFT CENTER WITH SWORD), VICE-MINISTER OF WAR
With his personal staff.

had given him for another month's arrears only ten days before. "Gone," said his Excellency; "all disbursed to the poor, starving troops of the army." "Have you none of that money left?" I said. "Not a kran remains in the war-chest," he replied. I thought it convenient at this point to pull out a private memorandum which I had brought with me, showing that His Excellency had deposited the last month's pay and several other sums for military purposes, in all 83,000 tumans, with a native banker, with whom it rested at that moment while the predicted rising of the troops was being staged by the Amir's gallant officers of the line.

Reading the dates and amounts of the deposits from my private memorandum, I asked him whether they were not correct.

His Excellency, Amir Azam, Vice and Acting Minister of War, lifted his two hundred and forty pounds of brain and adipose tissue to his full height of six feet, five. Placing his hand upon his heart, and looking proudly at his distinguished colleagues of the Council, he demanded to know whether his honor was being aspersed. As there seemed to be some doubt on that point, he passed on in his discourse, concluding his remarks with the statement that if he had 83,000 tumans to his credit, he was the last to know it. This latter statement apparently impressed the gentlemen of the Cabinet as the height of improbability, so that it was suggested that His Excellency summon his confidential accountant. This was done, and we sat around, at my request, until the accountant arrived. The Amir arose, stepped out, held a hurried conversation with his faithful keeper of the war-chest, and returning, with a metallic smile of joy and friendship upon his countenance, assured the Council and myself that I was right — in fact, correct — since he had just learned, to his intense surprise, that the preceding month's payment had not been made to the troops (although His Excellency had so directed some time ago), and it was *that sum* for which the army had been clamoring. It was all a *mauvaise intelligence*. By this simple means the rising of the troops was successfully postponed.

On this same evening our organization was strengthened by the arrival of Mr. F. S. Cairns, who had been appointed Director of Taxation and my principal assistant before we left Washington, but who had just been able to reach Teheran from the Philippine Islands, where he had been serving as Collector of Customs of the Port of Iloilo.

On June 23 the Sipahdar was reported to have telegraphed from Resht to the Regent, stating that he would return to Teheran and take up his duties if certain articles of the finance law of June 13 were modified, so as to allow him a greater participation in deciding upon the disposition to be made of the public revenues. There was loud mirth in the Medjlis when this statement was reported.

There were likewise rumors of the formation of an " Anti-American Society " among the Persians, principally among the so-called *Mustofis,* or Persian accountants, who had to do with the supervision of the *maliat* taxes in the provinces.

Strikes by the employees of the various ministries were engineered every day or so, and we were compelled to announce that any employee refusing duty would be permanently dropped from the rolls. In the meantime I had taken over all the offices and bureaus of the Ministry of Finance, leaving the Minister and Vice-Minister, with the Secretary-General and *Chef de Cabinet,* alone in their glory and undisturbed by the necessity of giving any orders or signing any Government obligations whatever.

Ever since the 13th of June, Mons. Mornard and the Russian Minister, Mons. Poklewski-Koziell, had been endeavoring by alternate threats and persuasions to get the Imperial Bank

of Persia to honor Mornard's checks, the principal one of
which was to be for a payment of 360,000 roubles said to be
due to the Russian Government for a shipment of second-hand
rifles which that bold financier, the Sipahdar, had purchased
some months previously in behalf of the Persian Government.
These arms were to be delivered to the Persian War Office in
Persia, but they had not yet reached the port of Enzeli.   The
price worked out about three times that for which the same
arms could be obtained on the market in Europe.   It may be
properly left to the Russian Government and the Sipahdar to
state where the difference went.

The Chief Director of the Imperial Bank declined, however, to do otherwise than obey the law of the Medjlis, and
as I had authorized him to state to the Russian Minister that
the sum would be promptly paid on delivery of the arms, the
latter and Mons. Mornard were forced to abandon their position.

Up to this time I had never seen Mons. Mornard, and as
the Cabinet, on June 29, had adopted a resolution calling upon
him to obey the law of June 13, which he had thus far failed
to do, I wrote to the Acting Premier, Mutashamu's-Saltana,
stating that I could no longer permit the situation to continue,
and that if immediate action were not taken to secure Mons.
Mornard's recognition of the authority of the Medjlis and its
laws, I would be compelled to lay the case before that body
direct.

On July 2 the Cabinet " resigned," but I soon learned that
its members expected to continue the performance of their duties.   The " resignation " of a cabinet in Persia is usually a
mere figure of speech, indicating at worst that some of the
members are vexed at something.

During this time the British Minister let it be known that
while he was not taking any part in the controversy with

4

Mornard, he favored the financial plans and organization which we were endeavoring to put into effect.

The entire Belgian force in the Customs department were threatening to resign *en bloc,* if they were to be placed under the control of the Treasurer-general, and this, coupled with the menacing attitude of the Russian Government, had made the Persian Cabinet extremely nervous. Furthermore, there were some members of the Cabinet, such as the Acting Premier and Minister of Foreign Affairs, Mutashamu's-Saltana, who I believe were not over-anxious that any serious change should be effected in the previous methods of conducting fiscal affairs. This distinguished Cabinet officer had already presented to me for payment a claim of his own, amounting to some 14,000 tumans, for unrewarded services while he was a member of the Turco-Persian Boundary Commission several years before. Indeed, there were not many Persian gentlemen who had ever been in political office who could not present any number of claims on the Government for divers services rendered, but not satisfactorily recognized by an ungrateful nation.

Finally, on July 8, the Council of Ministers demanded that Mons. Mornard should present himself and state whether or not he proposed to recognize and obey the law of the Medjlis of June 13, involving as it did the control by the Treasurer-general of all financial departments of the Persian Government, including the Customs service. Mons. Mornard presented himself at 10 o'clock in the morning. After a long discourse in French, in which he recounted the work of the Belgian Customs officials and expounded the difficulties of making any change whatsoever in their existing method of conducting the business, he stated that he, of course, had never had any other intention than that of obeying the law. The Acting Premier asked me whether I had anything to say, and I replied that I had not come to the Council to indulge in any "pourparlers" with any one as to whether any official of the Government would obey the law or not, but that, inasmuch as I had heard Mons. Mornard state that he did intend to obey the law, there appeared to be no need for further discussion and it only remained for him to do so. Immediately after this conversation ended, Mons. Mornard showed himself extremely polite and attentive, and evinced a desire to discuss the situation of the Customs service and the method of handling funds thereof, of all which I was very glad to talk with him. He promised to send a list of all deposits of Government funds which he had in the different banks and to submit the usual requisitions for expenses which had already been prescribed by my office.

I had by this time become acquainted with the Military Attaché of the British Legation, Major C. B. Stokes, whose four-year term of service in that capacity would shortly expire. I had been warned against Major Stokes by several people who claimed that he was a "scout" or spy of the British and Russian Governments, and was inimical to the aspirations of the Persian people. He was an officer in the British-Indian Army, and spoke, read and wrote Persian with facility, in addition to having made many trips throughout the country and being thoroughly acquainted with the manners, habits, customs and character of the people and with the different political elements throughout the provinces. I had for some time been formulating a project for the formation of a special gendarmerie force which should be under my direct orders and should assist and coöperate with the civilian officers of the Treasury in the collection of the different kinds of taxes throughout the Empire. It is true that the existing gendarmerie of the Persian Government was supposed to lend a hand in this task, but apart from the fact that they were almost as mythical a body as the Persian regular army, and, outside Teheran, were quite as apt to

make away with the taxes as to assist in their collection, they
were under the orders of the Persian Minister of the Interior
and commanded by some officers at Teheran who did not belong
to the elements desirous of seeing the finances of the country
put upon a solid basis.   It seemed vitally necessary, therefore,
that if any serious effort was to be made to collect the taxes due
to the Government in the places outside of the capital and two
or three other large centers, like Tabriz, Kazvin, Isfahan and
Shiraz, a new force would have to be organized especially for
this purpose.   I planned, therefore, to build up a department
to be known as the Treasury Gendarmerie, which should be an
integral part of the office of Treasurer-general.   It was hoped,
within a year, to enlist and instruct several thousands of men
for this purpose, and, in the course of several years, to increase
the force to 10,000 or 12,000, with which it would be possible
to practically assure the collection of the entire revenue nominally due the Government.   The Persian peasants, laboring-
classes and small property-owners are not intractable in the
matter of paying their dues to the Government, but the peculiar
condition in that country demanded that the Government
should be able to show the necessary force with which to exact
the taxes before it could hope to receive them on the mere demand of civilian officials.   After a number of talks with Major Stokes I became convinced that he was an ideal man to undertake the work of organizing and of instructing, along
technical lines, the officers and men who should compose this
force; and finding that he was loath to leave Persia, in whose
future prospects and regeneration he was sincerely interested,
I made the proposal to him, informally, that he should accept
the post of chief of this future gendarmerie organization, under
my own direct supervision and orders.   I thereupon wrote to
Sir George Barclay, British Minister, stating that, upon the
termination of Major Stokes' services as military attaché to

MAJOR C. B. STOKES, OF THE BRITISH-INDIAN ARMY.
Mr. Shuster sought to put him in charge of the Treasury Gendarmerie. The appointment was blocked through Russia's opposition.

COLONEL HJALMARSEN.
The Swedish officer who was placed in charge of the road gendarmerie of Persia.

the Legation, I would be pleased to secure him in some manner for the purpose of organizing the proposed Treasury Gendarmerie. After some correspondence with the Legation, I was informed, in writing, on July 22, by the British Minister, that he was authorized by his Government to tell me "that Major Stokes, before accepting the command of the gendarmerie, will have to resign his commission in the Indian Army." As the original tender made by me to Major Stokes contained no suggestion that he would be required, in order to accept it, to resign from the British-Indian Army, and as the situation would have been equally well met from the standpoint of the Persian Government by his being *seconded* for three years, I naturally assumed that on his tendering his resignation, in response to the condition thus made by his own Government,— a thing which he immediately did by cable,— it would be accepted. After two weeks, during which we had regarded the matter as practically settled, I was astonished to learn that the British Government had presented a *note verbale* on August 8 to the Persian Foreign Office "warning the Persian Government that it ought not to persist in the appointment of Major Stokes unless he is not to be employed in Northern Persia." This remarkable communication went on to say that "if the Persian Government does persist, His Majesty's [British] Government will recognize Russia's right [*sic*] to take such steps as she thinks are necessary in order that her interests in Northern Persia may be safeguarded."

This action was followed on August 19 by another note repeating "the warning given on the 8th instant."

Thus the British Government, presumably acting in its right senses, had received a request for the services of a British subject for a period of three years to take part in the reorganization of one branch of the Persian Government and had formally expressed its consent, requiring only that the individual in question should resign his commission in the British-Indian Army, and, upon his doing so, in good faith, had suddenly executed a complete *volte face* and without any change in the legal aspects of the situation or in the rights of the parties concerned, had not only receded from its promise and agreement, but had combined with another foreign government in a cold-blooded attempt to intimidate the Persian Government in the exercise of its most elementary sovereign rights.

I had desired to secure Major Stokes, not because he was a British subject, but in spite of that fact, and solely in the belief that he was the most efficient and capable man for the important work which was to be done, and because the prompt and thorough execution of this task was vital to my whole scheme of financial reform in Persia. The Treasury Gendarmerie was not to be a dress-parade feature which might adorn the fiscal organization which we were endeavoring to create, but it was an indispensable part thereof, since without a well-trained, well-equipped force to assist the tax-collectors, and, by their mere presence, to maintain a certain degree of order in the provinces and distant districts, there was no possible hope of getting in the revenues. I knew perfectly well that, through personal acquaintance with them, I could probably have secured the services of any one of a number of retired officers of the United States army who would have done everything possible under the circumstances; but Major Stokes met the requirements of the situation exactly and possessed qualifications which no other man lacking his experience could possibly have, however intelligent he might be, and it was for this reason alone that he was selected. To this day I have never discovered just what were those indefinite "interests" in Northern Persia on which so much stress was laid by both the British and Russian Governments. It seems clear that they were not defined in the Anglo-Russian Convention of 1907.

It is equally clear that the Persian Government did not know of them. Nor did the British Government know of them as late as July 22; as otherwise how could that Government have contemplated accepting Major Stokes' resignation from the British-Indian Army in order that he might sign the contract which I had offered him to serve as Chief of the Treasury Gendarmerie?

To complete the record of this affair it should be mentioned that the Russian Legation, on August 19, addressed a memorandum to the Persian Foreign Office stating that " the Imperial Government of Russia, for reasons explained at the time to the Persian Government, considers the engagement by the latter of Major Stokes as chief of the armed forces —called gendarmerie — for the collection of taxes as incompatible with its interests, and I am charged to protest against that appointment. Failing satisfaction, the Imperial Government would reserve to itself the right to take such measures as it might judge to be necessary for the safeguarding of its interests in the North of Persia."

On learning of the first note presented to the Persian Government by the British Legation, I expressed the following views to the British Minister at Teheran:

I beg leave to address you, unofficially, on a subject of great importance to my work here. I have been intensely surprised to learn this evening that your Government has conveyed to the Persian Foreign Minister a note of warning or protest against my proposed employment of Major Stokes in the Treasury Gendarmerie. You are doubtless aware of the course of this matter up to the present. Need I say that in view of the tone of the communication which your Government instructed you to address to me on July 22 last, in effect that Major Stokes could accept the position upon resigning from the Indian Army, the apparent *volte face* indicated by their note of to-day is almost incomprehensible.

. . . Does your Government quite realize the position in which it is placing me before the Persian people and their Government in now suddenly joining another power to prevent the exercise of the most elemental act of sovereignty by this country whose independence and integrity both of those foreign powers have solemnly pledged themselves, jointly and severally, to respect?

My personal feelings are of no importance, but the success or failure of my mission here is of moment both to Persia, which entrusted her financial affairs to my care, and to my countrymen who are not unnaturally interested in the creditable accomplishment of my task.

Before accepting this work I was given clearly to understand that neither of the two principal powers having interests here offered any objection to my undertaking it, and surely such a statement was something more than an empty pledge.

No one, I am assured, knows better than yourself that the choice of Major Stokes was actuated by no political motive in the faintest degree, and no thinking person could suspect me of any intention to engage in political jobbery here,— a thing which would only make me ridiculous and spell absolute ruin for my work.

What, then, am I to think when I see the first vital step which I undertake in the task of bringing order out of chaos here obstructed and relentlessly opposed by the very two nations who have time and again professed their sincere desire to see the progress and prosperity of the stricken country which I am seeking to serve?

Does your Foreign Office fully realize that in adopting its most recent attitude in this affair it is inevitably producing the impression on the Persian People that it is in reality opposed to the successful accomplishment of my work, in addition to forcing me to assume that I can count on no friendly moral assistance from your Government in a vital matter of this kind?

If this were a normal place, where well-trained, capable and experienced men could be had, in comparative abundance, the result (though not the principle) of your Government's objections might not be so bad, but here, where, as you know, good men are extremely scarce, the attitude adopted amounts to a virtual veto of my efforts and a nullification of my chances of success.

I hope and trust that in some manner your Government may be brought to see the matter in this light, apart from what I am frank to say seems to me a totally uncalled-for interference in the purely routine and internal affairs of the financial organization which I am endeavoring to build up.

Personally, I feel so strongly on the subject that I am forced to contemplate the necessity of setting right my own countrymen, at least with a formal public statement of all my experiences in this connection since arriving at Teheran. Needless to say, such a course would be much to my regret, but there is such a thing as just dealing even between Governments and individuals, and certainly in this case I feel that my own record is sufficiently clear to bear the light of the most thorough inspection.

From a review of this incident it is manifest that unless the Convention of 1907 was a farce and a deception, by its own terms it had no bearing whatever on the proposed appointment of Major Stokes as a financial aid to the Treasurer-general. First, because the preamble of that document, as published to the world, avows that Britain and Russia mutually engage to respect the integrity and independence of Persia, and declares the sincere desire of the two signatories for the preservation of order throughout that country and its peaceful development. Yet one of the primary elements of sovereignty is the right of a country to manage its internal affairs, at least within the limitations of the law of nations, and surely the appointment of its own officials by any country can be considered as nothing else. Secondly, the plain purpose of the Convention was that neither signatory power should seek for herself, or support in favor of her subjects, any concessions of a political or commercial nature — such as concessions for railways, banks, telegraphs, roads, transport, insurance, etc.— within the so-called sphere of influence of the other power. But this was no case of a " concession." Major Stokes is not a bank or a railroad, or a political or commercial concession of any kind, and the voluntary tender to him of any post in the Persian service could, by no stretch of the imagination, be converted into a " seeking " or " supporting " by Great Britain of such a concession.

The second fallacy in the position of the two powers lay in the fact that the British Foreign Office itself never thought of construing Major Stokes' appointment into a violation of even the so-called " spirit of the Convention " until Russia raised the point. The evidence of this has been cited above.

Without in any manner recognizing the application or validity of the Convention as relating to herself, Persia might well have pointed out that where the *language* of a document is plain and clear there is no room for interpretation of the *spirit*.

Between individuals such action as that taken by the British Government towards the Persian Government or the Treasurer-general would clearly be considered bad faith. Sir Edward Grey, British Secretary of State for Foreign Affairs, has on more than one occasion since sought to explain his action in failing to keep his plain agreement in regard to permitting Persia to utilize the services of Major Stokes, on the grounds that Major Stokes' appointment would be a violation of what he, Sir Edward Grey, chose to term the " spirit " of the Anglo-Russian Convention of 1907. The use of the expression " spirit " would seem to indicate clearly that there was nothing in the language of the document itself which could justify any such interpretation. Furthermore, if the appointment of Major Stokes would have been a violation of the so-called " spirit " of that Convention, might one not inquire why this proposed violation was not recognized by the British Foreign Office at the very outset of the negotiations, and how was it that the British Foreign Office consented to that violation on condition that Major Stokes resign his commission in the British-Indian Army ? The truth is that the Russian semi-official press, and particularly the *Novoe Vremya,* had begun to bluster about the appointment, doubtless inspired by the Foreign Office at St. Petersburg, and inasmuch as the tension in Europe over the Moroccan affair had greatly increased at this time, Sir Edward Grey apparently felt himself compelled to *invent some pretext* for withdrawing from his previous promise to allow Major Stokes' appointment lest he do anything to displease the Russian Government to which he undoubtedly looked for some form of support in case of unpleasant eventualities with Germany. Under these circumstances was born that novel and marvelous doctrine of the "spirit of the Convention" under which each of the powers signatory might interpret any action which the Persian Government contemplated taking as an infringement of the self-created interests, mentioned but never defined with any degree of accuracy in that famous document.

On Sunday, July 9, the flighty Sipahdar returned quietly to Teheran, and locking himself in his house and denying himself to all visitors except a few particular favorites and confidants, he allowed the rumor to spread that he was contemplating taking some drastic action against the Medjlis and the Treasurer-general, who he claimed had shorn him of the power and privileges which he had won with his sword at the head of the Nationalist forces in 1909. In the meantime the Prince Salaru'd-Dawla, brother of the ex-Shah, had entered Persia from Asiatic Turkey in the neighborhood of Bagdad, and was gathering Kurdish tribesmen about him in what he announced to be another attempt to establish himself upon the throne of Persia. The Government forces in the neighborhood of Hamadan seemed utterly unable to cope with him and the situation was getting so bad that I felt compelled to point out to the Regent that if some adequate measures were not taken to check this filibustering movement, the most serious consequences might follow.

On July 1, Mons. Mornard not having kept his promise to turn over his bank balance to me, I both wrote and wired to him at his summer residence outside Teheran, where he was staying, telling him that if I did not hear that all Customs balances had been transferred to my credit in the banks by four o'clock that afternoon, I would be compelled to report his refusal to do so to the Medjlis and to consider his action as a breach of faith. Shortly after sending this telegram and before the written message which I had despatched by a mounted gendarme had reached him, he wired me to take possession of the Customs funds in the bank and to exhibit his message as authority for doing so.

On July 13, fearing that the Russian Bank (Banque d'Escompte de Perse) might endeavor to discredit the new administration of the Treasurer-general by failing to transfer from the ample balance of Customs receipts, which they had on hand, the funds necessary to pay the instalment due on that day of the interest and amortization charges on the Russian debt, I went to the bank that morning, saw the Acting Manager, Mons. Diamantopoulos, and obtained his statement that the transfer had been duly made on his books and that the balance of this amount, in accordance with the loan agreement, had been placed to the credit of the Government in the name of the Treasurer-general.

The Medjlis had by this time approved several proposals which I had made to them for the employment, under contract, of a number of additional American assistants, and I was endeavoring to select suitable men to bring out for that purpose. I received several letters during the next few days from the British Legation asking whether I would not be willing to accept a Swedish officer to take charge of the Treasury Gendarmerie, or whether I would not agree to employ Major Stokes only in the so-called southern sphere of Persia. Neither suggestion was of any practical value, since the Swedish officer was not familiar with the language or the country. As to the second suggestion, it was perfectly well known that the Persian Government had steadfastly refused to recognize any division of the country into " spheres of influence." Indeed, one of the great difficulties which I had encountered in endeavoring to secure the authorization of the Medjlis for the employment under contract of Major Stokes had been the fear that I would do just what England now suggested — send him only into the South, thereby tacitly recognizing by my official

EPHRAIM KHAN, CHIEF OF THE POLICE AND GENDARMERIE OF TEHERAN.
He did more than any other to defeat Muhammad Ali. "Persia's Garibaldi,"
as he is called, was killed in battle May 19, 1912.

acts the so-called " spheres of influence " which Russia and
England had endeavored to impose upon the Persian Government.

On July 17 I was shown a note which another official of
the Diplomatic Corps had received from the British Minister,
conveying the contents of a cabled despatch from the British
Foreign Office which directed the British Legation to side with
the Russian Government in the dispute over the control of the
Customs funds. I was reliably informed that the British Minister had received a despatch from Sir Edward Grey, stating
that the general European situation (meaning thereby the Moroccan question) was such that the British Government felt
compelled to take this attitude. I heard that this despatch
had greatly disturbed the British Minister and he had felt
compelled to communicate to one of his colleagues its general
purport.

On July 18, when I had just begun to learn the source of
some of the Government revenues, a new and startling compli-
cation suddenly arose. Late that night the telegraph brought
us the news that Muhammad Ali, the ex-Shah of Persia, who
was supposed to be interned at Odessa under the watchful eye
of the Russian Government, had landed that day with a small
following at Gumesh-Teppeh, a port on the Caspian Sea — on
Persian soil, but very near the Russian frontier.[1] This was

---

[1] The news sent by the London *Times'* correspondent at Teheran on July
18 was as follows:

" The ex-Shah Mohammed Ali has landed at Gumesh Tepe with some
half-a-dozen followers, said to include his brother Shua-es-Sultaneh and the
notorious Ameer Bahadur Jang. He is expected to proceed on Thursday to
Astrabad, which is at present without a Governor.

" Since the ex-Shah lately left Odessa, ostensibly for Vienna and Carlsbad,
persistent rumors have circulated here of his approaching return to Persia.
The Persian Government drew the attention of Russia to these rumors, as
also to the presence of the Shah's agent, Arshad-ed-Dowleh, who recently
passed through Baku, rumor says, with a false passport and a large number of rifles and cartridges. The Russian Government refused Persia any
assistance, and Arshad-ed-Dowleh proceeded to the Turcoman country.

" The ex-Shah's intrigues with the Turcomans now extend over a period

the proverbial bolt from the blue, for while rumors of such a thing had been current ever since the incursion of his brother, Salaru'd-Dawla, into Western Persia, few people in Teheran believed that Russia would have the face to violate so openly the solemn stipulation which she had signed with Great Britain and with Persia less than two years before.

of nearly a year. *The Persian Government last autumn drew Russia's attention to them in connection with the question of payment of the quarterly instalment of his pension.* By the Protocol of 1909 Russia expressly undertook to prevent any such intrigues, and it was stipulated that in such an event the ex-Shah should forfeit his pension. The ex-Shah has now reached Persia in a Russian boat, and it is widely asserted that his movements through Russia must have been known to the authorities.

" *Satisfaction at the prospect of the ex-Shah's return is openly expressed in Russian circles here.* It appears to be assumed that the country is thoroughly disgusted with the Mejliss. The ex-Shah's agents secured the support of the Shahsevens and the Turcomans. His brother, Salar-ed-Dowleh, has now declared for him in Kurdistan; the Sipahdar at Teheran is also not averse to the return of an autocratic régime, and his recent journey to Resht is connected therewith. These calculations overlook the surprising unity which the Mejliss and the Press have recently displayed, apparently scenting danger. There is no reason to doubt the loyalty to the Mejliss of the 1200 Bakhtiari who are at present at Teheran, and should this continue the ex-Shah's attempt is not likely to succeed. He will find a difficulty in persuading the Shahsevens and Turcomans to operate outside their own districts. It is, moreover, unknown what financial resources he commands."

CHAPTER IV

THE ATTEMPT OF MUHAMMAD ALI MIRZA, EX-SHAH OF PERSIA,
TO REGAIN THE THRONE. RUSSIAN INTRIGUES AND CON-
NIVANCE. MILITARY OPERATIONS AGAINST THE EX-SHAH
AND HIS BROTHERS. SUCCESS OF THE NATIONALIST TROOPS.
DEFEAT AND DEATH OF ARSHADU'D-DAWLA.

THE first despatches regarding the landing of Muhammad
Ali at Gumesh-Teppeh stated that he would be at the town
of Astarabad by the following Thursday, two days later.

On July 19, the day after the news arrived, all the political
parties at Teheran came together and a coalition Cabinet was
presented to the Medjlis and approved. This was composed as
follows: Sipahdar, Premier (without portfolio), Samsamu's-
Saltana (the Bakhtiyari chieftain), Minister of War; Wuthuqu'd-Dawla, Minister of the Interior; Ghavamu's-Saltana
(brother of Wuthuqu'd-Dawla), Minister of Justice; Mushiru'd-
Dawla, Minister of Posts and Telegraphs; Hakimu'l-Mulk,
Minister of Public Instruction; Mauwinu'd-Dawla, Minister of
Finance; and Mutashamu's-Saltana, Minister of Foreign
Affairs.

On this same evening the Medjlis passed a rigorous law declaring a state of siege, and placing the execution of martial
law in the hands of the Council of Ministers and the Minister
of War.

Despite this brave show there was an absolute panic in all
quarters of Teheran. The Nationalists feared that the ex-Shah
was going to be restored to power by the Russians and that
the city would be given over to be pillaged by the Turcoman

tribesmen who were accompanying him. The Royalists, or reactionary element, equally feared that reprisals would be made on them by the Nationalists and that they might be arrested and dealt with at any moment.

At this time there was literally no Persian army except on paper. The gendarmes and police of the capital did not number more than 1800 and they were very inadequately armed and equipped. Practically all this force was absolutely necessary to maintain order in Teheran.

Reports continued to come in to the effect that the Turcomans on the northeastern frontier of Persia were flocking to the ex-Shah's standard, and it was generally feared that he would be at the gates of the city within a few weeks.

Salaru'd-Dawla, his brother, was making headway in the Hamadan district, where he was reported to have gathered many thousands of the Kurdish tribesmen, and before this double danger the newly formed Persian Cabinet fairly quailed.

Up to this time the Government had acted with a certain degree of energy and solidarity, but under the strain of increasing fears the official fabric began to give way, and within a few days there was left not a government, but a small group of men who had come to the front and shown themselves determined to uphold the Constitution and to take all steps necessary to repel the rebels who threatened it.

Chief among these was Ephraim Khan, the chief of the police and gendarmes at Teheran, of whom mention has been made before. Ephraim Khan is a Turkish Armenian, who had come to Resht several years before and been employed there in some very humble trade. Little was known of his antecedents, but the general belief is that Ephraim (as he is commonly called) was the real head and shoulders of the expedition from Resht, and that the great Sipahdar was largely a figurehead.

After the capture of Teheran in 1909 and the restoration of the Constitutional Government, Ephraim was made Chief of Police of the capital, a post which carries with it much more responsibility and dignity than it would in more civilized communities.

In this office Ephraim built up and held together the only organized and fairly equipped force which the Constitutional Government had ever possessed, and with it he maintained a high state of public order in the city.   He had the capacity for drawing men to him and retaining their loyalty, and despite his somewhat limited education he was a man of great resource, undoubted military genius and unflinching courage.

In the crisis which thus confronted the Persian people Ephraim came rapidly to the front.   Being a Christian, he was *kaffar,* or unbeliever, in the eyes of the Muhammadans, but despite this great handicap and the jealousies which his increased power and influence aroused, it was recognized that he held the safety of the city in his hand, to say nothing of the salvation of the Constitutional Government, against the forces of the ex-Shah.

On July 19 the Samsamu's-Saltana, by virtue of the proclamation of martial law, became, as Minister of War, the military governor of Teheran, and as such he practically had the power of life and death over all his countrymen.

One of the first steps suggested was that a considerable number of well-known reactionaries and intriguers left behind by the ex-Shah should be arrested, principally to prevent them· from propagating disloyalty to the Constitutional Government. A list of thirty or forty of these individuals was drawn up by the Cabinet, was shown to the Regent, and put into Ephraim's hands to make the arrests.

On July 20 the Regent sent for me and we had a long conference as to the situation.   I suggested to him that some force

5

Facsimile of the Proclamation issued by the Persian Constitutional Government on the 3rd Shaban, 1329 (July 29, 1911), putting a price of 100,000 *tumans* (about $90,000) on the head of Muhammad Ali Mirza, ex-Shah of Persia, and 25,000 *tumans* (about $22,500) on the head of each of his brothers, Princes Shuau's-Saltana and Salaru'd-Dawla. (See opposite page.)

should be despatched at once from Teheran against the ex-Shah, principally for the moral effect which it would have on the doubting individuals in the capital and elsewhere, who were inclined to believe that no resistance would be made by the Government. The Regent approved this idea, and directed a conference between the Samsamu's-Saltana, Ephraim and myself. I also recommended to the Regent that the Medjlis should pass a law, declaring the ex-Shah and his two brothers who were in arms against the Government, to be outlaws, and offering a large reward to any one who might deliver them up, dead or alive. His Highness thought this a very good idea and promised to urge it on the Cabinet and Medjlis. The Regent also stated that a number of the more notorious reactionaries would be arrested by Ephraim in a day or so. I advised that it should be done at once, as each day increased the fear, doubt and confusion in the minds of the general public.

I had learned that morning, in a very confidential manner, that a despatch had come from the British Government to its Legation at Teheran, stating that England would protest to Russia against the ex-Shah's being allowed to regain the throne in violation of his own agreement and promises and of the formal stipulations of the Protocol signed with the Constitutional

---

TRANSLATION OF THE PROCLAMATION ON THE OPPOSITE PAGE.

AN ACT

relating to the proscription of Muhammad Ali Mirza and his brothers.

ART. 1.   As Muhammad Ali Mirza, the ex-Shah, is a "spoiler and corrupter on the earth," and as his proscription is necessary, The Council of Ministers is authorized to pay to such person (or to the heirs of such person) as destroys or captures Muhammad Ali Mirza, the sum of one hundred thousand *tumans*.

ART. 2.   The Ministry of War is authorized to pay to such person (or his heirs) as destroys or captures Salaru'd-Dawla the sum of twenty-five thousand *tumans;* and twenty-five thousand *tumans* to such person (or his heirs) as destroys or captures Shuau's-Saltana.

Government by the two powers in September, 1909. I therefore felt safe in informing His Highness that even the British
Government could hardly overlook the very evident bad faith
of Muhammad Ali's act and that he might count on its disap-
proval being expressed in some form. He was greatly encouraged by this.

That same evening Sipahdar received a telegram from
Muhammad Ali, directing him to assume charge of the Government at Teheran and to maintain order there until he, Muhammad Ali, could arrive. The Sipahdar gave out to the public
that he had wired back to the ex-Shah: " The people will
never endure your yoke." Whether he actually did so has remained a matter of considerable doubt.

By this time it had become perfectly evident that some members of the Cabinet, including Sipahdar, Mutashamu's-Saltana
and Muawinu'd-Dawla, were not putting their whole hearts
into the preparations for resistance. The Sipahdar remained
passively outside Teheran at his summer residence at the
Shimbran, and postponed from day to day the execution by
Ephraim of the orders for arrest. The people of Teheran
promptly grew very suspicious of the Sipahdar's loyalty, and
the Cabinet practically ceased to exist.

On July 21 I had a talk with the Samsamu's-Saltana in
which he stated that 2000 of the Bakhtiyari tribesmen had
been ordered to assemble at once at Isfahan, preparatory to
marching to Teheran, a journey which would consume about
ten days for a force of that size. I wired funds to the Bakhtiyari Khan who was Governor of Isfahan, to cover the preliminary expenses. Samsamu's-Saltana also promised to urge in
the Council and Medjlis that a price of 100,000 tumans be put
on the head of Muhammad Ali, and 25,000 tumans on the head
of each of his brothers, Prince Salaru'd-Dawla and Prince
Shuau's-Saltana. The Minister of War was so enthusiastic

PRINCE SHUAU'S-SALTANA, BROTHER OF MUHAMMAD ALI.

The confiscation of the Prince's estates by the Constitutional Government was made the subject
of the first Russian ultimatum.   A price of 25,000 tumans ($22,500) was put on his head by the
Persian Medjlis.

over this idea that he declared his willingness to raise the
money from his personal estates if the Medjlis felt any hesitancy on that score.

Samsamu's-Saltana was a man in the sixties, very tall and
straight, of very slight education, but of great personal pride
and with a very simple, almost childish mind. He had a good
heart, but soon fell under the influence of his intriguing brothers
and relatives. He felt keenly at this time the unaccustomed
responsibilities which had been thrust upon him and was anxious
to acquit himself of them in a creditable manner. His brother,
Sardar-i-Asad, had left for Europe a few weeks before, and
Samsamu's-Saltana therefore remained the real head in Persia
of the Bakhtiyari clans.

In this same conversation he told me that he was so devoted
to the Constitution that he had that very morning offered to
the Regent to go, ostensibly as an envoy, to Muhammad Ali,
and gaining his presence, to put a pistol to his breast and kill
him. " I am an old man," he said, " and I am more than willing to sell my own life, if I could thus rid my country of that
cruel tyrant." The Regent, however, had rejected the plan.

Samsamu's-Saltana then asked whether, as Military Govern-
or, he had the authority to direct expenditures for the public
defense, and on my stating that I so understood the law, he asked
me to employ up to 100,000 tumans to send envoys to kill
Muhammad Ali and his brothers. I told him that I thought
such steps had best be taken by the military authorities and
the police. He expressed his distrust of Sipahdar, Mutashamu's-Saltana and Muawinu'd-Dawla. He likewise agreed that
thereafter I should pay the so-called " central army " at Teheran
direct; that is, after actual inspection of the troops, and not
on payrolls made up and submitted by the War Ministry.
This meant cutting down the monthly allowance from 42,000
tumans to about 12,000 tumans.

By this time a number of the reactionaries had taken *bast* or refuge in the village of Zargundeh, where the summer quarters of the Russian Legation are located, since that territory was held by Russia to be free from interference by the Persian Government. From this secure position these men continued to plot against the Constitutional Government throughout the ensuing military campaign.

There was in Teheran a Bakhtiyari force, supposed to be about 600 men, who were kept by the Bakhtiyari Khans as a guard of honor and dignity, but were actually paid by the Government each month. These were now formed into the nucleus of an expedition.

Ephraim explained to me his plan for an expedition against the ex-Shah, but said that he dared not confide it to any of the Ministers, as he did not trust them. He had his men engaged in reloading the fixed ammunition for the Schneider cannon, as he did not dare accept it in the shape in which it had been delivered to him by the Cossack brigade. He said the Sipahdar should be hanged or shot, and was angry with the Medjlis because it had not yet voted the small pension which he had requested for Major Haase, the German Maxim gun expert, who had been wounded while serving Ephraim's orders the year before. Haase's services were needed on the coming expedition towards Astarabad, but he was dissatisfied with the treatment he had received. As he was only employed as an artillery instructor, the question of his participation in actual fighting rested with him alone. I was able to arrange a pension for him shortly afterwards and he agreed to accompany Ephraim.

Perhaps the most patriotic of the real Persian leaders at this time was the *Nawwab,* a man whose character and attainments would win for him a high place in any land and under any conditions. He had served as Minister of Foreign Affairs

HUSAYN KULI KHAN, NAWWAB.
Ex-Minister of Foreign Affairs, and leader of the Constitutionalists in Persia.

until he was forced out in December, 1910, by the insulting conduct of the British and Russian Legations, and since that time, steadfastly refusing any political office, he continued to work day and night for the betterment of conditions in Persia.

He was a man of about fifty-five, of distinguished appearance, possessing a thorough European education, speaking English, Persian and French with equal facility and, what is most remarkable of all, he had the reputation of being absolutely honest in both his official and personal affairs. He was a Democrat in politics, and had become generally recognized as the real head of the Democratic party in Persia, though many others, both in and out of the Medjlis, were much more prominent. During my entire acquaintance with him up to the day I left Teheran I never found him to be anything but a high-minded gentleman and a patriot of unfailing devotion to the interests of his country.

In the conversation which took place at the Nawwab's house, Ephraim explained that he had received an order only that morning from the Council of Ministers directing the arrest of some twenty reactionaries whose names were given, but that an hour later, before the order could be executed, Sipahdar (who was still nominally the Premier) had called him on the telephone and directed that it be suspended. About this time one of Ephraim's officers was brought in and reported that the police had arrested a man named Nizamu's-Saltana and a number of other reactionaries, but that they had claimed to be *organizing a volunteer* force by orders of Sipahdar. Ephraim said that he would undoubtedly get orders from Sipahdar to release these people, and that if he did not do so and defied Sipahdar, the latter, who was on good terms with some of the *mullahs,* would brand him as *kaffar* (unbeliever) and become a hero with a certain class of Muhammadans. He thought that

Sipahdar should be arrested, but hesitated to take the step himself for the special reasons just stated.

We discussed my plan for the formation of a Treasury Gendarmerie, but it was plain that Ephraim ingenuously suspected in it some idea of partitioning Persia between Russia and England, especially if Major Stokes were to be in command.

At this meeting arrangements were made to raise a special force of mounted volunteers to be under Ephraim's orders.

On the following morning, July 23, Samsamu's-Saltana and Arbab Khaikosro came to the Atabak Park to discuss plans. The former complained bitterly that Sipahdar was a traitor and that the Regent was weak and vacillating. He stated that he had presented to the Cabinet the plan for proclaiming rewards for the capture of the ex-Shah and his brothers, but that Ministers claimed to be afraid to send it to the Medjlis, as it was "so unusual." He said that he had telegraphed to Isfahan for 3000 more Bakhtiyaris to come to Teheran. Nor was the Cabinet willing to put before the Medjlis my proposed bill granting to Major Stokes, after the expiration of his services in Persia, the pension which he was compelled to give up on resigning his commission in the British-Indian Army.

The situation in Teheran at this time was growing steadily worse. The sentiment in certain quarters in favor of the ex-Shah was increasing, the new coalition Cabinet, of which so much had been expected, was squarely split, the three supposed Moderates, Sipahdar, Mutashamu's-Saltana and Muawinu'd-Dawla, being openly antagonistic to their four Democratic colleagues. There had been an utter failure to arrest and punish well-known traitors who were openly acting against the Constitutional Government; and to make matters worse Sipahdar still controlled a sufficient number of deputies in the Medjlis to prevent any decisive action against him being taken.

I had given instructions to enlist 500 Treasury gendarmes

at once, and the next two days were spent in getting uniforms and equipment under preparation. During this time I had frequent conferences with the leaders of both parties in the Medjlis, and they seemed to have begun to realize that some positive action must be taken to save the situation.

On July 25 the deputies in the Medjlis by a large majority voted to get rid of Sipahdar and Mutashamu's-Saltana, and immediately sent a committee to the Regent to demand that he accept the resignation of these two ministers, which was done. That cleared the air somewhat and steps were taken to form a new Cabinet which should really work for the maintenance of the Constitutional Government.

Majdu'd-Dawla, who had been arrested two days before by Ephraim's men, having been condemned by military order to be hung as a traitor, was to be executed on the 25th, but shortly before the appointed time the British Minister, Sir George Barclay, wrote to the Persian Government, demanding that this man should be given a formal trial, and clearly indicating that his execution would be displeasing to the Legation. The grounds for this step were that Majdu'd-Dawla was a K. C. M. G., an order to which the British Minister also belonged.

The effect of this intervention, while doubtless not so intended by Sir George Barclay, was exceedingly bad, as it convinced a number of timorous people that the British Government as well as the Russian Government was secretly favoring the plans of the ex-Shah. Even Ephraim Khan believed that such was the case. While the arrest of Majdu'd-Dawla was being made, one gendarme and two servants—one a woman—had been killed.

On July 26 a new Cabinet was formed as follows: Premier and Minister of War, Samsamu's-Saltana; Minister of Foreign Affairs, Wuthuqu'd-Dawla; Minister of Finance, Hakimu'l-Mulk; Minister of Justice, Mushiru'd-Dawla (brother of the President of the Medjlis, Mutaminu'l-Mulk); Minister of Public

Instruction, Alau's-Saltana; Minister of the Interior, Ghava-mu's-Saltana; Minister of Posts and Telegraphs, Dabiru'l-Mulk.

On the next day the news reached Teheran that the advance guard of Muhammad Ali's forces had arrived within a few miles of the important town of Sharud, to the northeast of the capital. My tax-collector at that place also wired that he had received an order from Prince Shuau's-Saltana, directing him to collect the taxes without delay and to pay them, under pain of death, to the governor just appointed by the ex-Shah. This loyal Constitutionalist telegraphed the message himself and begged me not to reply to it as the receipt of a telegram by him from me would cause his death. The day following he again wired stating that 400 Turcomans had ridden suddenly into Sharud, and had pillaged all the Government offices as well as his private house. He had succeeded in escaping with his family to the house of an Armenian friend.

On July 28 all the Ministers had signed the bill providing for Major Stokes' contract, so that I was able to purchase a sufficient amount of Imperial Bank Loan of 1911 bonds to provide for Major Stokes' pension after his resignation should be accepted.

On this same day one of the deputies of the Medjlis brought before me a Persian *fidai* (whose name is omitted for obvious reasons) and informed me that the man had just confessed to him that he had come from an interview with a certain Russian Vice-consul at Teheran, who had urged him, as a means of gaining Russian protection and good-will, to shoot or poison me, as " I was balking Russia's plans in Persia." The original purpose of the interviews was to enable the Russian Consulate General to send a secret message to Muhammad Ali, of which my informant was to be the bearer. The story seemed not

SIPAHDAR-I-AZAM (Greatest of the Marshals).
He was the Prime Minister holding the portfolio of War when Mr. Shuster arrived at Teheran.
He was a Russian protégé and was strongly suspected of conspiring with Muhammad Ali
in his attempt to gain the throne.

improbable, but I had it suppressed, as it could only have complicated my work.

On a later occasion a Persian named Farajoolah Khan, at one of the " salaams " being held at the *Darbar,* was heard to state that he was a member of a band which had been formed for the purpose of killing Mr. Shuster in the same manner as Saniu'd-Dawla was assassinated. Some Persians informed Ephraim's police agents, and the valiant gentleman was flogged and put in chains.

On July 29 the Medjlis passed the law putting the price of 100,000 tumans on the head of Muhammad Ali and 25,000 tumans on the head of each of his two brothers. The law granting Major Stokes' pension was likewise approved. Later that afternoon the Russian Minister called at the Foreign Office and demanded that the contract with Major Stokes should not be signed, threatening that his Government *would exact heavy compensation!* The Persian Minister of Foreign Affairs was so frightened that he sent me a note to the effect that the law would not be operative until it was signed by the Regent, which we both well knew to be untrue. That, however, in Persia is called " keeping up official appearances."

Some time before this the consignment of Russian rifles and ammunition which Sipahdar had contracted for with the Russian Legation had arrived at Enzeli and they were being transported over the Resht road to Teheran. Their arrival had been so timed that there was the gravest danger of their being seized by agents of the ex-Shah, but the greater part of the boxes had now 7000 rifles and 4,000,000 cartridges, and, as it turned out, they reached Kasvin and were comparatively safe. These made a most welcome addition to the military stores at Teheran. Without them the Constitutional Government would have been almost without arms. I took 1500 rifles and 600,000 cart-

ridges and stored them in the cellars of our residence at Atabak
Park, for safe-keeping until the Treasury Gendarmerie had use
for them. Fire-arms have a strange and mysterious way of
evaporating in Persia, no matter how many official records are
kept of them, so if one really expects to need them they should
be kept in sight all the time.

Up to this time little has been said of the attitude of the
Russian Government towards the attempt of Muhammad Ali
to seat himself on the throne of Persia. Russian officials, however, had been neither idle nor passive.

The Russian Government, acting for herself and Great
Britain, had two years previously assumed the responsibility of
keeping the ex-Shah to his agreement not to indulge in any
political agitation against the Constitutional Government of
Persia. This was in accordance with Article XI of the Protocol
of September 9, 1909, signed by both powers. By permitting
Muhammad Ali to escape from Odessa, to cross through Russia,
to embark on a Russian steamer, traverse the Caspian and land
on Persian territory, Russia failed utterly " to take efficacious
measures " to prevent not only political agitation but actual
hostile steps against the Persian Government. The fact is that
he traversed the entire Russian passport system with a suite of
uniformed officers, a false beard and a consignment of guns and
rapid-fire cannon, said to have been labeled " mineral water."
This fact, together with his false passport describing him as a
merchant of Bagdad named " Khalil," was alleged to have been
sufficient to throw the unsuspecting Russian passport officials
off their guard. The Russian Government would apparently
have the world believe it was not at any pains to keep posted as
to Muhammad Ali's movements.

He had been in Vienna for some time, buying arms and
making preparations for his expedition. Some things which
happened there were afterwards made clear in the ante-mortem

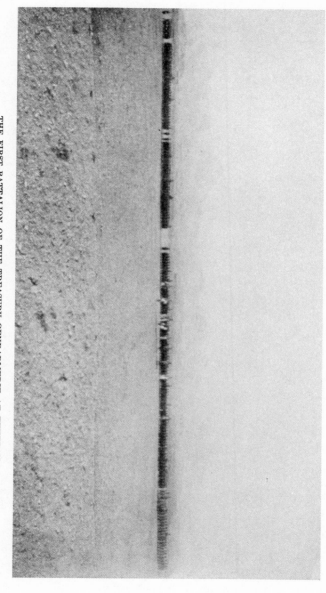

THE FIRST BATTALION OF THE TREASURY GENDARMERIE AT TEHERAN.
This force was created by Mr. Shuster to assist in the collection of taxes.

statement of Arshadu'd-Dawla, the ex-Shah's principal general, who accompanied him to Persia and was captured and shot by the forces under Ephraim Khan.

Mr. W. A. Moore,[1] the London *Times* correspondent at Teheran, who was present at the military council the night before Arshadu'd-Dawla was shot, gives the following account of his statements on this point:

Then Muhammad Ali and I met in Vienna. The Russian Ambassador [1] came to see us, and we asked for help. He told us that Russia could not help us. Russia and England had an agreement with regard to Persia, from which neither would depart. They had resolved not to intervene in any way, internally, " But, on the other hand," he said, " the field is clear. If we can do nothing for you, we equally will do nothing against you. It is for you to decide what are your chances of success. If you think you can reach the throne of Persia, then go. Only remember we cannot help you, and if you fail we have no responsibility." " Well, there is something you can do for us," we answered. " Lend us some money."

[1] Mr. Moore understands Persian very well, and based on this testimony, it seemed safe to state that the Russian Ambassador at Vienna had held these reported conversations with the ex-Shah and his general. After I had published this statement, however, in my open letter to the London *Times* of October 21, the Russian Government in an official *communiqué* denied that its Ambassador at Vienna had ever said these things, claiming that they were pure invention. This denial, when it was subsequently mentioned in the British House of Commons, was greeted with laughter.

I learned, subsequently, however, that it was very probable that this time, at least, the Russian official denial was justified — that is, so far as it went,— taken literally. It seems that it was *not* the Russian ambassador at Vienna who had held these interviews with the ex-Shah and his general. In the Persian language the word for "ambassador" and for "minister" is the same, and when Arshadu'd-Dawla had stated in the presence of Mr. Moore and the officers of the Persian Nationalists the night before his death that these interviews had taken place with the Russian "diplomatic representative" (using the common Persian expression therefor) at Vienna, Mr. Moore and the others had naturally assumed that he was referring to the Russian Ambassador at that place. It seems, however, that the Russian diplomatic representative to whom reference was made was the famous Mons. de Hartwig who had formerly been Minister at Teheran and had done everything in his power to retain Muhammad Ali on the throne and who, at the time that these interviews took place at Vienna, was accredited as Russian Minister to Belgrade, from which place he came up to Vienna on several occasions and had these interviews with the ex-Shah and Arshadu'd-Dawla. I did not learn these facts until after I had reached Vienna on my way back from Persia last January.

" No, it is quite impossible," he replied.   And though we begged much and had a second interview, he rejected our proposal.   Only he suggested that, if Muhammad Ali had a receipt for some jewels which were in the keeping of the Russian bank at Teheran, money could be raised on that receipt. But Muhammad Ali had not got the document, and so nothing came of that.

The ex-Shah embarked, with his party and munitions of war, upon the Russian steamer *Christoforos* from a Russian port just north of Baku, and, crossing the Caspian Sea, landed at Gumesh-Teppeh.   In spite of the improbability of such being the fact, the world might give the Russian Government the benefit of the doubt and assume that this escape of the ex-Shah was entirely accidental, so far as Russia was concerned, and that the Russian Cabinet had not been advised by its diplomatic representative at Belgrade or at Vienna of Muhammad Ali's intentions to take this step, if it were not for other abundant evidence which demonstrates that in reality the ex-Shah's filibustering expedition to regain the throne of Persia was not only known in the highest circles of the Russian Government but that it was well known throughout the entire bureaucracy of that country.   Ten days before Muhammad Ali landed upon Persian soil the Russian Minister at Teheran took occasion, at a dinner party at which a large number of people were present, to state that, within a few weeks, the Persian Constitutional Government would cease to exist.   The statement created considerable surprise at the time, but when, on July 18, the news of Muhammad Ali's arrival reached the capital, those who heard it fully understood the reference.   It is notorious that the Consular representatives of Russia throughout Persia received the news of the ex-Shah's landing with unconcealed joy; they made no effort whatsoever to hide their real feelings and sympathies and, not content with this, they took united and decided action in a dozen different localities to aid and facilitate the forces and agents of the ex-Shah in their endeavor to overturn the Constitutional Government. Muhammad Ali was regarded by Russian officials as the best possible means for the forwarding of their policy of aggression and assimilation in Persia. They had found that the Constitutional Government, principally through the existence of an elective body of eighty members, was much less tractable than a single despot upon the throne, who could be intimidated by threats or bought over to serve the purposes of the Imperial Russian Government.

On July 23 the Persian Government addressed a note to all the legations in Teheran informing them of a law which had just been passed, declaring a state of siege. Most of the legations replied in the usual manner, merely calling attention to certain provisions in the Treaty of Turkmanchay, but the Russian Legation adopted from the very outset a far different and most unfriendly tone, claiming among other things the right to arrest directly, at any time, so-called "illegal Russian subjects," defined in the Legation's note, "who might take part in the events actually going on in the country." The patent object of this claim put forward at this time was to give the Russian Legation and Consuls throughout Persia the excuse to arrest, on the mere allegation that they were a kind of Russian subjects, any Persian fighting-men of known reputation who might take the side of the Government against Muhammad Ali. If this threat to arrest all Russian subjects "who might take part in events" had been literally executed, it would have been necessary, as things turned out, to have arrested most of the Russian Consuls and consular employees themselves.

At Resht the Russian Consul went further and actually informed the Persian Government of his intention to arrest any one on suspicion of his being a Russian subject, to investigate the matter at his leisure, and to hold him until the end of the troubles.

On July 31, when Muhammad Ali had barely put foot on

Persian soil and had made no appreciable advance towards subjugating the country, Britain and Russia addressed to the Persian Government the following *indentique de facto* recognition of the ex-Shah's belligerency:

" Seeing that the ex-Shah, contrary to the advice frequently given him by the Governments of England and Russia, in effect that he should forbear from any agitation whatever in Persia, has now landed in Persia, the British (Russian) Government declares that the ex-Shah has now forfeited his right to the pension fixed by the Protocol. But, on the other hand, the British (Russian) Government believes that as the ex-Shah is now in Persian territory, the British (Russian) Government cannot intervene. Therefore the British (Russian) Government states that in the conflict that has unfortunately arisen in Persia *they will in no way interfere.*" [1]

The Constitutional Government of Persia was therefore plunged into throes of civil strife through the criminal negligence or the connivance of at least one government which had solemnly pledged itself to prevent exactly this contingency. When the fact became known, and the so-called declaration of neutrality which has just been described was made by the two powers, even then the Persian Government could have speedily extricated itself from the difficulties thus thrust upon it, had that " neutrality " been faithfully observed. How well the Russian officials in Persia observed the neutrality which their Government had proclaimed, the following incidents may serve to show.

On July 29 the Russian Acting Consul at Isfahan, proceeding upon his conception of neutrality, wrote to the Persian Foreign Office:

According to information received by this Consulate the Government of Isfahan intends to hold a meeting of the clergy, nobles, prominent citizens and merchants, for the purpose of framing a telegram to the representatives

1 The italics are the author's.

of foreign powers to the effect that they, the people, do not desire Muhammad Ali, and to protest against his arrival in Persian territory. I request you in advance to inform the proper quarters that as this matter concerns Persia and the Persians, it would be useless to give trouble to the Imperial Legation and the Consulates of Russia..

Later he wrote:

You must not uselessly give trouble in the matter of Muhammad Ali Shah to the Imperial Russian Legation and Consulates. It is the duty of the Persian Foreign Office representative and of the Government to restrain and prevent any such incidents and they must fulfill it.

One Rashidu'l-Mulk, a Persian subject, formerly Governor of the district of Ardebil, had been placed in command of some Government forces. He treacherously fled before an inferior number of Shahsevens, tribesmen who had always remained supporters of the ex-Shah. He was accused of high treason, arrested and confined at Tabriz. On July 27 the Russian Consul-general at Tabriz,[1] having demanded his release of the Persian Acting Governor, and having been informed that Rashidu'l-Mulk was held by orders of the Constitutional Government, sent 300 Russian soldiers, fully armed, to the Governor's palace, beat off the Persian guards, insulted the Acting Governor, liberated Rashidu'l-Mulk and took him away. Shortly afterwards he joined the rebel forces of Shujau'd-Dawla [2] which were threatening Tabriz.

[1] To the formal protest lodged by the Persian Government over this affair the Russian Legation replied, officially admitting responsibility for the orders given to the Russian Consul-general at Tabriz to " take necessary steps " to prevent certain punishment, which was alleged to be threatened, from being inflicted on Rashidu'l-Mulk. We have seen what steps the Russian Consul-general took,— steps which in the case of two equal powers would have meant immediate war. The sole justification attempted by the Russian Legation for this outrage was that " the representatives of the Government of Russia have accorded a certain protection to Rashidu'l-Mulk." As a matter of fact no sentence at all had been passed on Rashidu'l-Mulk, though even if it had the outrage would have been none the less.

[2] Shujau'd-Dawla is the title adopted by the bandit, Rahim Khan, mentioned in the Introductory Chapter. He was protected constantly by the

There were numerous other [1] examples of the hostile interference on the part of the officials of the Russian Government
with the affairs of Persia, a friendly sovereign nation. Almost
any one of them, occurring between two governments of relatively equal strength, would have brought about war. In every
case a diplomatic protest was duly prepared and presented by
the Persian Government to the Russian Minister at Teheran.
Similar representations were made by the Persian Legations at
St. Petersburg and London. But in not a single instance that
has been recorded was the slightest notice of these protests taken
by the Russian Government, nor was a single Russian official
punished for his acts.

On the afternoon of July 30 I received a visit from a Persian
military gentleman, of imposing presence, who informed me that
he had been charged by the Government with leading the first
expedition against the ex-Shah. His name was Sardar-i-Muhiy,
though he has formerly been known as Muizzu's-Sultan. He
had taken part in the advance on Teheran of the Nationalist
forces under Sipahdar in 1909, and was accounted a brave
fighter. He came into my office literally covered with automatic
pistols and cartridges, of which latter 300 or more were
garlanded in belts across his chest, waist and shoulders. He was
a large man and wore long, bright yellow boots. He had agreed
to form and lead several hundred volunteer cavalry against the
Turcomans at Sharud, and as a preliminary he drew forth and
presented a requisition signed by the Minister of War calling
for about 26,000 tumans. This sum was largely made up of
his salaries as military commander and as governor of the town
of Astarabad (a place which there was no probability of his

Russian troops in the neighborhood of Tabriz, and fraternized with the
Russian officers. Russia made his presence the pretext for keeping her
soldiers in Azarbayjan.

[1] For further instances see the Author's letter to the London *Times*
contained in Appendix C.

SARDAR-J-ASAD.

The Bakhtiyari chieftain who led the Persian forces from Isfahan in 1909 and with Sipahdar-i Azam
captured Teheran from Muhammad Ali and the Cossack Brigade.

reaching), as well as a large " contingent fund " to be expended by him personally. This gentleman had already been paid by the Government the sum of 6000 tumans advance salary as Governor of the district of Kirman, for which place he had never even started. After some rather warm correspondence with the Cabinet, I paid the sum demanded, but soon found that this was but the first of a series of onslaughts which were commenced by the Cabinet on the public treasury and continued up to the time that I left Teheran over five months later. There seemed to be hardly any one with any sort of a pretext for demanding money who did not secure the approval of the Cabinet or the Ministry of War and present his claim to the Treasury. The stream began and never stopped. In truth, it must be said that the efforts of the Cabinet to defeat the ex-Shah were tinged with a decided desire to see their favorites generously compensated.

About this time the Bakhtiyari tribesmen, with their *Khans,* began to arrive at Teheran from the South, and the demands which most of them made for money were so preposterous and out of all proportion to a just compensation or to what their actual needs were that I was forced several times during the following months to threaten to resign if the Cabinet continued to sanction such wholesale attempts at looting the Treasury. Even the Minister of Finance, Hakimu'l-Mulk, expressed his shame at the actions of the Bakhtiyari chieftains, and declared that he also would resign if the Cabinet continued to support them. The first Bakhtiyaris to reach Teheran were commanded by Muin-Homayun, one of the young Khans, who later displayed real p.. ..tism and great bravery in the campaign.

By August 3 the Prince Salaru'd-Dawla had reached the town of Kirmanshah in Western Persia, and having ordered the merchants to stop paying the Customs taxes, had promptly demanded of them a "loan" of 50,000 tumans. He made a similar demand on the branch of the Imperial Bank there, but was refused.

The Cabinet, including the Premier, Samsamu's-Saltana, now began to show marked hostility towards me on account of my protests against the official plundering which was going on, and the Premier refused to keep his promise to assist in the organization of the Treasury Gendarmerie by allowing me to have barracks and other equipment in the possession of the Ministry of War.

The Government's forces at this time consisted of an indefinite number of unorganized Bakhtiyaris who were distributed in Isfahan, on the road to Teheran, and at Teheran, and 1200 police and 500 gendarmes at the capital. There were also 500 gendarmes under one of Ephraim's lieutenants at Kasvin, and some 200 Armenian volunteers, or "professional fighting-men," as they were called.

On August 8 the news came that Arshadu'd-Dawla had defeated a force of Government troops which had been stationed at Damghan, to the northeast of Teheran. A number of the Government troops on this occasion deserted to the ex-Shah. The Sipahdar, while he was Minister of War, had stationed these men there, with two cannon. These cannon, together with the other supplies and munitions, had fallen into the hands of the ex-Shah's troops. There were many who believed that the unfortunate affair was the result of a pre-arrangement by Sipahdar, whose treachery to the Constitutional Government was now generally acknowledged.

During the month of August a number of Nationalist expeditions were sent out against the ex-Shah and his lieutenants in Northern Persia. The first substantial success which the Government troops obtained was at Firuzkuh, in the mountains to the northeast of Teheran. Here, in a narrow pass, the young Bakhtiyari chieftain, Muin-Homayun, defeated and captured Rashidu's-Sultan and killed sixty of his men.

On the night of August 15, 800 horsemen of Prince Salaru'd-Dawla's force occupied the town of Hamadan. There was no resistance by the Government troops of the regular army who were supposed to be stationed there.

The movements and whereabouts of the ex-Shah himself were at this time a matter of great uncertainty. He was reported to have become panic-stricken on learning that a price of 100,000 tumans had been put upon his head, and rumor had it that he immediately reëmbarked on the steamer which he had kept anchored off the coast ever since his landing. Ephraim had in the meantime been despatching small forces of picked men to guard the mountain passes leading to Teheran, and was hoping to get a force in Muhammad Ali's rear and cut him off from the sea. Ephraim himself, in view of the critical situation in Teheran, had decided not to go out against the ex-Shah's main forces until they were within striking distance of the capital.

On August 11, I went to Gulhak to a dinner given by Colonel H. R. Beddoes, the representative of Messrs. Seligman Bros. of London. The other guests were Sir George Barclay, the British Minister, his Russian colleague, Mons. S. Poklewski-Koziell, and Mr. W. A. Moore, correspondent of the London *Times*. The conditions in Persia were freely discussed and the Russian Minister was at no pains to conceal his belief that the ex-Shah would shortly be victorious and capture Teheran. The question of Major Stokes' appointment was gone into at length. After dinner we had several rubbers of bridge, and my good fortune in that game seemed to impress the Russian Minister with the ability of American financiers.

During the course of the evening the Russian Minister and I strolled out on the balcony of the house. Mons. Poklewski-Koziell was a very engaging man. He again referred to the incapacity of the Constitutional Government and asked me bluntly whether I would not be willing to remain under Muhammad Ali, when he was restored to power, and be Treasurer-general or *Vazir* with full powers such as I then possessed. He assured me that if I would do so, I would have the full support of the Russian Government and would be suitably compensated. All that I needed to do in order to signify my acceptance of this offer was to remain passive until the change took place. The proposal was delicately worded, but its import was unmistakable. I am quite sure that the Russian Minister regarded it as a highly proper suggestion, and that no insult was intended. Stripped of all diplomatic trimmings and phraseology, however, it was plainly proposed that I should cease to aid or advise the existing Persian Government, allowing it to hurry into bankruptcy and ruin, and take service under a cruel and vicious monster who would be the cringing slave of the St. Petersburg cabinet. I told the Minister that I had agreed to serve the Persian Government to the best of my ability, and that whatever the outcome might be, I would not think of remaining under Muhammad Ali.

It has occurred to me since that the Russian diplomats at Teheran and Vienna displayed too much active interest in the success of the ex-Shah for the representatives of a government which the British Foreign Office officially declared to have been innocent of either knowledge of, or participation in, the violation of the Protocol of September, 1909.

On August 15, in a long conversation, the Regent painted a very gloomy picture of the situation of Persia. He expressed, however, his satisfaction at the manner in which the Government's finances were being controlled, and stated that there were always loud complaints in Persia when any effective supervision of the funds was attempted.

Three Swedish officers who had been engaged by the Persian

SARDAR-I-BAHADUR, SON OF SARDAR-I-ASAD.

A young and patriotic Bakhtiyari chieftain who was devoted to the Constitution when the rest of his clan were deserting it.

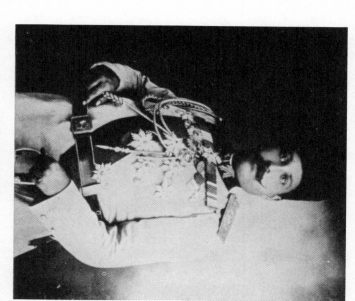

ARSHADU'D-DAWLA.

Muhammad Ali's principal general in his campaign to regain the throne during the summer of 1911. He nearly captured Teheran with 2000 Turcomans, but was wounded, captured, and shot on the field of battle.

Government arrived at the capital to take up their duties with the Ministry of the Interior in instructing the gendarmerie of that department.

After several long debates which I had been having with the Cabinet, it was now agreed that the payment of the troops of the so-called " central army " should be effected by the Treasury direct instead of by the Ministry of War. This enabled me to effect decided economies.

On August 20 the Prince Salaru'd-Dawla was reported to be at Hamadan with 10,000 men preparing to march on Teheran. At that time the total Nationalist forces in and about the capital did not exceed 3000 and there was another panic.

Tuesday, August 22, was the young Shah's fourteenth birthday, in honor of which a great *salaam,* or public reception, was held at his summer palace outside Teheran. I was unable to attend, but my principal assistant, Mr. Cairns, made the trip and presented His Majesty with a narwhal tusk, which Admiral Peary had brought back from his last polar expedition. It was signed with the famous discoverer's name, and had been sent to the Shah through the Persian Chargé d'Affaires at Washington, who had entrusted the valuable souvenir to Mr. Cairns for delivery.

Sultan Ahmad Shah had never before seen Mr. Cairns, and through some mistake of the interpreters he for some time labored under the impression that Mr. Cairns was the discoverer of the North Pole who had come to present the tusk in person. The proper explanations were finally made, much to Mr. Cairns' relief.

Life in Teheran at this time was not particularly pleasant. The heat, though dry, was quite severe, but the most annoying feature was the thick dust which arose early in the morning when traffic on the streets and roads began, and never settled until late at night. Fortunately, the Atabak palace was provided, as most large Persian houses are, with underground chambers which duplicated the entire first floor. These were always cool, even during the hottest part of the day, and in them I had established my personal offices. During the entire summer, from the middle of June until the end of September, all the foreign legations, most of the European residents of Teheran, and many wealthy Persians, move out of the city to the different summer resorts eight or more miles away on the slopes of the mountains, but as I had just started the work of organizing the Treasury, I felt it incumbent upon us to remain in town where the Government offices were located.

During the latter part of August the demands for money made by the Bakhtiyari chieftains at Teheran became so outrageous that I was compelled to refuse to honor any further requisitions in their favor until some definite military operations had been conducted by them. They realized that the Government, through the utter incompetency of its regular army, was in a very tight place, and they evidently proposed to make the most of the situation. Their purely mercenary attitude was so plainly apparent that a great deal of bitter feeling was aroused against them at Teheran.

In the course of visits from the Russian and British Ministers, we talked of the loan of £4,000,000 which I had been discussing for some time with the representatives of Messrs. Seligman Bros., of London.

Later, Sir George Barclay spoke of the embarrassment which the condition of the southern trade routes was causing his Government, and asked whether something could not be done to better things. I explained to him that the withdrawal of the Bakhtiyari tribesmen from these districts as a result of their being called to Teheran to take part in the defense of the Constitutional Government against the attacks of the ex-Shah had of course left many portions of the trade routes unguarded, a thing for which the Persian Government could hardly be held morally responsible under the circumstances. Sir George Barclay then proposed that I should take charge of the policing of these roads or should at least furnish from the newly organized Treasury Gendarmerie a sufficient force to restore order there. He stated that if he could cable his Government that I would undertake this task, it would relieve the British Foreign Office of great embarrassment as it was being constantly questioned and attacked in the House of Commons for the failure to properly look out for British commercial interests in that portion of Persia. I replied that if the British Government would assist in the speedy formation of an adequate force of Treasury Gendarmes I would be entirely willing, with the approval of the Persian Cabinet, to undertake this work, but that the main factor in the organization of this gendarmerie was the services of Major Stokes, and that so long as his valuable assistance was denied the Treasury we did not see how we could undertake an additional difficult task of this kind, however desirous the British Government might be of seeing it accomplished.

During this conversation I referred to what I considered the unjustifiable attitude of the British Government in refusing to keep its promise with regard to Major Stokes' services and in siding openly with the Russian Government in its attempt to interfere with Persia's most elementary sovereign rights. I laughingly suggested that since the attitude of these two powers was so manifestly hostile to Persia's welfare, it might be found advisable to offer certain concessions to German interests, which had for sometime previously been seeking an entry into the western part of Persia. The British Minister's horror at this grim joke was so real that I hastily changed the subject.

At this time there was a force of Bakhtiyari tribesmen under the command of Amir-i-Mufakhkham, located near Hamadan for the purpose of opposing the advance of Salaru'd-Dawla's troops.

The Bakhtiyaris of this force had already been paid for their services, but the chieftains at Teheran — and especially one of the brothers of Samsamu's-Saltana, named Sardar-i-Jang — demanded the payment of a further amount of 60,000 tumans, before they would give the orders for Amir-i-Mufakhkham to take the field. This attempt to gouge the bankrupt Persian Government was so flagrant that I felt compelled to inform the local press of the situation, and it was soon known in Teheran, to the great discomfiture of the Bakhtiyari chieftains.[1]

On August 28 the Turcomans under the command of Arshadu'd-Dawla advancing along the road to Teheran had reached the town of Aiwan-i-Kaif, where they met and defeated a smaller force of irregular troops of the Government. This was about fifty-six miles from the capital. Some reënforcements were immediately despatched under the command of Amir-Mujahid, a younger brother of Samsamu's-Saltana.

On September 4 word came that Arshadu'd-Dawla was advancing upon Teheran and that he was very near the town of Imamzadeh-Jaffar, about forty miles to the southeast of Teheran. Ephraim left Teheran immediately with 350 picked men, accompanied by Major Haase, the German artillery instructor, in charge of a Maxim gun and three Schneider quickfirers. The report was that the Bakhtiyari forces under Amir-Mujahid had been defeated. Messrs. Moore and Moloney, the correspondents of the London *Times* and of Reuter's News Agency, respectively, and Mr. J. N. Merrill, an American assistant who had shortly before arrived at Teheran and was in

[1] In addition to this the loyalty of Amir-i-Mufakhkham himself was a matter of serious doubt. Two years before, in 1909, he had taken the side of the ex-Shah against the Nationalist forces. Sometime later these suspicions as to his real intentions were confirmed by his cowardly actions in an engagement which took place between a portion of Salaru'd-Dawla's troops and the Bakhtiyaris under his command, in which the Government forces were utterly routed and fled without offering any real resistance to the rebels.

THE EX-SHAH'S GENERAL, ARSHADU'D-DAWLA, A FEW
MINUTES BEFORE HE WAS EXECUTED.

ARSHADU'D-DAWLA, ON HIS KNEES, WAITING TO RECEIVE THE
SECOND VOLLEY FROM THE FIRING PARTY.
Although twenty men fired the first time, he was only wounded once. A
donkey strolled behind him in the interval and had to be driven away.

charge of the Treasury Gendarmerie, left in an endeavor to catch up with the Government forces and see the engagement.

On Tuesday, September 5, at 11 o'clock in the morning, the Nationalist forces under the command of Ephraim attacked the ex-Shah's forces composed of about 2000 Turcomans and Persians under Arshadu'd-Dawla. Fourteen hundred of the enemy were mounted. The Government forces consisted of about 500 Bakhtiyaris, about 180 Armenian volunteers and gendarmes, three Schneider cannon and one Maxim gun. The Bakhtiyari cavalry were under the direct command of Sardar-i-Bahadur and Sardar-i-Mutashem. The other Government forces, under Amir-Mujahid, were still facing Arshadu'd-Dawla about two miles south of Imamzadeh-Jaffar. They consisted of about 400 Bakhtiyaris and a few gendarmes. An hour before noon Arshadu'd-Dawla was posted on a hill about one-half mile square, defended by four cannon. He had sent 300 Turcomans into the village of Veramin to create a panic there. When the Government troops under Ephraim had reached the neighborhood early that morning they had. heard firing between the troops of Amir-Mujahid and the Turcomans.

Ephraim sent Major Haase with the Maxim gun and Sardar-i-Bahadur and his cavalry to an elevation around the right flank of Arshadu'd-Dawla's forces. They reached a commanding position unobserved and opened fire with the Maxim gun on the Turcomans. According to the story of Arshadu'd-Dawla himself (who was subsequently captured), the barking of the Maxim gun frightened the Turcomans terribly and threw them into confusion. Their commanders were unable to restore order and when the Bakhtiyari cavalry led by Sardar-i-Bahadur charged them, they broke and fled in confusion. Arshadu'd-Dawla was wounded in the foot and was unable to escape. He was captured by a party of Bakhtiyaris.

The Turcomans left 60 or 70 dead and between 300 and 400

prisoners and wounded. The rest fled precipitately to the south, to gain the Meshed Road and return to their territory on the northeastern frontier. The fight was over at one in the afternoon of Tuesday. The Bakhtiyaris did not pursue the enemy, it is said because they were exhausted by the long ride of the previous night and morning.

Arshadu'd-Dawla was brought to Ephraim's headquarters about midnight Tuesday and was treated with extreme politeness by the Nationalist chiefs. He received medical attention for his wound, was made comfortable and supplied with food, drink and cigarettes. He reclined in the midst of a circle composed of Ephraim, Major Haase, the Bakhtiyari chiefs, and Messrs. Moore, Moloney and Merrill.

Arshadu'd-Dawla was then asked about the movements of the ex-Shah in Vienna and after leaving there. He replied that at Vienna Muhammad Ali Mirza and he had twice interviewed the Russian Ambassador there, who had told them that neither Russia nor England could take any part in the internal struggle which would result from Muhammad Ali's entering Persia to regain the throne, but that if he was able to do so the road was clear. Arshadu'd-Dawla said Muhammad Ali asked for men, arms and money, but the Russian Ambassador replied that this could not be granted. The Russian Ambassador, however, apparently gave them some assurances, since they were able to take with them three Austrian cannon, packed in boxes, through Russia, from Vienna to Baku, without any difficulty made either on the score of their passports or their baggage. When asked how these boxes of heavy war materials were taken all the way across Russia without detection, he explained that they were marked " mineral water." He also stated that Muhammad Ali had traveled with a false passport describing him as a merchant of Bagdad named Khalil.

Arshadu'd-Dawla had quantities of ammunition, his men

were armed with Austrian carbines of good type and he had a case containing a considerable sum of Persian money.

During his talk with the chiefs he pleaded very strongly, though not in so many words, for his life. He asked pitifully not to have the meeting break up, but they assured him that he could have a good night's sleep and be ready for the morrow.

Early the next morning, some twenty gendarmes, under orders, led him, unbandaged, up against a wall and fired· upon him. He fell forward throwing up his hands in a dramatic manner, but upon examination was found to be still alive, only one bullet having hit him. He was left on the ground for a short time while a file of Armenian volunteers was marched up, the Persian troops had proven suspiciously poor marksmen. A donkey which had strolled in between him and the wall was driven off. While this was happening Arshadu'd-Dawla got upon his knees and exclaimed in Persian: *" Zindabad Muhammad Ali Shah!"* (Long live Shah Muhammad Ali!) When the second volley was fired he was hit in a number of places and instantly killed.

Neither Ephraim nor any of the chiefs were present at the execution, but Messrs. Moore, Moloney and Merrill were.

Arshadu'd-Dawla died without fear or any sign of regret for his actions against the Government. He requested that his body be sent to Teheran to his wife and that the golden locket and necklace, which he wore, should be buried with him. His body was brought to Teheran on September 6, and on the next day was exposed publicly in the *Maidan* (public square). It was propped up against an ordinary cart, and a large crowd of people viewed the spectacle. The reason for this rather unusual proceeding was the necessity which the Government felt of convincing the people that this well-known general had actually been killed and his Turcomans defeated. Ephraim afterwards told me that the reason for having him executed at once on the field of battle was that, if he had been brought to Teheran, some pretext would undoubtedly have been found by the Russian Legation for interceding in his behalf.

This defeat was generally regarded as a death blow to the ex-Shah's chances of capturing Teheran. Arshadu'd-Dawla was his bravest and most skilful general, and had succeeded by a very remarkable and courageous dash in getting within forty miles of the capital. If he had not been intercepted and defeated by Ephraim's forces, Teheran would have fallen into his hands without effectual resistance of any kind, and the city would have been given over to the Turcomans to plunder and pillage. The results of turning several thousand barbarians into the city with permission to wreak their wills would have been too frightful to contemplate. A large number of Turcoman prisoners — many of them old men with white beards — were brought to Teheran within the next few days, as well as the four captured cannon and a considerable number of rifles. The main body of the Turcomans who escaped retreated up the Meshed Road at full gallop. They evidently expected to be pursued by the Bakhtiyari cavalry, and although not a single horseman went in pursuit of them they pushed on until a large number of their horses dropped with fatigue. There are a number of small telegraph stations along this road belonging to the Meshed branch of the Indo-European Telegraph Company. The British telegraph official at Teheran in charge of this branch, learning immediately of the defeat of the Turcomans, had instructions wired to his operators all along the road to inform the Turcomans as they passed that the Bakhtiyaris were " just behind them." As a result of this trick the rebels were kept in full flight and prevented from pillaging the country people and small villages along the road, as they had been doing and would doubtless have done upon this occasion.

At this time the city of Tabriz was reported to be seriously

ARSHADU'D-DAWLA, THE FAMOUS GENERAL OF THE EX-SHAH, ABOUT TO BE SHOT AS A REBEL. After his defeat and capture by the Nationalist troops under Ephraim Khan in September, 1911.

BODY OF ARSHADU'D-DAWLA JUST AFTER HIS EXECUTION.

threatened by Shujau'd-Dawla with a large force of Shah-sevens. With the defeat of Arshadu'd-Dawla, however, the only remaining force upon which the ex-Shah and his followers could base their political hopes was that of his brother, Prince Salaru'd-Dawla, in the district of Hamadan.

CHAPTER V

MILITARY OPERATIONS AGAINST PRINCE SALARU'D-DAWLA. HIS DEFEAT BY THE GOVERNMENT FORCES. THE INCIDENT ARISING FROM THE CONFISCATION BY THE GOVERNMENT OF THE ESTATES OF PRINCE SHUAU'S-SALTANA. MY LETTER TO THE LONDON "TIMES."

DURING the early part of September the Government forces under the Bakhtiyari chieftain, Amir-i-Mufakhkham, had been defeated near the town of Malayer by the troops of Prince Salaru'd-Dawla. The Bakhtiyaris lost in killed and captured, 200 men and a number of rifles, cannon and cartridges. Their treacherous commander claimed also to have lost the sum of 15,000 tumans which he had shortly before received from the branch of the Imperial Bank at Hamadan. Another Government general, Amir-Nizam, had also surrendered, under very suspicious circumstances, to Salaru'd-Dawla, several big guns which the Government had entrusted to him for the defense of Hamadan.

On September 11 another engagement occurred between the government forces at Sabatkuh under Muin-Homayun and the troops which were accompanying the ex-Shah and his brother Shuau's-Saltana. The ex-Shah's forces were completely routed and he and his brother escaped with great difficulty under cover of a thick fog. He was reported at this time to have fled to Gumesh-Teppeh with only seven followers.

By September 18 Prince Salaru'd-Dawla was advancing from Hamadan towards Teheran apparently unopposed by any Government forces. In his proclamations to the people he styled

himself " King," and telegraphed from one place to both the
Medjlis and Council of Ministers, addressing them as " my
Medjlis " and " my Ministers." On September 27 the Bakhtiyari forces of the Government, having been joined by Ephraim
with his volunteers and artillery, met and defeated the main
army of Prince Salaru'd-Dawla at a small village called Bagh-
i-Shah between the towns of Qum and Nuvaran, about ninety
miles to the southeast of Teheran. With Ephraim were the
Bakhtiyari chiefs Sardar-i-Buhadur, Sardar-i-Mutashem, and
Sardar-i-Jang. The Prince Salaru'd-Dawla had about 6000
men, all told. He lost 500 in killed and wounded and 200 prisoners. The Nationalist forces were less than 2000 men. Their
losses were reported to be the surprisingly small number of two
killed and six wounded. Six cannon and a large quantity of
ammunition were captured. The Prince Salaru'd-Dawla
retreated in full flight toward the southwest, and his chances of
capturing Teheran and establishing himself upon the throne
promptly vanished. Had he been energetically pursued by the
Government forces, he would undoubtedly have been captured,
as at one time he was but a few miles in the lead.

By the early part of October, therefore, the Nationalists had
been successful in two campaigns, as a result of which both the
ex-Shah and his brothers were in flight and their forces completely shattered.

The credit for these two victories is almost entirely due to
the skill, energy and courage of Ephraim Khan. On his return
to Teheran he was presented by the Medjlis with a gem-studded
sword, was given a pension of 300 tumans a month, and the
post of " Commander of the Army of the North."

There still remained some small bodies of the ex-Shah's followers near Astarabad, and against these Muin-Homayun was
despatched with 500 Government troops about October 8.

The famous old bandit, Naib Husayn, was again making trou-

7

ble for the Government near the town of Kashan, which lies directly south of Teheran, between Qum and Isfahan. Against him the Government at my suggestion, sent 250 troops of the Cossack Brigade with some Russian officers, to coöperate with a Bakhtiyari force of 300 coming up from Isfahan. The Cossacks, however, finally returned to Teheran without accomplishing any practical results.

On October 4 the Council of Ministers transmitted to me an order for the confiscation and seizure of the estates and property of Princes Shuau's-Saltana and Salaru'd-Dawla, directing that I, as Treasurer-general, should execute the same, and convert the properties into the Persian Treasury.

The issuance of such an order was, of course, perfectly lawful and proper, as the three persons against whom it was directed had not only violated their agreements with the Constitutional Government, but had engaged, at the head of armed forces, in open and notorious rebellion.

When the Persian Government decided to take this step it sent an official of the Ministry of Foreign Affairs to notify the British and Russian Legations of the contemplated measures, as a mere matter of courtesy, with the information that if any foreign interests should be found to exist in connection with these estates, all rights of foreigners would be fully safeguarded and guaranteed by the government. Neither Legation offered the slightest objection.

The order of confiscation contained a clause to the same effect.

On Monday, October 9, I gave the necessary instructions for its execution. Not anticipating the slightest difficulty in the actual seizure of the estates, under these circumstances, I despatched in all six parties, each composed of a civilian official of the Treasury, an officer of the Treasury Gendarmerie, and five gendarmes. They were ordered to seize, in the name of

THE MOUNTAIN GUN DETACHMENT STARTING ON AN EXPEDITION.
Major Haase, the German artillery instructor, is in the center on horseback.

THE QUICK-FIRING GUNS OF EPHRAIM'S GENDARMES AT TEHERAN.

the Government, the different properties in and about the city of Teheran.

The principal estate was the park and palace of Prince Shuau's-Saltana, situated in the city proper, not very far from Atabak Park. It was a very magnificent building, filled with rare and costly furniture, tapestries, rugs and bric-à-brac, and surrounded by a large garden, enclosed with a massive wall. In it some of the wives and children and the mother of Prince Shuau's-Saltana continued to reside.

What happened upon the arrival of the seizure parties at these different properties can be best shown by the following translation of the official report which I made on the affair to the Council of Ministers on October 10. The translation, from the French original, is as follows:

TEHERAN, October 10, 1911.

To the Council of Ministers:

I have the honor to present to the Council of Ministers the following report of the incidents connected with the execution of the order of confiscation, dated October 4, 1911, transmitted to me by the Council of Ministers, whereunder I was to take possession of all the properties of the rebels Shuau's-Saltana and Salaru'd-Dawla, in the name of the Imperial Government.

In conformity with this order I gave the necessary instructions to six parties of gendarmes, each composed of a civilian official, an officer of the Treasury Gendarmerie, and five gendarmes, indicating to them the six properties belonging to these two rebels, and the spot to which each party should proceed.

There were first four properties belonging to Shuau's-Saltana, to-wit, a garden situated in the city of Teheran, a garden near Gulhak, called "Chizeh," and two estates situated outside Teheran, called Dawlatabad and Mansuriabad, respectively; there were also two properties belonging to Salaru'd-Dawla, to-wit, one situated in the district of "Chariar," and the other called "Mardabad."

The instructions given to my agents were to the effect that they should take peaceable possession of these properties in the name of the Imperial Government, making known to the persons who might be found in actual charge of the estates the terms and conditions of the order of confiscation issued by the Council of Ministers, and calling special attention to the fact that any contracts which might exist with foreign subjects would be fully respected by the Imperial Government, but that in case there should be a rental agreement with any foreign subject, the rent for the property to be paid in accordance with the agreement should be remitted to the Treasurer-general of the Government until the expiration of the term.

I also informed my agents, in the clearest possible way, that in case any unforeseen incident should arise, they should act with the greatest discretion, and display all possible patience, and that they should under no circumstances use violence without having obtained from me further instructions.

Yesterday, October 9, about ten o'clock in the morning, one of these parties, composed of a civilian official, two agents of the Cadastre, an officer of the Treasury Gendarmerie and four soldiers, proceeded to the gate of the park of Shuau's-Saltana, situated in the city of Teheran.

I insert here the translation of the report dated October 9 and signed by Ali Asghar, officer of the Treasury Gendarmerie, and by Muhammad Nazar, the civilian official: —

To Mr. Shuster,
        Treasurer-general of Persia.

This 15th of Chawal, at 10 o'clock in the morning, I, the undersigned, accompanied by Mirza Ali Asghar Khan, two agents of the Cadastre, and four gendarmes, proceeded to the park of Shuau's-Saltana. Arrived before the gate of the park some Persian Cossacks told us not to enter. After having communicated to them the order to confiscate all the property of Shuau's-Saltana, we entered the garden, placed a gendarme at the gate, and commenced to open the rooms and make an inventory of the furniture.

In the meantime one of the Cossacks had communicated by telephone with the Cossack Brigade, and we next saw two Russian officers enter the apartments, saying with fury that we had no right to enter the park and that we should depart immediately.

As soon as Mirza Ali Asghar Khan had stated in Russian that we had received the order of the Government to be there, they commenced to threaten us, declaring that if we did not leave at once, they would have us beaten by the Cossacks; in fact, they called up a dozen Russian Cossacks who were waiting behind and gave them the order to attack us. In vain Mirza Ali Asghar wished to telephone.

Not being authorized to resist beyond this point, we called our men and left the garden. Nevertheless the Russian officers and Cossacks followed us to the end of the street, threatening us if we did not hasten our departure.

(Signed) MUHAMMAD NAZAR,
ALI ASGHAR.

According to the details furnished by these two officials in their verbal report, their lives were threatened by the two officers of the Russian Consulate (who were in full uniform) and by the armed Russian Cossacks who were under their orders.

On leaving the garden the Persian officials came to give me their report of the affair. About 11:30 A. M. I sent to His Excellency, Mr. Poklewski-Koziell, Russian Minister, the following telegram in English: —

His Excellency,
    S. Poklewski-Koziell,
        Russian Minister, Zargundeh.

I regret to have to inform you that this morning about nine o'clock I sent my representatives to seize the properties of Shuau's-Saltana in accordance with the order of confiscation given by the Imperial Government, and that after my representative had taken possession of the garden and while he was making an official inventory two Russian officers from your Consulate with ten Russian Cossacks appeared at the garden and ordered my representative and guard to leave, threatening to fire on them if they did not do so; and to fire on them if they again appeared in the neighboring street. My representatives then left under menace of being fired on. I feel sure that your Excellency will recognize that this action by your Consular officers is wholly unwarranted and unlawful and I therefore request you in this friendly manner to give immediate orders to your Consulate to have their force withdrawn and to inform me of their withdrawal.

W. MORGAN SHUSTER,
Treasurer-general.

After having dispatched this telegram I wrote a letter to Mons. Poklewski-Koziell, confirming my telegram and adding the following paragraph which I insert here in its original English text:

As the order given me by the Council of Ministers is explicit and imperative, and as I have no alternative but to execute the same at once, I feel that I should inform you that I will send my representatives there to-morrow morning at ten o'clock to take possession of the garden in question, and I sincerely trust the necessary arrangements will have been made to avoid the possibility of any unpleasant incident of any description.

Again expressing my personal regret that any misunderstanding should have arisen on this matter, I beg to remain, dear Mr. Minister, with kindest regards, etc. . . .

Towards eleven o'clock in the evening I received from Mons. Poklewski the following reply to my telegram:

Private.

Mons. Morgan Shuster, Teheran.

Your wire, letter received. Dawlatabad is a property rented by two Russian subjects and no measures against it ought to have been taken without previously assuring Consulate-general that all rights of Russian subjects will be safeguarded and their contract not interfered with. It is on this explicit condition that measures taken by Persian Government against property of Shuau's-Saltana will not be opposed by Russian Legation which will also hold Persian Government responsible for any claims subjects may have against Shuau's-Saltana.

(Signed) POKLEWSKI.

I invite the special attention of the Council of Ministers to the fact that not only did His Excellency the Russian Minister not reply at all to the request which I had made in my telegram concerning the withdrawal of the force sent into the garden of Shuau's-Saltana in Teheran, but he referred in his reply to the estate of Dawlatabad, which is outside the city and of which I had made no mention in my two communications.

After having notified His Excellency the Russian Minister that at 10 o'clock this morning I was going to send my representatives to the garden of Shuau's-Saltana in Teheran, to take possession of the property, and had received no reply on this subject, nothing remained but to carry out that intention.

This morning then, at 10 o'clock, I sent my representative, Mr. Cairns, with a force composed of fifty Treasury gendarmes, commanded by five Persian officers, and fifty gendarmes of the city police, commanded by three officers. This force was placed under the direct orders of one of my American assistants, Mr. Merrill.

I had given personally to Mr. Merrill and to the other officers strict instructions by the terms of which they were to take possession of the garden of Shuau's-Saltana, peaceably, if possible; if forcible opposition was made to the execution of the orders, they were under no circumstances to fire the first shot, but on the contrary to allow the Cossacks to fire first upon them. Under any circumstances, they were to carry out their orders and take possession of the property.

COMPANY OF "AMNIEH," PERSIAN ROADGUARDS, WITH THEIR OFFICERS.

EPHRAIM KHAN AND SARDAR-I-BAHADUR DURING THE CAMPAIGN AGAINST THE SHAHSEVENS.

After having received these instructions, and having arrived in front of the garden, Mr. Cairns and Mr. Merrill entered the Russian Consulate, which was near by, with an officer of the Treasury Gendarmerie who speaks Russian, and having been received by Mons. Pokhitanof, the Russian Consul-general, Mr. Cairns explained to him the object of their visit, reading to him the order of confiscation and repeating the instructions which he had received, at the same time assuring him that the rights of any foreigners would be respected, etc. Mr. Cairns then requested the Consul-general to withdraw the force which had been placed in the garden.

After some discussion the Russian Consul-general refused absolutely to withdraw this force. I should state here that the Consul-general during the entire conversation gave Mr. Cairns and Mr. Merrill the impression that the force which was in the garden was stationed there by the instructions of the Consul-general himself, and, I repeat, the Consul refused absolutely to withdraw it. Mr. Cairns thereupon notified him that he would take possession of the garden by force.

The necessary orders having been given, the Government gendarmes proceeded to an iron gate of the garden and saw inside some six or seven Persian Cossacks, armed with rifles. Demand was made upon them to open the gate and they were told that if they did not allow the Government gendarmes to enter peaceably, force would be employed. The Persian Cossacks replied that they did not have the key; the Government gendarmes, not wishing any further delay, went to another gate which they found a short distance away, and by this entered the garden. They took the arms from the Persian Cossacks and informed them that if they would withdraw without resistance, they might do so in peace. The Persian Cossacks accepted, and their arms having been surrendered, they departed, leaving the Treasury gendarmes in complete possession of the garden.

Strict orders were given concerning the taking of an inventory of the furniture, etc., and the superintendent was informed that the women who were living in the Anderun would not be incommoded and that they could either remain there or leave at their convenience. Furthermore, I sent a member of the family which resided in the Anderun to express regrets at the necessity of taking any steps which might inconvenience them, but that they might be sure of not being annoyed in any manner and that they might remain there a sufficient time to permit them to make new arrangements.

This afternoon, about 2:30 o'clock, I received a telephone message from the Persian officer who had been left in charge of the garden, informing me that a few minutes previous three officers in uniform and armed, two of whom seemed to be from the Russian Consulate, the other being Ayoub Khan, a "*Sarhang*" of the Cossack Brigade, drove up before the gate. The sentries signaled to them with their hands that no one could enter. The Cossack officer having stepped out of the carriage, the Russians called to him, saying, "They are going to fire on you," to which the Cossack officer replied, "No," and the sentries likewise said that they were not going to fire. The Russian officers, according to my information, then began to insult and threaten the officers and gendarmes of the Government. After some time they went away from the gate without further incident.

Yesterday evening, about 6 o'clock, I received the verbal reports of the officers and officials who had been sent to take possession of the properties of Dawlatabad and Mansuriabad.

After having arrived with their respective detachments at these two places and after having read the order of confiscation to the persons whom they found there, the representatives of the Government took peaceable possession of the two properties, and the two officers, after posting sentries, entered the houses; but, sometime later, two officers of the Russian Consulate, in uniform, arrived with fourteen or fifteen Russian Cossacks and suddenly entered the house at Dawlatabad; one of the Consular officers seized the Treasury Gendarmerie officer by one arm, while a Russian Cossack seized the other, and demanding to know whether he carried any weapons, they searched him. The Cossacks thereupon made the gendarmes prisoners, one after another, at their different posts, and took possession of their arms. They were then locked in a room under a guard of three Cossacks. The detachment of Cossacks then went to Mansuriabad, about two kilometers away, where the same scene was enacted. Having assembled the prisoners, the Russian Consular officials made the officers enter carriages with them, caused the gendarmes to mount donkeys, and conducted the party under arrest, surrounded by Cossacks, to the Russian Consulate in Teheran.

There the Russian Consular officials warned them not to repeat their actions in connection with the properties of Shuau's-Saltana and Salaru'd-Dawla, "who are Russian subjects." After having further enjoined them, they gave back to the gendarmes their arms and cartridges and allowed them to go.

Regarding the property of "*Chizeh*," near Gulhak, the party which was sent there to take possession informs me that they executed the order without difficulty; at the present time they are in peaceable possession.

Regarding the properties of Salaru'd-Dawla, which are some distance away, I have not yet received any news.

I cannot conclude this report without expressing my clear conviction that, in this entire affair, the Russian Consulate-general and its officials have acted in a totally unjustifiable manner and absolutely contrary to the laws and the sovereignty of the Imperial Government. At the same time I should state that in my opinion my representatives have comported themselves throughout in a thoroughly proper and dignified way, under peculiarly difficult conditions.

After this incident took place there was a Russian *communiqué* to the press, suggesting that Mr. Cairns had broken off a conference with the Russian Consul-general or that a " conference " was going on when the final seizure was made.

There was of course no " conference " whatever in the sense evidently intended in that statement. There was a courteous call by Mr. Cairns on Mons. Pokhitanof, in an endeavor to prevent what might have been very regrettable occurrences. Finding, however, that no possible explanations or assurances could dissuade this insubordinate official from the attitude he was bent on adopting, Mr. Cairns departed, expressing the hope that there would be no trouble when he took the property.

It will be noted that two hours after the Treasury officials were in peaceable possession of this place, MM. Petroff and Hildebrand, the same two Russian Vice-consuls who had led the first assault by the Russian Cossacks the day before, drove up to the gate and commenced abusing the Persian sentries there, telling them that they would be killed, and employing vile insults — all in an endeavor to provoke these ignorant guards into losing their temper and taking some action which these Consular officials could construe into an insult to the Russian Government. In other words, finding that they had been thwarted in their effort to obtain, however illegally, the possession of these properties, these Russian officials deliberately sought to involve their Government in the dispute.

Fortunately, the Treasury gendarmes had received such strict instructions that they kept perfect control of themselves and

refused to be entrapped into noticing the insults and impre-
cations which were addressed to them by these valiant Consuls,
who thereupon drove away and reported, with absolute falsity,
that the affront had actually occurred which they had gone
there to provoke.

These false statements were reported to St. Petersburg by
Mons. Pokhitanof independently of his Minister, who, I have
the strongest reason to believe, entirely disavowed the Russian
Consul-general's actions in the whole affair.   The position officially taken by the Russian Government shortly thereafter, however, showed the truly remarkable absence of all discipline or
coördination in the Russian Ministry of Foreign Affairs.   Here
was a plain case calling for careful investigation and recommendation by the diplomatic representative at Teheran, yet, dis-
regarding every element of truth and justice, the St. Petersburg Cabinet, in which the " forward party " had obtained the
complete ascendancy with the appointment of Mons. Kokovtsoff,
now upheld its insubordinate Consul-general, to the notorious
discredit of its Minister, merely because it suited the secret purposes of the Cabinet to act on Pokhitanof's false reports.

The low esteem in which Mons. Pokhitanof was held both by
his own Minister and by the British Minister was notorious
in Teheran.   Sir George Barclay would not receive him socially and declared his actions in the Shuau's-Saltana affair to
have been those of a crazy man.   Relations between Pokhitanof
and Mons. Poklewski-Koziell thereafter became so strained that
neither the Consul-general nor his staff nor family attended the
annual official ball given at the Russian Legation on December
19, although practically every other member of the European
colony was present.

The afternoon of the day that Pokhitanof's Cossacks drove
out the Treasury gendarmes from Shuau's-Saltana's garden,
Mons. Poklewski-Koziell, who was at his summer quarters in

ARTILLERY BELONGING TO EPHRAIM'S GENDARMERIE AT TEHERAN.

SIPAHDAR-I-AZAM WITH HIS STAFF.

Zargundeh some miles outside the city, called the Consul-general on the telephone and demanded to know why he had interfered in the matter. A heated argument took place over the wire, at the conclusion of which the Russian Minister demanded to know what justification Pokhitanof had for his actions. The latter replied that he had his reasons. Poklewski then said that if he (Pokhitanof) had no excuse, he had better find one very shortly, as I had telegraphed a complaint. Pokhitanof then stated that he would " send up some papers." [1]

A messenger was at once despatched by Pokhitanof to the *Banque d'Escompte* to get a certain fictitious obligation which Shuau's-Saltana had executed to the Bank several years before at the time when the terms of Muhammad Ali's deposition were being arranged. Shuau's-Saltana had given this instrument in the hope that the Russian Bank, acting in collusion with him, would be able to collect some 225,000 tumans from the Constitutional Government on the grounds that Shuau's-Saltana (the deposed Shah's brother) was indebted to the Bank to that extent. It was notorious, however, that far from owing the Bank anything, he was its creditor to a considerable extent — a fact which I was subsequently enabled to prove by an authenticated copy of his will made just before he left Persia. This attempt by the Russian State Bank to defraud the Persian Government of a large sum was so flagrant that the British Minister took sides with the Persians, and the scheme failed. It was this same fraudulent paper which Pokhitanof relied on to establish his contention that the *Banque d'Escompte* held a mortgage on Shuau's-Saltana's garden. The exact status of the Bank's accounts with Shuau's-Saltana was immediately conveyed to me from a confidential source, as well as the fact that Pokhitanof had obtained from the Bank that day the paper in

---

[1] This entire conversation was reported to me that same evening by a Persian telephone employee — who understood Russian and had overheard the discussion.

question. The Russian Government never presented the slightest evidence in support of its claim that the *Banque d'Escompte*
had any interest in the Shuau's-Saltana's property.[1]

Ever since the 8th of August when the British and Russian
Governments had attempted to intimidate the Persian Government into renouncing any effort to secure the services of Major
Stokes for the organization of the Treasury Gendarmerie, I had
been carrying on very friendly but purely informal negotiations with both Mons. Poklewski-Koziell and Sir George Barclay in the endeavor to bring their Governments to see the benefits which would accrue from the withdrawal of their opposition, as well as the injustice of their attitude, toward Persia.
I think that it is not going too far to say that both these gentlemen became thoroughly convinced that my request was a most
reasonable one and that it arose from no other motive than a
desire to secure efficient help for a rather difficult task.   The
St. Petersburg Cabinet, however, had far different things in
mind than the rapid reorganization of Persia's finances.   The
Russian Government had become convinced by one or two incidents, which I somewhat doubt the propriety of my mentioning at this time, that it could not expect the American finance

---

[1] Articles IV and VI of Shuau's-Saltana's last will and testament read as
follows:

IV.   " A cette date, je possède à la Banque d'Escompte une somme de
18.000 Tumans au comptant, en compte courant, et je possède également
une somme de près de 20.000 tumans à la Banque Impériale, qui, à cause
d'une certaine différence, ne me l'a pas payée et qui retient injustement
mon solde créditeur.   Mes executeurs testamentaires tâcheront évidemment
à poursuivre cette affaire et à ne point laisser se perdre le droit de mes
héritiers mineurs."

VI.   " Mon unique dette, à cette date, consiste en une obligation de
46.000 tumans envers ma mère Nozhat-es-Saltana, sur laquelle obligation
j'ai déjà payé 3.000 Tumans.   Il reste donc un solde de 43.000 tumans
dont je suis redevable à ma mère d'après cette même obligation imprimée
et rédigée de la main de Montakhab'd-Dawla (le . . .).

Outre cette dette due à ma mère, je ne dois plus rien absolument à personne à quelque titre que ce soit.   Et si une obligation venait à etre ex-
hibée par une personne quelconque, *elle doit etre reconnue comme fausse et
falsifiée.*

Je suis absolument quitte detoutes dettes outre celle relatée ci-dessus."

officials in Persia to follow the lines marked out for themselves by the Belgian Customs officials.

On October 15 Mons. Poklewski-Koziell wrote me finally that his Government would not withdraw its opposition to Major Stokes' appointment. This step, coupled with the attitude adopted by Russia in the Shuau's-Saltana affair, to say nothing of her having taken steps which defeated all chance of Persia securing on satisfactory terms the loan of the £4,000,000 which I had been informally negotiating with the representatives of Messrs. Seligman Bros., convinced both the leaders of the Medjlis and myself that Russia had determined to take full advantage of the still disturbed European situation and the only too apparent weakness of the British Foreign Office in all its relations with Russia concerning Persian affairs.

The loss of Major Stokes' services and the blocking of the permanent improvements and revenue-producing expenditures which were to be financed with the funds derived from the proposed loan of £4,000,000 practically nullified all hope of my accomplishing any constructive financial work in behalf of Persia. I deemed it but fair that these facts should no longer remain hidden, and, on October 17, in the course of an interview with the correspondents of the London *Times* and Reuter's News Agency, I took occasion to say that the final refusal of Russia to withdraw from her unwarranted attempt to coerce the Persian Government in the case of Major Stokes and the complete acquiescence of England in the coercion plainly showed that there was no genuine friendly feeling on the part of those two Governments towards the financial reformation and the general progress of Persia. This seemed a very mild statement of the facts to those on the ground who were really acquainted with what had been done to thwart our efforts, but the London *Times,* in its issue of October 19, chose to characterize my statements as unjust and unfounded. As this well-known journal is commonly recognized as the semi-official organ of the British Foreign Office, I felt obliged to defend myself from this attack and actually to give the facts to the British public, in the hope that the British Government might still be persuaded to insist upon Persia's being allowed that independence and sovereignty which both powers had solemnly bound themselves to respect.

I therefore prepared a partial statement of the situation, and on October 21, after consultation with a number of prominent Persians, and with the unofficial sanction of the Cabinet, I mailed an open letter [1] to the *Times* with a request for its publication.

The letter was printed in two sections in the *Times* of November 10 and 11. When the press despatches from London on the former date brought word of the publication of this communication, the British Minister sent over and asked me for a copy, which I immediately sent him. This communication was received with varying comments by the British press, and was made the basis for a number of questions put to the Secretary of State for Foreign Affairs in the House of Commons.

[1] See Appendix C.

SATTAR KHAN, ONE OF THE DEFENDERS OF THE CITY OF
TABRIZ WHEN IT WAS BESIEGED BY THE FORCES OF
MUHAMMAD ALI SHAH.

SARDAR-I-MUHIY, THE "WALKING ARSENAL."
He was foremost in the attacks made on the Persian treasury when
the irregular forces were formed to fight against the
ex-Shah during the summer of 1911.

CHAPTER VI

B Y the end of October the Russian Government was landing troops at Enzeli, and assembling a still larger force
at Baku. England at this time notified the Persian Government that she was sending two squadrons of Indian *sawars* to
Bushire, on the Gulf, whence they would proceed to Shiraz as
" Consular guards."

The yellow-booted military gentleman, Sardar-i-Muhiy, who
had presented to me the first requisition for war funds, was
defeated by the Turcomans at Bender Djez, and both Russian
gun-boats and the Russian Consul openly aided the rebel forces.

On November 2 Mons. Poklewski-Koziell, the Russian Minister, called at the Persian Foreign Office and made a verbal
demand, in the name of his Government, that the Treasury gendarmes should be immediately withdrawn from the park of
Shuau's-Saltana, and that Persian Cossacks from the Cossack
Brigade should be put in possession of the estate. He also
demanded an apology for the " insult " which his Government
alleged had been offered to its Consular officers. He refused to
pay any attention to Persia's protest against the violation of
her sovereignty and the interference with her internal affairs,
and actually returned the written protest lodged by the Persian
Government, though he had previously received and acknowledged the same.

The Russian Minister stated that his instructions were to

obtain an immediate answer, " yes " or " no," from the Persian
Cabinet.

The Persian Minister of Foreign Affairs stated that he could
not take action in such an important matter without consulting
his colleagues.

After two days' discussion the Cabinet consulted me as to
their best course, and while disclaiming any desire to intervene
in purely political affairs, I gave my opinion that Russia was
without law or justice in her demands, and that if the Cabinet
was going to stand at all on the rights of Persia, this seemed a
very strong case for them.

On the same day that this verbal ultimatum was presented
another incident took place.

After many fruitless attempts to get certain wealthy grandees
in Teheran to pay their taxes, I sent small parties of Treasury
gendarmes to exact them by force, as had always been the procedure in Persia. One of the most flagrant tax-evaders was
Prince Alau'd-Dawla, a member of the royal family and former
governor of Shiraz.

After he had insulted and driven out the last tax-collector
sent to his house, I had the latter return there, accompanied by
five Treasury gendarmes, who posted themselves at the gates and
informed the prince that his property was seized until he paid
his dues to the Government. Alau'd-Dawla left by another
gate and rushed to the house of Samsamu's-Saltana, the Bakhtiyari Premier, who lived near by. With tears in his eyes the
Prince described the brutal treatment which he had received
from the Treasury officials, and he so played on the feelings of
his friend, the Premier, that the latter's brother, Amir Mujahid,
a Bakhtiyari chieftain, was sent to drive away the Treasury
gendarmes. Amir Mujahid had become my bitter enemy, principally because I had refused to honor a number of heavy
demands for money for his forces. He went to the residence

of Alau'd-Dawla, with the latter's son, a colonel in the regular army, and some Bakhtiyari guards, and rushing upon the unsuspecting gendarmes, beat them with his heavy stick and had their guns wrested from them. This was late in the afternoon.

The next morning I received a note from the Premier, advising me of the step he had taken. I replied at once, demanding a full written apology for the affair, the punishment of the guilty parties and the immediate payment of the taxes. The following day the Premier made a very manly apology in the Council, sent me a written one, and said that he was an excitable old man and "had gone quite out of his head when the great Prince Alau'd-Dawla had rushed in with tears in his eyes."

The guns of the Treasury gendarmes were restored to them publicly by the Premier's military aide, and the taxes were paid in full. The effect of this incident was most valuable, as the prestige of the Treasury was greatly enhanced, and a number of other grandees and princes who had hoped to continue evading the law, promptly paid their taxes. If the insult to the Treasury force had been allowed to pass unnoticed, we might as well have closed up the office. Such little incidents are given great importance in Persia, where above all things a man or a government must keep prestige.

After some days of discussion, the Cabinet, on November 6, sent a Foreign Office official to the Russian Legation to convey the verbal reply to Russia's ultimatum. The reply was a dignified exposition of the attitude of the Persian Government, coupled with an offer to abide by an impartial and complete investigation of the facts of the Shuau's-Saltana incident.

In the meantime the press despatches described a sinister threat by Russia to seize the Province of Ghilam and the district of Talich, in Northern Persia. The Russian Government was undoubtedly surprised by Persia's firm attitude and the tenor of her reply.

On November 7 I received a note from Sir George Barclay, the British Minister, stating that he desired to call and read me a telegram from his Government. He did so the next day. The telegram was from Sir Edward Grey and instructed Sir George to inform me that my assignment of Mr. Lecoffre, a British subject, to Tabriz to inspect the finances there would result in a protest by Russia " to preserve her interests there," and would create the danger of her seizing Northern Persia. It was perfectly apparent, even from the British Minister's manner, that Russia had instigated this action by the British Foreign Office. As a matter of fact I had, some weeks previously, decided to send Mr. Lecoffre to Tabriz to investigate the misappropriation of nearly 1,000,000 tumans of the taxes there during the preceding two years. He was one of my few European assistants who could speak Persian, who understood the intricacies of the Persian taxation system, and he had been at Tabriz before and knew the situation there. I frankly confess that I was surprised to find that even Russia had raised any objection, since Mr. Lecoffre had been in the Ministry of Finance at Teheran for nearly two years, and was occupying a rather important and influential position there. Teheran, of course, is in the so-called " Russian " or " Northern Sphere " of Persia, and by sending Mr. Lecoffre to Tabriz on a special mission I was merely transferring him from one point in Northern Persia to another.

I replied to Sir George Barclay that I always had been and was still most anxious to observe all the legitimate interests of Russia and the other powers in Persia, but that I could not, as he well knew, in this case any more than in the Stokes' case, recognize the existence in Persia of foreign " spheres of influence " — a thing which the Persian Government had officially refused to do, and had actually forbidden me to do on more than one occasion. I added that if the Russian Government would show a single friendly action towards my work in Persia, I could guarantee that it would be reciprocated to the fullest extent.

Sir George went through the delivery of his message like a man taking medicine, and left without entering into any argument.

On November 11 the Medjlis unanimously passed a law authorizing me to employ under contract ten more Americans as financial assistants.

At noon the same day Mons. de Giers, the Oriental Secretary of the Russian Legation, presented a written renewal of the original demands of the Russian Government on Persia. Mons. de Giers stated that if the demands were not complied with within forty-eight hours, diplomatic relations between the two countries would be broken off.

The London *Times* published an editorial on my open letter, accusing me at the end of having " thrown in my lot " with the Persian Nationalists. I am unable to understand with whom the *Times* thought I should have thrown in my lot while I was working in the service of the Constitutional Government.

It was about this time that my letter to the *Times* was printed in Persian, in the form of a pamphlet, and circulated quite widely. A local newspaper, *Tamadun,* publicly admitted having printed and circulated this pamphlet as soon as I was charged with having done so — which I had not.

By November 11 the Persian Cabinet, having been thoroughly frightened by the extensive preparations which Russia was evidently making for occupying Northern Persia, consulted the British Government as to what course should be pursued. Sir Edward Grey promptly cabled his advice to accept the Russian ultimatum, and apologize as was demanded.

The Premier, Samsamu's-Saltana, sent me a letter demanding that I should remove all my gendarmes from the park of Shuau's-Saltana. I should mention that this simple-minded old chieftain had been subjected for several days to some very strong Russian influences, and some suspicion of his entire loyalty had already been aroused among the deputies of the Medjlis.

When, therefore, I received this order, but signed only by him as Premier, instead of by the entire Council of Ministers, as the original order of confiscation had been, I had no choice but to reply that the order of the Council could be revoked only by a similarly authoritative document. I insisted either that my agents should be left in charge of the properties, or that I should be relieved of all responsibility for them.

The usual Cabinet " crises " were occurring during these days. One might meet the Finance Minister on the street and hear from him that he had " resigned," but he would be found at the Council chamber the following morning.

On November 18 the Russian Legation informed the Persian Government that as the ultimatum had not been accepted, diplomatic relations were thereby broken off, but that commercial matters would continue to be handled by the Russian Consuls. It was reported that 4000 Russian troops were en route from the Caucasus for Persia.

The Cabinet, having reflected on Sir Edward Grey's advice to yield to the Russian demands, decided to do so and accordingly sent me a written order to deliver the estates of Shuau's-Saltana to their representatives and to recall my gendarmes. I had this order executed, taking receipts in full for everything that we had seized.

It was evident by this time that the British Foreign Office had become alarmed by Russia's threatening attitude and that the

WUTHUQU'D-DAWLA, MINISTER OF FOREIGN AFFAIRS DURING MOST OF THE TIME MR. SHUSTER WAS IN PERSIA.

He was foremost in urging the acceptance of Russia's demands, and in bringing about the destruction of the Medjlis on December 24, 1911

GHAVAMU'S-SALTANA, MINISTER OF THE INTERIOR, AND BROTHER OF WUTHUQU'D-DAWLA.

advice to Persia to yield at once was actuated by a desire to stay the advance of Russian troops lest Parliament should criticize Russia's violation of the Convention of 1907.

In the meantime a new Persian Cabinet had been formed and it was voted to apologize to Russia.

On November 24, therefore, the Persian Minister of Foreign Affairs, Wuthuqu'd-Dawla, drove in full uniform to the Russian Legation. Seizing the Russian Minister by the hand he said: "Your Excellency, I am instructed by my own Government to apologize in its name for the affront put upon the Consular officers of Your Excellency's Government in the Shuau's-Saltana affair." Then followed the grim diplomatic jest which only a Russian Cabinet with its utter disregard for fairness or decency would think of perpetrating.

The Persian Ministers evidently believed that their self-abasement and the delivery of the estates would appease even Russian anger and settle the whole affair. They reckoned, however, without knowledge of the true plans of Russian bureaucracy. A compliance by Persia with Russia's demands was the very last thing that the Russian Cabinet desired. Had Russia merely been seeking to uphold the dignity of her insubordinate Consular officials, Wuthuqu'd-Dawla's apology would have ended the affair. What Russia plainly wanted was *to have some pretext for continuing to occupy Northern Persia with her troops* — a thing which she had *started to do* before her ultimatum to Persia had even been presented. Sir Edward Grey had assured the Persian Cabinet, through the British Legation at Teheran, that if an apology was made to Russia, the Russian troops which were already entering Persia would be withdrawn. It was upon this assurance made by Sir Edward Grey — with what authority has not been disclosed — that Persia yielded to Russia's demands.

Thus we understand clearly why the Russian Minister, in replying to Wuthuqu'd-Dawla's apology, stated that Persia's agreement to the demands of the first ultimatum was accepted, but that he was instructed to give notice that *in the meantime another ultimatum was being prepared!*

It should not be difficult to picture the surprise on the face of Persia's representative at this bit of ghastly humor. The meeting had been arranged by the British Minister. Absolutely nothing new had occurred in the interior to give grounds for such a novel procedure. It was only too plain that Russia proposed to keep pouring her Cossacks into Northern Persia, whatever the British or the Persian Governments might do or say. The long-expected chance to start the outflanking movement on India and to edge towards the Persian Gulf had arrived. The embers of the Moroccan diplomatic conflagration still glowed sufficiently to make her sure that no serious protest would be made by England.

True to its promise, on November 29, at noon, the Russian Government presented to Persia its second ultimatum, demanding its acceptance within the space of just forty-eight hours.

The language of this remarkable document is important enough to be quoted in full:

TRANSLATION OF THE TEXT OF THE SECOND RUSSIAN ULTIMATUM.

In the course of our interview on Friday (November 24) I had the honor of explaining to Your Excellency the reasons which impelled the Imperial Government of Russia to put several further proposals before the Persian Government, and I have been waiting for my Government's instructions on the subject.

Those instructions have now reached me and I have the honor to make on behalf of the Russian Government the following proposals:

(1) The dismissal of Mr. Shuster and Mr. Lecoffre; the status of the other persons who have been invited into service by Mr. Shuster will be determined in accordance with the second proposal.

(2) An undertaking by the Persian Government not to engage in the service of Persia foreign subjects without first obtaining the consent of the Russian and British Legations.

(3) The payment by the Persian Government of an indemnity to defray the expenses of the present despatch of troops to Persia. The amount and manner of payment and compensation will be fixed after the receipt of the Persian Government's reply.

(EXPLANATIONS BY RUSSIAN MINISTER)

I consider it my duty to explain that the reasons for these measures are:

(1) The absolute necessity of obtaining compensation owing to the fact that the Imperial Government had been forced to send troops to Persia and owing to the recent insulting acts of Mr. Shuster towards Russia.

(2) The earnest desire of the Imperial Government is now to remove the principal source of conflict which has arisen and in the future to lay the foundations upon which the two Governments can firmly build up friendly and stable relations, *and to give a prompt and satisfactory solution to all the Russian matters and questions still pending.*[1]

(3) In addition to the above facts I have to point out that the Imperial Government will not wait longer than forty-eight hours for the execution of the aforesaid proposals, and during this interval the Russian troops will remain at Resht. If no reply or an unsatisfactory reply be received at the expiration of the said period, the troops will advance and it is evident that this will increase the indemnity to be paid by Persia to Russia.

The impression which the modest " proposals " made on the Persian Cabinet, Medjlis and general public can be better imagined than described.

The language of the document, which was Persian, is purposely ambiguous, especially in those parts speaking of " compensation " and " prompt and satisfactory solution to all Russian matters and questions still pending."

At the same time that this ultimatum was handed in, a note was presented by the Russian Minister informing the Persian Government that " in consideration of a telegram sent by the

---

[1] The italics are the author's.

Lady Nizatu's-Saltana, the mother of Shuau's-Saltana, to Their Imperial Majesties, the Czar and Czarina of All The Russias, the aforesaid Lady and *her property* are henceforth placed under the protection of the Government of Russia."

The lady in question was a Persian subject. The Russian Government relieved her of this disability by telegraph.

CHAPTER VII

THE BREAD RIOTS. THE MEDJLIS REJECTS RUSSIA'S ULTIMA-
TUM. INVASION BY RUSSIAN TROOPS. PERSIA PLANS FOR
RESISTANCE. PART PLAYED BY PERSIAN WOMEN. ABOLISH-
MENT OF THE MEDJLIS BY COUP D'ETAT, DECEMBER 24.

IN the Russian ultimatum of November 29 the name of the
British Government was used, though the British Minister
apparently had nothing to do with the affair. The acceptance
by Persia of the demands thus made upon her would have been
almost tantamount to a cession of her sovereignty to Russia
and Great Britain. Shortly after the presentation of this
ultimatum Sir Edward Grey was asked in Parliament to explain why the name of the British Government was used. He
replied that he agreed with the Russian demands, with the
possible exception of the indemnity clause, to pay which might
cripple Persia's force for policing the southern trade route, thus
prejudicing British commerce. This was apparently the only
possible objection which the British Foreign Office could see,
or urge against the ultimatum. In the course of his remarks
Sir Edward Grey accused me of having endeavored to " set the
clock back " in Persia. This, he said, was the reason of my
failure, and I must go.

The Regent sent for me in the early afternoon of the 29th,
some two hours after the ultimatum had been delivered. I
found him surrounded by the Cabinet, including my old friend,
Mutashamu's-Saltana, who had in some mysterious manner
succeeded in gaining favor with the Premier, Samsamu's-
Saltana.

The Regent said that the Government was very nervous about the " bread situation." In Persia cheap and plentiful bread is the test by which administrations and Cabinets stand or fall. Wheat bread is the principal food of the people, especially in the cities and large towns. It is not, as a rule, baked at home, but in public bakeries, of which in Teheran there are several hundred. The bread comes out in large strips, about half an inch thick. These strips are handled very much as if they were wrapping paper. A Persian on the road is very apt to wrap up his bit of cheese and fruit in his strip of bread.

When the wheat is harvested in the summer the Government collects a proportion of it in taxes. In the districts around the capital and other large towns, this government wheat is supposed to be brought in and stored in public granaries, in order that the people may have a plentiful supply of good cheap bread during the winter. The Persian Government has been doing this from time immemorial. If it did not do so, and sold its wheat when collected, the grandees and rich owners of wheat-producing districts would combine, control the supply sent each day to the public markets for sale to the bakers, and force up the price. Bread would immediately become scarce and dear, and there would be a serious *chuluk* or riot. To prevent this it was the custom of the Government to deal out, commencing in the fall, a certain amount of wheat at a fair price to the bakers; this procedure, together with the knowledge that the Government had wheat in reserve, kept the price reasonable and, as a rule, prevented private combines.

It was the wheat or bread situation which was causing the Regent and the Cabinet trouble at this time. There had been a poor crop in Northern Persia, especially around Teheran. This was due partly to a drought and partly to the general disorders, destruction of crops and pillaging which had been going on ever since Muhammad Ali had made his entry into

Persia. Then the fighting which had been going on during the summer, and the continued presence of large numbers of Bakhtiyaris and other irregular troops in the neighborhood of the capital, had frightened away the muleteers and cameldrivers on whom every one depended to bring the wheat into the city.

The regular function of the Treasury in regard to wheat was merely to see that the taxes payable in this grain, as those payable in rice, barley, cotton and straw, were collected, and that the wheat was transported to the cities and stored. Foreseeing a serious situation, however, and knowing that the government wheat stores had always been a fruitful source of graft for the Governor and other officials of the capital, the Cabinet had asked me to keep a close watch on the supply and on its destination.

I had accordingly been making extraordinary efforts to get wheat in from the outlying districts before the roads should become blocked. I was also endeavoring to prevent the Teheran municipal officials from making their usual annual fortunes at the expense of the bread supply. A " ring " had been formed by a number of reactionary grandees for the two-fold purpose of enriching themselves and embarrassing the Constitutional Government.

I told the Regent and the Cabinet that if they desired me to deal with the situation and would appoint an honest Governor of Teheran, I would accept the responsibility. They promised to make the changes needed, but as usual procrastinated until matters grew much worse. There were a number of small bread riots from time to time, but they had been easily suppressed.

In connection with the bread supply a rather gruesome incident occurred. The chief baker in Teheran was one of the principal grafters in the " municipal bread-ring " and a great trouble-maker for the Treasury. He was a man of evil record, and reputed to have baked an offending subordinate to death in his own oven on more than one occasion. Speaking of him and his intrigues one day to several prominent Nationalists I remarked that he was the cause of most of the trouble with the bread supply in the capital, was feeding inferior bread to the people, and that he should be " gotten rid of." A morning or so afterwards, on entering my office rather late, I was informed by one of my Persian assistants that " the chief baker had been killed in accordance with my wishes!" I leave the reader to imagine my surprise and feelings. As a matter of fact he had been assassinated, and though I have no reason to believe that my own remarks had anything to do with his taking off, I determined thenceforth to be more cautious and precise in my language. The unfortunate man was a murderer, and had waxed wealthy by stealing from the poor, often starving people of the city, so no great injustice was, perhaps, done, but the interpretation put by my young Persian friend on his untimely end gave me quite a shock. From that time on the control of the bread became much easier.

The afternoon of November 29 an unusual incident occurred in the Medjlis. The Premier, Samsamu's-Saltana, after leaving the Regent's palace went to the Parliament to present for approval a new Cabinet which he had formed. Among the names was that of Mutashamu's-Saltana, designated as Minister of Justice. Even deputies long accustomed to approving ministers of threadbare reputation revolted at this. The Premier had been growing very friendly with the Russian Legation and his insistence, against the advice of his colleagues, on having Mutashamu's-Saltana in the Cabinet was due to the latter's close relations with well-known Russian emissaries and protégés.

When the aged Premier in reading his list of names came to

TAQI-ZADA, THE FAMOUS CONSTITUTIONALIST DEPUTY FROM TABRIZ.

He was forced into exile on account of his political views.

PRINCE SULAYMAN MIRZA, LEADER OF THE DEMOCRATS IN THE MEDJLIS.

He was an ardent and patriotic Nationalist

the new Minister of Justice things commenced to happen in that dignified assemblage.

Prince Sulayman Mirza, the leader of the Democrats, mounted the tribune and declared that the Premier possessed the confidence of the deputies, but that the Democrats could not accept a member of the traitorous Cabinet of the Sipahdar. Amid cries of anger from the Moderates, the Premier ascended the platform and commenced a violent harangue against the Democrats. He was called to order by Mutaminu'l-Mulk, the President, whereupon he rushed from the Chamber declaring that he would call his Bakhtiyaris and kill all the Democrats. The chief priest of Teheran then attacked the President and the Democrats. The President then employed the Persian equivalent of the sergeant-at-arms and the mace; he solemnly called the chief priest to order three times, the utterance of the last word meaning imprisonment for the offender. At this point the assemblage broke up in an uproar and the one really undignified session of Persia's Parliament was recorded.

This scene and the reports of the Russian ultimatum threw the capital into tumult. Nothing but the fact that Ephraim was in charge of the police and gendarmes saved an outbreak by the disorderly and fanatical elements. At this time the Treasury Gendarmerie consisted of about 800 men,— practically all stationed in Teheran. They were well drilled, fully equipped and in charge of four American officers, three of whom had recently arrived.

The Premier's attempt to get Mutashamu's-Saltana into the Cabinet and his threats to use the Bakhtiyaris against the Democrats had convinced the latter that Russian intrigues had been at work on the Ministers, and that the Constitutional Government was again to be threatened. It had been discovered that Prince Alau'd-Dawla, who had refused to pay his taxes until force was used, was plotting with a number of well-known reactionaries to ask the Russian Government to restore Muhammad Ali to the throne. The police seized a formal petition to that effect bearing the signature of this grandee and a number of others.

On the day after the ultimatum was presented I received a call from the Nawwab and Ephraim. They asked my advice on the situation. I told them that they could inform the Medjlis and the Cabinet that I desired them to take whatever decision they considered best for the Persian people, without any thought of myself or of my American assistants. During the afternoon and evening a large number of deputies called and asked my advice. To all I made this same reply, explaining that as the action which the Government might take would so vitally affect my own reputation and future, I did not care to influence them in any manner. I promised that the Americans would abide loyally by the decision of the Medjlis as to the Russian ultimatum, whatever that decision might be.

The next morning, December 1, on entering my office I learned that Prince Alau'd-Dawla had just been shot as he was leaving his house, by three men who were on a neighboring balcony watching for him. He died shortly thereafter.

Another attempt at assassination was directed against Mushiru's-Saltana, a former prime minister of Muhammad Ali, while he was out riding. He was wounded in the leg, but his nephew who was with him was killed.

These crimes were undoubtedly the result of the conviction which had taken possession of the members of the secret *anjumans* (societies) in Teheran that a well-organized campaign was on foot to strangle the Constitutional movement in Persia and restore despotism and vengeance in the form of Muhammad Ali. The fact that the reactionaries were known to be practically selling the country to Russia only increased the bitterness of the Nationalists. The anjumans, which had in previous years played such an important and even heroic part in Persia's struggle towards free institutions, had not ceased to exist. They were passive while the Constitution seemed in no danger, but they sprang vigorously into action the moment that their ideal was threatened. Their members were in many cases known as *fidais* (self-devoted), and they were always prepared to take up arms in defense of their principles.

The effect of the killing of Prince Alau'd-Dawla was tremendous, and before the shock of horror which the assassination caused had subsided, a panic seized every public official and grandee who felt that his conscience was not entirely clear in his actions towards the land of his birth.

When the Samsamu's-Saltana learned of the death of his friend, the Prince, he broke into tears and swore an impassioned oath to annihilate the elements which he believed were responsible for the act. "I will kill twenty Democrats for this!" he said.

The last Russian ultimatum was claimed to be based on two pretexts which were at best rather puerile, even if true. Incidentally the facts alleged, namely, that I had appointed Mr. Lecoffre, a British subject to be a tax-collector in the Russian sphere of influence, and that I had caused to be printed and circulated a Persian translation of my letter to the *Times,* were totally devoid of truth.

Nevertheless, the Russian demands, with all the hypocritical attempts made to justify them, fairly stunned the people of Persia. Accustomed as the Constitutional Government had been in recent years to the high-handed and cynical actions of the St. Petersburg Cabinet, the Ministers had not looked for such a blow as this.

The Cabinet had been realizing dimly that the peace of Europe was being jeopardized by the open and increasing hostility between England and Germany, and that the tension over the Moroccan affair, while subsiding, was still very marked. They felt also that Sir Edward Grey's preoccupation with the European crisis had driven from his mind whatever conception he might have had of the importance of Asiatic problems to the British Empire. This situation, it was clear, was leaving Russia absolutely free to push forward her long-cherished plans for the absorption of Persia and the establishment of a naval base on the Persian Gulf. Russia could work her will in Persia so long, at least, as she even pretended to acknowledge the Anglo-Russian Convention of 1907, and by this patent subterfuge relieved the British Foreign Office of the embarrassment of explaining in Parliament why Russia had not been held to her signed agreement.

Despite all this the Persians, as events have shown, had far too much confidence in the sacredness of treaty stipulations and the solemnly pledged words of the great Christian nations of the world to imagine that their whole national existence and liberties could be thus menaced overnight, and on a pretext so shallow and farcical.

Their disillusionment came too late, though it is difficult to see what they could have done, even had they realized the truth earlier than they did. If Russia had not adopted the pretext which she did, she would have soon found or manufactured others. The trap which closed around Persia had been set by the hands or by the fate which brought about an unexpected move on the European chess-board during the summer of the year 1911, and the Bear's paw had been skilful enough to spring the trap before the opportunity was lost.

In the sudden crisis which now confronted the Persian Government nearly every man began to suspect his neighbor. The administration split immediately into two factions. The Cabinet, under Samsamu's-Saltana, adopted one course, and more or less carried the Regent with it. The deputies of the

GROUP OF AMERICAN AND PERSIAN OFFICIALS OF THE TREASURY.
Taken at the entrance to the office-building next to Atabak Palace.

Medjlis, on the other hand, sincerely believing themselves to
represent the patriotic aspirations and sovereignty of the
Persian people, were inclined to meet their responsibilities
face to face.

The Persian statesmen and chieftains who formed the
Cabinet at this time, whether because they perceived the naked
steel behind Russia's threats more clearly than their legislative
compatriots, or whether they suffered from that abandon and
tired feeling which comes from playing an unequal and always
losing game, quickly decided that, despite the betrayal of their
trust thereby involved, they would accept this second ultimatum
with all its future oppression and cruelty for their people.

On December first, therefore, shortly before the time limit
of forty-eight hours fixed by Russia for the acceptance of the
terms had expired, the Cabinet filed into the Medjlis to secure
legislative approval of their intended course.

It was an hour before noon, and the Parliament grounds
and buildings were filled with eager, excited throngs, while the
galleries of the chamber were packed with Persian notables of
all ranks and with the representatives of many of the foreign
legations. At noon the fate of Persia as a nation was to be
known.

The Cabinet, having made up its mind to yield, overlooked
no point, which would increase their chances of securing the
approval of the Medjlis. Believing, evidently, that the ridiculously short time to elapse before the stroke of noon announced
the expiration of the forty-eight-hour period would effectually
prevent any mature consideration or discussion of their proposals, the Premier, Samsamu's-Saltana, caused to be presented
to the deputies a resolution authorizing the Cabinet to accept
Russia's demands.

The proposal was read amid deep silence. At its conclusion
a hush fell upon the gathering. Seventy-six deputies, old men

9

and young, priests, lawyers, doctors, merchants, and princes, sat tense in their seats.

A venerable priest of Islam arose.   Time was slipping away and at noon the question would be beyond their vote to decide. This servant of God spoke briefly and to the point: "It may be the will of Allah that our liberty and our sovereignty shall be taken from us by force, but let us not sign them away with our own hands!"   One gesture of appeal with his trembling hands, and he resumed his seat.

Simple words, these, yet wingéd ones.   Easy to utter in academic discussions; hard, bitterly hard, to say under the eye of a cruel and overpowering tyrant whose emissaries watched the speaker from the galleries and mentally marked him down for future imprisonment, torture, exile or worse.

Other deputies followed.   In dignified appeals, brief because the time was so short, they upheld their country's honor and proclaimed their hard-earned right to live and govern themselves.

A few minutes before noon the public vote was taken; one or two faint-hearted members sought a craven's refuge and slunk quietly from the chamber.   As each name was called the deputy rose in his place and gave his vote; there was no secret ballot here.

And when the roll call was ended every man, priest or layman, youth or octogenarian, had cast his own die of fate, had staked the safety of himself and family, and hurled back into the teeth of the great Bear from the North the unanimous answer of a desperate and down-trodden people who preferred a future of unknown terror to the voluntary sacrifice of their national dignity and of their recently earned right to work out their own salvation.

Amid tears and applause from the spectators, the crest-fallen and frightened members of the Cabinet withdrew, while the deputies dispersed to ponder on the course which lay darkly before their people.

By this vote the Cabinet, according to the Constitution, ceased to exist as a legal entity.

Great crowds of people thronged the *Lalezar,* one of the principal streets of Teheran, shouting death to the traitors and calling Allah to witness that they would give up their lives for their country.

A few days later, in a secret conference between the deputies of the Medjlis and the members of the deposed cabinet, a similar vote was given to reject the Russian demands. Meanwhile thousands of Russian troops, with Cossacks and artillery, were pouring into Northern Persia, from Tiflis and Julfa by land and from Baku across the Caspian, to the Persian port of Enzeli, whence they took up their 220-mile march over the Elburz mountains towards Kasvin and Teheran.

In the Government at Teheran conference followed conference. Intrigues against the deputies gave way to threats. Through it all, with the increasing certainty of personal injury, the members of the Medjlis stood firmly by their vote.

It is impossible to describe the days and nights of doubt, suspense and anxiety which followed one another during this dark month of December in the capital. There was a lurking dread in the very air, and the snow-covered mountains themselves seemed afflicted with the mournful scenes through which the country was passing.

A boycott was proclaimed by the Islamic priests against Russian and English goods. In a day the old-fashioned tramway of the city was deserted on the mere suspicion that it was owned in Russia, while an excited Belgian Minister rained protests and petitions on the Persian Foreign Office in an endeavor to show that the tramway was owned by his countrymen. The cars ran absolutely empty for the day. Crowds of youths,

students and women filled the streets, dragging occasional
absent-minded passengers from the trams, smashing the
windows of shops which still displayed Russian goods, seeing
that no one drank tea because it came from Russia, although
produced in India, and going in processions before the gates of
foreign legations to demand justice of the representatives of
the world powers for a people in the extremity of despair.

One day the rumor would come that the chief *mullahs* at
Madjef had proclaimed the *jihat* or holy war against the Russians; on another that the Russian troops had commenced to
shoot up Kasvin on their march to Teheran.[1]

The boycott of English goods in the South became so serious
that at Shiraz it was exceedingly difficult for the British Indian
troops to obtain food supplies, and the chief-priests having declared the notes of the Imperial Bank of Persia — a British
corporation — to be unclean, they were turned into the bank for
redemption in government-minted coins at the rate of 20,000
tumans a day.

At one time two men were arrested by the secret police, who
had been informed of a conspiracy to kill the Treasurer-general.
Their house was raided and a bomb-making plant found, together with a number of nitroglycerin bombs. Under police
examination they confessed that they had been paid by certain Persian reactionaries to blow me up while I was driving
through the streets.

Life in Teheran during this period did not seem to me to be
particularly healthful. It was not uncommon while sitting in
my office to hear bullets whistling over the garden from the

---

[1] On December 13 the chief *mujtahid* at Najaf, Mullah Muhammad
Kazim al-Khorasani, died suddenly, under very suspicious circumstances as
he was on the eve of starting for Teheran, as it was rumored, to preach the
"holy war" against the Russians. He was commonly believed to have
been poisoned by Russian agents. He and his two colleagues, Hajji Husayn
ibn Khalil and Mullah Abdullah al-Mazandarani, had been foremost among
the Islamic clergy in supporting the Nationalist cause in Persia.

TYPICAL PERSIAN AND ARMENIAN "FIGHTING MEN."

PERSIAN ARTILLERY LEAVING TEHERAN TO TAKE THE FIELD.

different street fights which were taking place in the neighborhood. A Mauser pistol serenade occurred nearly every night. Russian officers, from the additional detachment of Cossacks which had arrived from Kasvin, reconnoitered Atabak Park in the early morning hours and made faces at the guards at the gates. Of course the fact that Russia had sent a large army into Persia for the express purpose of expelling me, coupled with the virulent attacks directed against me by the Russian semi-official press, was a virtual invitation to numerous bad characters and political renegades from the Caucasus (of which there were hundreds in Teheran) to do me harm in the belief, whether justified or not, that they would thereby regain the Russian Government's favor and protection, as had the assassins of Saniu'd-Dawla.

One evening, just as I was preparing to go to a small dinner party with my wife, I was brought word that three Caucasians were on the watch for me in a neighboring street. The information proved to be accurate, and I thought it advisable to remain indoors.

About this time some of the Persian Nationalists asked me to allow them to organize a personal bodyguard to protect me against attempts on my life. I consented and from that time on these volunteer protectors never allowed me out of their sight day or night, except when I retired to sleep.[1]

On December 14 Major Stokes left Teheran to return to his regiment in India.

The next day the Russian Legation informed the Persian Government that if within six days the conditions of the ultimatum had not been complied with, the Russian troops at Kasvin, about 4000 in number, would start for Teheran. A few days later, under cover of the Russian advance to Kasvin, some

---

[1] One of these men, I greatly regretted to hear, was hung some weeks after my departure, on the ground that he was a dangerous *fidai*.

2000 Turcomans advanced towards the capital from Mazandaran, and actually got as far as Damghan, whence they threatened the city. Teheran at the time could not spare more than 600 men to oppose them. A force of this size was sent out under one of Ephraim's lieutenants to hold them in check.

Telegrams and messages of encouragement and sympathy from Muhammadan societies all over the world poured into Teheran. Some of them must have heaped coals of fire on the heads of the devoted Cabinet which had from the outset favored a surrender to Russia.

The Persian Defense Society of Calcutta telegraphed the Cabinet as follows:

" Do not submit to the new proposals, but take advantage of the impression produced in Manchester and among the Moslems of the world. Even the Indian women are excited. The pressure from the North is for a railroad concession. Have no confidence in the advice of the South. Increase the relation with America." [1]

At one time a touch of grim humor was added to the situation by a declaration of the Turkish Minister of Foreign Affairs at Constantinople, in reply to a question in the Parliament. This Ottoman wag replied that Persia's independence could not be in danger, because it was *guaranteed* by the Anglo-Russian Agreement. At the time some 12,000 Russian troops were occupying the entire northern part of the Empire.

Various proposals were considered by the Medjlis as a way out of the apparent *impasse*. One of the most novel ideas presented was that of affording the United States Government a pretext for taking a hand in Persia. One night a number of

---

[1] This semi-cryptic message showed a remarkable grasp of the actual situation in England, Teheran and elsewhere. It was commonly believed in Persia that if the Medjlis granted Russia certain railroad concessions, she would withdraw her troops and come to some more favorable settlement of the ultimatum The last sentence refers to the Author.

the party leaders and prominent members of the Medjlis came to my office with a request that I should draft a short law, giving a concession to build a number of important railways which had been discussed. The name was to be left blank, the law was to be passed immediately, and I was to fill in the name of some American capitalist or of some group of capitalists, telegraph the concession to New York, and have the American concessionaires demand the protection of their Government. I admired the breadth of the conception, but explained that I could not take part in such a transaction.

Mushiru'd-Dawla, who was nominally Minister of Justice, although he had kept entirely out of the Cabinet's proceedings since the ultimatum, sent to me to ask whether I would undertake to arrange terms with Russia and England, if the Medjlis granted me full powers. He said that his brother, the President of the Chamber, was anxious to present such a measure, and that the majority of the deputies favored it. I thanked him, but said that I thought such affairs properly belonged to the Cabinet and not the Treasurer-general, particularly as I was one of the subjects of the ultimatum. Several of the deputies also proposed that the Government should comply with Russia's demand for my dismissal as Treasurer-general, but that I should be retained as a " general adviser " to the Medjlis.

When the Medjlis, in desperation, sent a committee of twelve to wait on the Regent and inform him that, having no confidence in the personnel of the Cabinet, the Medjlis was about to adopt a resolution authorizing the Regent to enter into negotiations with Russia and England, and to make terms with those powers in behalf of Persia, His Highness turned deathly pale, flew into a panic, and threatened to call his carriage and start for Enzeli in half an hour, if they dared to mention such a thing again.

At one time all four political parties in Persia — Democrats,

Moderates, Union and Progress and the *Dashnaktiyoon,* or
Armenian party — met, through representatives, and decided to
resist the further advance of the Russian troops towards the
capital. The total available forces which Persia could have
sent on this errand were some 2000 Bakhtiyaris, about 300
Armenian fighting-men, with a few machine-guns, and perhaps
some 3000 fidais or " faithful ones "— patriotic volunteers who
had sworn to uphold and defend the Constitutional Government
of Persia. The entire force would have been an unorganized
and unequipped body of brave men. That they would have
been able to hold successfully the mountain passes leading to
Teheran, even against 15,000 Russian troops, there can be no
doubt, and that the fidais were more than anxious to meet the
Russians was fully shown by the heroism and gallantry of their
brothers who but a few weeks later sustained for six days an
equal conflict at Tabriz against Russian troops and artillery at
odds of one to five, with two batteries of modern artillery
against them and none in their possession.

In addition to these forces, there were now 1100 Treasury
gendarmes, instructed by four brave and skilful American
officers. They were the pick of the Young Persia patriots who
really desired to serve their country, and I had taken care that
they should be well-drilled, equipped and armed. When,
later on, the thirty-five Persian officers who commanded them
heard of the overthrow of the Medjlis, they came and begged
to be allowed to fight for their country, and I had ample evidence that they were more than eager to go against the Russian
troops.

Late on the night that the decision was taken by the leaders
of the four political parties to resist the Russian advance I was
visited by a committee of safety who sought my advice as to the
best means of carrying out their purpose. I recall very well
the unreality of the interview. A dozen men, of different

walks in life, the chosen leaders of a strange and wholly alien people, consulting one whom they considered an " infidel " as to whether they should take a step obviously heroic and dramatic, yet which would spell danger and death for thousands of their people and incredible physical disaster in the end.

We spent three hours in conference, and they finally compelled me to express the reluctant opinion that if a single hostile move were made against the Russian troops north of Teheran, the 50,000 Cossacks who would be poured into Persia when the snows melted the following spring would crush out the last spark of Persian liberty and leave, perhaps, not even widows and orphans to mourn at soldiers' graves.

It was a strange, sad talk. Probably they had no right to place the responsibility for such a decision on a foreigner, but I am glad to recall that I pointed out to them the unavoidable distress which would follow any aggressive action on their part.

When they filed out, having yielded to the idea of only passive opposition to Russian demands, another humble chapter had been written among many which mean little to the world at large yet which are potent with consequences for those to whom the drama is very real.

It was at this time, when rumors were flying about Teheran that the Medjlis would yield to the threats and bribes which well-known Russian emissaries were employing with many of the deputies, that the Persian women performed the crowning act of the noble and patriotic part which thousands of their sex had been playing since Persia's *risorgimento* began.

The Persian women since 1907 had become almost at a bound the most progressive, not to say radical, in the world. That this statement upsets the ideas of centuries makes no difference. It is the fact.

It is not too much to say that without the powerful moral force of those so-called chattels of the oriental lords of creation the ill-starred and short-lived revolutionary movement, however well conducted by the Persian men, would have early paled into a mere disorganized protest. The women did much to keep the spirit of liberty alive. Having themselves suffered from a double form of oppression, political and social, they were the more eager to foment the great Nationalist movement for the adoption of constitutional forms of government and the inculcation of Western political, social, commercial and ethical codes. Equally strange is the fact that this yearning by the people received the support of large numbers of the Islamic priests,— a class which stood to lose much of its traditional influence and privilege by the contemplated changes.

During the five years following the successful but bloodless revolution in 1906 against the oppressions and cruelty of Muzaffaru'd-Din Shah, a feverish and at times fierce light has shone in the veiled eyes of Persia's women, and in their struggle for liberty and its modern expressions, they broke through some of the most sacred customs which for centuries past have bound their sex in the land of Iran.

I had ample opportunity to observe the frequent manifestations of the influence and high purposes of the Muhammadan women.

We of Europe and America are long accustomed to the increasingly large rôle played by Western women in business, in the professions, in literature, in science, and in politics, but what shall we say of the veiled women of the Near East who overnight become teachers, newspaper writers, founders of women's clubs and speakers on political subjects ? What, when we find them vigorously propagating the most progressive ideas of the Occident in a land until recently wrapped in the hush and gloom of centuries of despotism ? Whence came their desire to play a part in the political and social regeneration of their country and their unwavering faith in our political and

social institutions? That it came and still exists there can be
no possible doubt, and with it was born the discriminating intelligence which is as a rule acquired only by long years of
practical experience.

The Persian women have given to the world a notable example of the ability of unsullied minds to assimilate rapidly
an absolutely new idea, and with the *élan* of the crusader who
has a vision, they early set to work to accomplish their ideals.

I had been fortunate enough shortly after reaching Persia
to win the confidence of the National Assembly, or Medjlis, a
body which fairly represented the hopes and aspirations of the
great mass of the Persian people. This point gained, I was
soon made aware that another great, though secret, influence
was watching my work with jealous but kindly eyes. It was
well known in Teheran that there were dozens of more or less
secret societies among the Persian women, with a central
organization by which they were controlled. To this day I
know neither the names nor the faces of the leaders of this
group, but in a hundred different ways I learned from time to
time that I was being aided and supported by the patriotic
fervor of thousands of the weaker sex.

A few examples may suffice. While sitting in my office one
morning last summer, I was told that one of the Persian clerks
in the Treasury department wished to see me on an important
matter. Information comes unexpectedly and from such
curious sources in the Orient that no offer can be safely rejected. This young man came in. I had never seen him. We
spoke in French, and after receiving permission to talk freely,
with many apologies he said that his mother was our friend;
that she had commissioned him to say that my wife should not
pay a visit to the household of a certain Persian grandee, by
whose family she had been invited, since he was an enemy to the
Constitutional Government and my wife's visit would make

the Persians suspect me. I thanked him, and at the time did not myself know of the contemplated call, but soon learned that it was planned, and, of course, advised against it. I called the young Persian again and asked him how his mother knew of this purely private social affair of my wife's; he said that it had been known and discussed in the secret society to which his mother belonged, and that it was decided to warn me against it.

On another, more recent occasion, a large crowd of poor women came to the Atabak Park to demonstrate against me because the Treasury had been unable to pay the Government pensions, on which there was over a million dollars then due. The available funds had been necessary for the volunteer troops who had been fighting against the ex-Shah. I sent one of my Persian secretaries to see these women and ask who had told them to come and make this demonstration. He returned mentioning the name of a famous reactionary grandee who was at the time well known to be favoring the cause of Muhammad Ali. I had them told that they would be given an answer on the following day if they dispersed quietly, which they did.

I then sent to one of the women's societies a simple explanation of our financial straits and the impossibility of paying these pensions because of the needs of the Constitutional Government, with a request that they prevent any further agitation against the Treasury. Though it did not become possible to pay the pensions, there was never another demonstration by women on this account.

They have a saying in Teheran that when the women take part in a *chuluk* (riot) against a Cabinet of the Government, the situation has become serious.

When the confiscation of the properties of the estates of Shuau's-Saltana took place, the Russian Government, finding that its Consul-general had had no excuse, either in law or

A PERSIAN WOMAN.

in fact, for his conduct, concocted and gave out the pretext that the park of Shuau's-Saltana in Teheran was mortgaged to the Russian Bank at Teheran, and that its former owner owed the bank some $225,000. Every one knew that the claim was both false and absurd, but as there is no recognized system for recording mortgages and as the rebel Prince himself would doubtless have sworn to the transaction in order to save his property from confiscation, I was at a loss how to disprove this claim. To all demands that the Russian Bank should produce its books and other proofs of the debt a deaf ear was turned.

It was then that I received a striking proof of the courage and patriotism of a Persian woman, and of the practical value of her support.

One of my principal Persian assistants, a very highly educated and patriotic man, came to see me and said that his sister was one of the wives of the Prince Shuau's-Saltana, and that she had obtained one of the copies of the Prince's last will and testament, executed within the year, just before he had left Persia, and in compliance with all the ceremony and formality required by law and the Muhammadan religion for a man of that rank.

She had informed him that this document, as was required, contained full lists and inventories of all the Prince's lands and property, and a statement of all debts due to him or by him — in fact, a complete and solemn report of his financial situation. The sister of my informant had told him to bring me this document — though at enormous risk to the lives and property rights of herself and her children — because she believed it was her duty to her country. I received the document, and with it was able to refute the last falsehood on which the Russian Government had depended to justify the hostile and unlawful acts of her Consular officials in this affair.

With the dark days when doubts came to be whispered as

to whether the Medjlis would stand firm, the Persian women, in their zeal for liberty and their ardent love for their country, threw down the last barriers which distinguished their sex and gave striking evidence of their patriotic courage. It was rumored more than once that in secret conclave the deputies had decided to yield to Russia's demands. The bazars and people of the capital were torn with anxiety. What could the Nationalists do to hold their representatives to their duty?

The Persian women supplied the answer. Out from their walled courtyards and harems marched three hundred of that weak sex, with the flush of undying determination in their cheeks. They were clad in their plain black robes with the white nets of their veils dropped over their faces. Many held pistols under their skirts or in the folds of their sleeves. Straight to the Medjlis they went, and, gathered there, demanded of the President that he admit them all. What the grave deputies of the Land of the Lion and the Sun may have thought at this strange visitation is not recorded. The President consented to receive a delegation of them. In his reception-hall they confronted him, and lest he and his colleagues should doubt their meaning, these cloistered Persian mothers, wives and daughters exhibited threateningly their revolvers, tore aside their veils, and confessed their decision to kill their own husbands and sons, and leave behind their own dead bodies, if the deputies wavered in their duty to uphold the liberty and dignity of the Persian people and nation.

Though the Medjlis was destroyed by a *coup d'état* executed by Russian hirelings a week or two later, it passed out of being, stainless of having sold its country's birthright.

May we not exclaim: All honor to the veiled women of Persia! With the constraining traditions of the past around them; with the idea of absolute dependence upon the fancy and caprice of men ever before them; deprived of all opportunity

to educate themselves along modern ideals; watched, guarded
and rebuffed, they drank deep of the cup of freedom's desire,
and offered up their daily contribution to their country's cause,
watching its servants each moment with a mother's jealous eyes,
and failing not, even in that grim, tragic hour when men's hearts
grew weak and the palsying dread of the prison and its tortures,
the noose and the bullet had settled on the bravest in the land.

When neither threats nor bribes availed against the Medjlis,
Russia decreed its destruction by force.

In the early afternoon of December 24, the deposed Cabinet,
having been themselves duly *persuaded* by well-known methods
to take the step, executed a coup d'état against the Medjlis, and
by a demonstration of gendarmes and Bakhtiyari tribesmen,
succeeded in expelling all the deputies and employees who were
within the Parliament grounds, after which the gates were
locked and barred, and a strong detachment of the *Guard
Homayoon,* the so-called Royal Regiment, left in charge. The
deputies were threatened with death if they attempted to return
there or to meet in any other spot, and the City of Teheran
immediately passed under a *de facto* government and military
control. The self-constituted *directoire* of seven who accomplished this dubious feat, had first ascertained that the
considerable force of Bakhtiyari tribesmen, some 2000 in number, who had gathered in the capital after the defeat of the ex-
Shah's forces in September last, had been duly " fixed " by the
same Russian agencies who had so early succeeded in persuading the members of the ex-cabinet that their true interests lay
in siding with Russia. It is impossible to say just what
respective proportions of fear and cupidity decided the members
of the deposed Cabinet to take the aliens' side against their country, but both emotions undoubtedly played a part. The
Premier was one of the leading chiefs or Khans of the Bakhtiyaris, and another chief, Sardar-i-Mutashem, was the self-styled

Minister of War.   These chieftains have always been a strange and changing mixture of mountain patriot and city intriguer — of loyal soldier and mercenary looter.   The mercenary instincts, possibly aided by a sense of their own comparative helplessness against Russian Cossacks and artillery, led them to accept the stranger's gold and fair promises, and they ended their somewhat checkered, but theretofore relatively honorable career, by selling their country for a small pile of cash and the more alluring promise that the " Grand Viziership " (i.e., post of Minister of Finance) should be perpetual in their family or clan.   When they had decided to take arms against the Medjlis, which had always distrusted them, the other armed force of the Constitutional Government — the gendarmes of Teheran — headed by Ephraim Khan, had apparently lost heart, and this brave Armenian fell in with the plans of the Cabinet.   Between the two forces, they abolished the last vestige of constitutional rule in Persia, and left their country at the mercy of seven oriental statesmen who had already sold out to the Russian Government.   It was a sordid ending to a gallant struggle for liberty and enlightenment.

That same afternoon a large number of the " abolished " deputies came to my office.   They were men whom I had grown to know well, men of European education, in whose courage, integrity and patriotism I had the fullest confidence.   To them the unlawful action of their own countrymen was more than a political catastrophe; it was a sacrilege, a profanation, a heinous crime.   They came in tears, with broken voices, with murder in their hearts, torn by the doubt as to whether they should kill the former Ministers and drive out the traitorous tribesmen who had made possible the destruction of the Government, or adopt the truly oriental idea of killing themselves. They asked my advice, and, hesitating somewhat as to whether I should interfere to save the lives of notorious betrayers of

THE MEDJLIS BUILDING.
After its bombardment by the Cossack Brigade under the Russian Colonel Liakhoff.

ENTRANCE TO THE PARLIAMENT (MEDJLIS) GROUNDS.

their country, I finally persuaded them to do neither the one nor the other. There seemed to be no particular good in assassinating even their treacherous countrymen, as it would only have given color to the pretensions of Russia and England that the Persians were not capable of maintaining order.

When the last representative element of the Constitutional Government, for which so many thousands had fought, suffered, and died, was wiped out in an hour without a drop of blood being shed, the Persian people gave to the world an exhibition of temperance, of moderation, of stern self-restraint the like of which probably no other civilized country could show under similar trying circumstances.

I have often been asked whether the Persians were really capable of reforming their government; whether they were not mere degenerates, and if there was any true national spirit among them. We all know how easy it is to give forth patriotic utterances in piping times of peace, in the heart of a conventional and orderly community, when there is no danger involved in the most fiery defiance of the powers of evil. But when a body of seventy Muhammadan representatives, in momentary dread of the prison or a worse fate at the hands of an overwhelmingly superior force, withstood day by day the intrigues, bribes and threats which the agents of a powerful nation were freely employing, and when these seventy men went down into oblivion and private terror still refusing to sign away the honor and sovereignty of their nation, I think the question as to national spirit may be considered to have been thereby fairly answered.

No one who knew these representatives of a stricken race in those dark days could fail to love the Persian people, or to sympathize with their just aspirations. Their faults are well known; they are principally those of environment and tradition.

10

The very capacity of the Persians to govern themselves has been speciously attacked in those quarters where the denial outstrips the query. That the Persians were unskilful in the practical politics and in the technique of representative constitutional government no one could deny; but that they had the full right to develop along the particular lines of their customs, character, temperament and tendencies, is equally obvious. Five years is nothing in the life of a nation; it is not even long as a period for individual reform; yet, after a bare five years of effort, during which the Persian people, with all their difficulties and harassed by the so-called friendly powers, succeeded in thwarting a despot's well-planned effort to wrest from them their hard-earned liberties, the world is told by two European nations that these men were unfit, degenerate and incapable of producing a stable and orderly form of government.

With a knowledge of the facts of Persia's downfall the scales drop from the eyes of the most incredulous, and it is clear that she was the helpless victim of the wretched game of cards which a few European powers, with the skill of centuries of practice, still play with weaker nations as the stake, and the lives, honor and progress of whole races as the forfeit.

CHAPTER VIII

FROM the time that the Cabinet of Samsamu's-Saltana had, on December 1, proposed to the Medjlis the acceptance of Russia's ultimatum, the attitude of the Ministers toward me had noticeably changed. Having apparently made up their minds not to resist the Russian demands in any manner, they were anxious that I should make that course easy for them by resigning at once, thus making it unnecessary for them to obtain the consent of the Medjlis.

While, personally, I was entirely willing to take this step, the idea had not even been suggested to me until the Medjlis had twice, by a formal vote, resolved to reject the Cabinet's proposal. For me then to have resigned would have clearly been a usurpation by me of the right of the Medjlis to decide a question vitally affecting the sovereignty of the country. Nevertheless, I held frequent conferences with leading deputies and other prominent officials, in which I plainly told them that I had come to Persia to aid the Persian Government, and that if I could better assist them by resigning, I was more than ready to do so. The invariable reply was that I was the employee of the Medjlis and that if I forced their hand by resigning, they would be compelled to regard it as a breach of faith. I received daily visits from great numbers of Persians, officials and private individuals, who all implored me not to resign under any circumstances, as in their opinion it would mean the end of all hope of a constitutional government in Persia.

Under the law, the Cabinet of Samsamu's-Saltana ceased to have any legal status at noon on December 1, in view of the overwhelming vote of lack of confidence given by the deputies. Nevertheless, as the Bakhtiyari chieftains had been tasting power for many months through the possession of the Premiership by their chief, Samsamu's-Saltana, they were most indisposed to retire again to private life. Furthermore, there had recently been a decided *rapprochement* between the Bakhtiyari chieftains and the Russian Legation, and it was perfectly evident that the Russian Government had persuaded them to take its view of the case.

After the formal rejection by the Medjlis of the Russian demands — an event which the Russian Government probably did not really anticipate — the Russian officials and well-known emissaries in Teheran tried other means to bring about at least a colorable acceptance of their ultimatum. During the days of excitement and ferment large sums of money were spent among the poor people in the name of the Russian Government. In several mosques where numbers of people had congregated, as they are accustomed to do during winter, especially if the bread supply is short, meals were served to thousands of Persians with the information that Russia was furnishing the money to do so, and that only the hostility of the Medjlis to Russia was the cause of the scarcity of bread. It was said that no less than 100,000 roubles was expended for this purpose.

The afternoon of December 1, after the assassination of Prince Alau'd-Dawla and the rejection of the Cabinet by the Medjlis, I was informed that several of the more bitter and hostile Bakhtiyari Khans, inspired by Amir Mujahid, Sardar-i-Jang and the treacherous Amir Mufakhkham, had discussed

AMIR-I-MUFAKHKHAM.

SARDAR-I-ZAFFAR.

AMIR MUJAHID.

SARDAR-I-JANG.

Four Bakhtiyari Khans at Teheran who took part in bringing about the destruction of the
Medjlis on December 24, 1911.

making an attack on my residence and offices at Atabak Park, with a view to seizing the Treasury, burning the records, and driving the Americans from their posts. Amir Mujahid and several others had received large sums of money for military purposes during the preceding summer, and I had been seek-ing to obtain an accounting from them.

When this news reached me, I sent a Persian friend to the Bakhtiyari headquarters to inform the Khans that if they contemplated anything so foolish, they had better think twice about it. My purpose, of course, was to let them know that I was aware of their attitude. I had the guard of Treasury gendarmes at Atabak Park increased by fifty men, making a total of one hundred and fifty on duty there. The Bakhti-yaris never came.

Shortly after this, grave dissensions occurred between Eph-raim and the Bakhtiyari chieftains, and for several days an armed collision between Ephraim's police and gendarmes was hourly expected. Ephraim then resigned as head of the city police. It was rumored that the Bakhtiyaris, who were each day showing themselves more completely under Russian influ-ence, were plotting to disarm Ephraim's men and take charge of the policing of Teheran, with the assistance of the Cossack brigade under the Russian Colonel Vadbolski. This sinister suspicion greatly increased the unrest and disorder in the city. Serious rioting and bloodshed were momentarily expected, and the fidais, to the number of 2,000, gave out that they were pre-pared to take part in the proceeding.

The dispute between Ephraim and the Bakhtiyaris was sub-sequently patched up and the former resumed charge of the police.

At Atabak Park we had the honor of being reconnoitered from time to time by Russian officers, one of whom, on Decem-ber 4, endeavored to insult the guards at the gate.

In the attitude of Wuthuqu'd-Dawla, Minister of Foreign Affairs, and his brother, Ghavamu's-Saltana, Minister of the Interior, I now noticed a marked coldness, though these two had previously been friendly to me. The change occurred when they learned that I had despatched Mr. Lecoffre to Tabriz to investigate the gross frauds and malversations of the revenues which had been going on there for a year before and ever since my arrival in Teheran. The revenues of this province of Azarbayjan were computed to be about 1,000,000 tumans. Yet for months before I took charge, and during the entire summer while I was Treasurer-general, *not a single cent* had been collected there for the Government, according to the Persian *pishgar,* or tax-collector. This was the more remarkable as the summer is a favorable time for collecting the revenues. Private information came to me that the tax-collector had already made his fortune, and that he sneered at the Central Government at Teheran, including the Treasurer-general. That he thought himself safe in so doing was perhaps due to his being the father of the two ministers just referred to: Wuthuqu'd-Dawla and Ghavamu's-Saltana. That they should become suddenly hostile to me on learning of Mr. Lecoffre's mission to Tabriz, is perhaps explainable by that same relationship.

Intrigues are so deep and personal interest so strong in Persia that it is perfectly easy to conceive how these two ministers were favorably inclined even to the acceptance of the Russian ultimatum, when we remember that one of its clauses demanded " the immediate dismissal of Mr. Lecoffre " from the Persian service!

The above facts are cited to show the situation between the Cabinet and myself after their *coup d'état* was executed against the Medjlis on December 24.

The Medjlis was my employer. That body had directed my

THE PERSIAN NATIONALIST TROOPS AT TABRIZ, UNDER THE COMMAND OF PRINCE AMANULLAH MIRZA ZIYAU'D-DAWLA.

engagement, approved the contract under which I undertook the financial work, and had on June 13 passed a law, one of the express objects of which was to make me in my task independent of the influence or control of any Cabinet which might come into being. The same idea and motives brought about this step as produced the status of the officials of the "Ottoman Debt."

When, therefore, the Medjlis was destroyed by force, the Americans were left without an employer or status, unless they chose to recognize the purely *de facto* Cabinet, which had merely arrogated to itself police powers, as the lawful government of Persia. I neither felt authorized nor desired to take such a step. With the abolition of the Medjlis the last hope of doing any effective work in behalf of the Persian people had gone, and I was compelled to regard our task as at an end.

Prior to December 24, the Cabinet had several times proposed to me, through various emissaries, that I should resign. As inducements to this course they offered me personally, in addition to the compensation due me under my contract with the Government, the " Order of the Lion and the Sun " of the first class (theretofore given only to potentates), a formal testimonial as to my services to the people of Persia, the privilege of nominating my successor, and varying honorariums. To these proposals I replied that unless and until I could obtain some authentic expression (even though unofficial) to the effect that the deputies of the Medjlis would not consider my resigning to be a betrayal of their interests, I would not resign, and that as to the other inducements I was content to forego the diamond-studded " Order," the parchment, and other rewards, unless they should come from the lawful representatives of the Persian people, to whom alone I was content to look for any recognition of my services. I was informed that my reply was not favorably received by the members of the Cabinet.

Several days before the *coup d'état* of December 24, the Cabinet adopted an attitude of open hostility, and the Bakhti-yari Khans renewed their threats to attack my residence and pillage the Treasury.

The destruction of the Medjlis was the end of the Constitutional Government in Persia.

On the afternoon of the next day, Christmas, I received a call from the *Chef de Cabinet* of the Ministry of Foreign Affairs, who delivered to me a letter in Persian of which the following is a translation:

The Honorable Mr. Shuster:

As you are aware, the Commission elected on the eve of the 29th of Jilharjeh, 1329, and invested with plenary power by the Medjlis for the purpose of dealing with the question of the ultimatum of the Russian Government, decided, on the last day of the same month, with the coöperation of the Council of Ministers, on the acceptance of the terms of the ultimatum, and the purport of the said decision has been duly communicated to the Russian Legation.[1]

Seeing that the stipulations of the aforesaid ultimatum necessitate the recall of your honorable person from the service of the Persian Government and the severance of your connection with matters financial, we hereby inform you of the situation, and as regards the office of the Treasury-general and the individual to whom you will hand over the books and the service, as well as the status of the American functionaries who have been invited to the service of the Persian Government, the decision of the Government will be transmitted to you later.

This was signed by seven former Ministers, including the Samsamu's-Saltana and the Wuthuqu'd-Dawla.

On receipt of this entirely illegal order of dismissal, I had one of three courses open to me: to accept it, to forcibly

---

[1] This Commission was never legally elected, nor was any such decision ever taken by the body of men who were said to compose the Commission. The author has the entire documentary history of the matter, but the most striking proof that no such authority was granted by the Medjlis is the fact that the Ministers felt it necessary to destroy the Medjlis before attempting my dismissal.

resist it, or to make no reply, leaving the next move to the de facto Cabinet. Had I chosen the latter course, I might have been in Persia still, on one pretext or another. To have resisted the order of the Cabinet, however illegal as regards me, would have meant severe rioting and bloodshed in Teheran. The people were terribly incensed at the destruction of the Medjlis, and if I had adopted an attitude of open defiance of the *directoire* who pretended to exercise the powers of government, it is impossible to say what the consequences would have been.

A large majority of the deposed deputies were planning to meet and declare the dissolution of the Medjlis to be unconstitutional, the Regent to be false to his oath, and the Ministers to be traitors. Nothing but the most stringent police measures taken by Ephraim, and the presence in Teheran of over 2,000 Bakhtiyaris, large bodies of whom were patroling the streets, kept the people from breaking out into serious disorders. Ephraim and the Ministers, especially the Wuthuqu'd-Dawla, had large guards around their residences, and nothing but the thought of the Cossack brigade and a large recent addition of Russian troops to the Consular force in the capital, together with the existence of a Russian army only eighty miles away at Kasvin, kept the people from attacking the Ministers and others whom they felt had betrayed them.

Under these circumstances, and after careful consideration, I decided that it was my duty to eliminate myself from the situation, and that no good could come from the Americans remaining longer in Persia. I accordingly notified the *directoire,* on December 26, as follows:

In reply I have the honor to state that the notification of the termination of my contract with the Imperial Government of Persia to serve as Treasurer-general of Persia will be acted on by me in proper form and manner upon the settlement of the question of the individual to whom I am to transfer the official responsibilities of my office and upon the arrangement of the question of the status of my fourteen American assistants,[1] as to which matters it is stated that I will receive a further communication from the Honorable Council. The future status of my American assistants is at present the principal object of my solicitude.

Some days before Christmas I had been notified that the American instructors and Persian officers of the Treasury Gendarmerie desired to call in a body and pay their respects on the day. This was before there was any suspicion that the Cabinet was going to take the action which it did against the Medjlis on December 24.

I received the officers early Christmas afternoon, at the time appointed, but realizing what a rumor-loving place Teheran was, and the excitement over the Cabinet's action the day before, I was careful to inform them in a little address that they should be scrupulously mindful of the fact that they were officials of a purely financial administration, and that they should refrain from all acts or public dissensions of a political nature. This was in the presence of a number of servants and onlookers. Nevertheless, as I had feared, the news immediately spread that I had called the Treasury Gendarmerie to arms and intended employing them to restore the Medjlis. A few hours later I received the communication from the Ministers which has been referred to above.

On December 24 a message was received from the Acting Governor at Tabriz, stating that the Russian troops stationed there had started to massacre the inhabitants. Shortly after

[1] In addition to Messrs. Charles I. McCaskey and Bruce G. Dickey, who went with me to Teheran, and Mr. F. S. Cairns, who arrived on June 19, the following Americans, whose engagement by me under contract had been authorized by the Medjlis at different times, had arrived: Messrs. Loring P. Jordon and Robert R. Brott, secretaries; Messrs. Frank G. Whitney and P. J. Fitzsimmons, accountants; Messrs. J. N. Merrill, Oscar Preuss, John F. Green and E. P. Lowry, Treasury Gendarmerie instructors; and Messrs. W. J. O'Donovan, Turin B. Boone and D. J. Waters, office assistants. The majority of these men did not reach Teheran until November and the early part of December.

THE "ARK." A CITADEL IN TABRIZ.

This was attacked and bombarded by 4000 Russian troops in December, 1911. It was
defended by 1000 Persian "fidais" (self-devoted) who held out for four days.
The American Consulate General (see flag) was in the line of fire.

VIEW OF THE CITY OF TABRIZ.

Capital of the province of Azarbayjan.

this the Indo-European lines were cut (by bullets, it was afterwards alleged) and news ceased. Additional Russian troops were on the way to Tabriz from Julfa. The exact origin of the fighting at Tabriz is not clear. It was reported that some Russian soldiers claiming to be stringing a telephone wire, mounted the roof of the police headquarters about 10 o'clock at night, on December 20, were challenged by the Persian sentries, and replied with shots. Serious street fighting commenced the next morning, and continued for several days. The Acting Governor reported that the Russian troops indulged in terrible brutality, killing women and children in the streets and hundreds of other non-combatants. There were about 4,000 Russian troops and two batteries of artillery around the city. About 1000 of the Tabriz fidais took refuge in an old citadel, called the "Ark." They were without artillery and poorly armed. The Russians bombarded the place for some time, killing a large number of the fidais. The superior numbers and the artillery of the Russians finally conquered, and there then ensued a period of terrorism during which no Persian's life or honor was safe. At one time Mons. Poklewski-Koziell, the Russian Minister at Teheran, telegraphed to the General in command of the Russian troops at Tabriz, telling him to stop fighting, as matters were being arranged at the capital. The General replied to the Minister that he (the former) took his orders from the Viceroy of the Caucasus at Tiflis, and not from Teheran.

On New Year's Day, which was the 10th of *Muharram,* a day of great mourning and held sacred in the Persian religious calendar, the Russian Military Governor, who had hoisted Russian flags over the Government buildings at Tabriz, hung the Sikutu'l-Islam, who was the chief priest of Tabriz, two other priests, and five others, among them several high officials of the Provincial Government. As one British journalist put

it, the effect of this outrage on the Persians was that which
would be produced on the English people by the hanging of
the Archbishop of Canterbury on Good Friday. From this
time on the Russians at Tabriz continued to hang or shoot any
Persian whom they chose to consider guilty of the crime of being a " Constitutionalist." When the fighting there was first
reported a prominent official of the Foreign Office at St. Petersburg, in an interview to the press, made the statement that Russia would take vengeance into her own hands until the " revolutionary dregs " had been exterminated.

Many on reading this gruesome threat shuddered to recall
Russian vengeance in Turkestan, where in 1881 Skobeloff
massacred 8,000 defenseless Turcomans at Denghil Tepe on the
principle that with Asiatics the duration of peace is in direct
proportion to the number slain. And the fate of the Chinese
settlement at Blagovestchenk on the Amoor, where in 1900,
the Russians, desiring to strike terror into the Chinese and
save trouble in dealing with them in the future, told the inhabitants that they should move. When the Chinese explained
that they had no steamer or other means of conveyance, the
Russian humorists told them to move into the river, and thereupon drove the entire population into the water to drown.

With these incidents in mind it is not difficult to understand
the semi-official *Novoe Vremya's* utterance that " in this case
true humanity requires cruelty. The *whole population* of
Tabriz must be held responsible and punished. . . . There is
a limit even to Russian indulgence."

Experience has amply demonstrated that the Russian Government, having the power, never does *less* than it promises
in cases of this kind. It is safe to say that the horrors of
Tabriz will never become fully known. The Russians saw well
to that. Unrestrained shootings, hangings, tortures, blowing
of men from cannon, and the cynical butchery of women and

SULTAN AHMAD SHAH, THE PRESENT RULER OF PERSIA.

He succeeded to the throne on July 18, 1909, after the deposition of his father, Muhammad Ali. Behind him on the left is the Crown Prince. The others are royal teachers.

children in the streets of their town — and even worse things — make a fair record for the officers and troops of a nation whose ruler promotes peace tribunals and poses as the friend of mankind.

One significant fact: at the same time that the fighting broke out at Tabriz, the Russian troops at Resht and Enzeli, hundreds of miles away, shot down the Persian police and many inhabitants without warning or provocation of any kind. And the date happened to be just after the Persian Cabinet had definitely informed the Russian Legation that all the demands of Russia's ultimatum were accepted,— a condition which the British Government had publicly assured the Persians would be followed by the withdrawal of the Russian invading forces, and which the Russian Government had officially confirmed, "*unless fresh incidents should arise* in the meantime to make the retention of the troops advisable."

In the light of these events is it probable that it was the comparatively helpless and foredoomed Persians who at Tabriz, Resht and Enzeli started simultaneous attacks upon vastly superior bodies of Russian soldiers?

During the interval between December 25 and the 7th of January there had been a steadily rising tide of indignation against the traitorous ministers who had sold their people. Protests by telegraph poured in from the provinces, denouncing the Regent and the Cabinet, for their attack upon the Constitutional representatives. I had sent word to the ministers time and again that their order of dismissal left affairs in the Treasury in chaos, and that if they did not promptly take the next step, I would turn over my office to my senior assistant, Mr. Cairns, designating him under the law of June 13, and leave Teheran. The Cabinet had promised, as had the Regent, that Mr. Cairns should succeed me as Treasurer-general, although he had no particular desire to remain. The

British and Russian Legations, however, threatened the Persians with severe measures if they allowed any one but Mons. Mornard, the Belgian Administrator of the Customs, to succeed me. After two weeks of a vain endeavor to get the Cabinet to take some proper step, I delivered over my office to Mr. Cairns on January 7, having notified them two days previously that in the absence of their providing, within forty-eight hours, some business-like method for my relief, I would take that step.

By afternoon the transfer to Mr. Cairns was formally made, the necessary receipts given, and the Ministers and banks notified. I left my power of attorney with Mr. McCaskey to act for me in any and all matters pertaining to my official papers and accounts as Treasurer-general of Persia.

Some hours later a representative from the Ministers telephoned that he was coming with an important communication. Later he arrived and read to me a manifestly pre-dated decree from the Regent and communication from the Ministers, appointing Mons. Mornard as " Acting Provisional Treasurer-general." I turned the communications over to Mr. Cairns, who had assumed the duties of Treasurer-general. This was a typical Persian method, though it came a little late in the day. The Ministers knew, of course, that I would not have turned over my office, under any circumstances, to Mons. Mornard, a man whose character was more than notorious and of whose gross irregularities in the conduct of his administration I had already become aware.

Mr. Cairns promptly informed the Ministers that he stood ready to turn over the Treasury to his successor and that he and his thirteen American associates, in view of the admitted violation of their contracts by the Persian Government, were desirous of leaving the country.

On January 9 the Regent sent word to me that he desired to

say farewell on the following day and that the young Shah desired to receive me in audience and thank me for my services.

On the following day I drove for the last time to the *Darbar* where His Majesty was to receive me. Arrived at the palace, I passed through long lines of aged and melancholic courtiers, glistening officers and obsequious attendants. The young Shah was very nervous, as is usually the case when giving a private audience. He spoke through an interpreter and thanked me very gravely for what I had sought to do for his country. I wished him success and prosperity, though the career of " merry monarch " hardly seemed in store for him.

His Majesty promised to send me a specially framed portrait of himself as a souvenir, but I hardly expect to see it.

From there I drove to the Regent's private residence and spent several hours with His Highness, who expressed great regret at my departure and much anxiety as to the future of the country.

In the meantime, Mr. Cairns had been in communication with the Russian and British Legations, whose Ministers both agreed that the contracts of the American assistants had been violated by the acceptance of the ultimatum and that they had a right to depart. As Mr. Cairns knew perfectly well that the Persian Ministers were merely executing the orders of the Russian Legation, he preferred to save time and settle all remaining questions direct.

My preparations for the journey having been completed, I left Atabak Park for Enzeli on the morning of Thursday, January 11. The Regent had placed at my disposal the new automobile which had but recently arrived for the use of the Shah and himself. In our party were Mrs. Shuster, our two little daughters and governess, and Mr. Edward Bell, the Secretary of the American Legation at Teheran, who was traveling to Paris on a short leave. Our trunks had gone on ahead and the only question remaining was whether we would get over the high mountain passes between Teheran and the Caspian before they became blocked with snow.

It was a beautiful morning. The mountains behind Teheran were white with snow; the sun shone brightly in a clear blue sky, and there was life tonic in the air. Nature favored, but our hearts were sad, for our task in Persia, to which we had looked forward with both pleasure and pride, had come to a sudden and very unpleasant end.

As I stood in a circle of gloomy American and Persian friends, about to step into the autmobile, I could not help recalling the evening of my arrival at the same spot just eight months before, and there swept over me the realization that the hopes of a patient, long-suffering Muhammadan people of reclaiming their position in the world had been ruthlessly stamped out by the armies of a so-called civilized and Christian nation.

We passed out the Kasvin gates of Teheran at half-past nine o'clock, with Mons. Varnet, the Shah's French chauffeur at the wheel.

I shall never forget my emotions as we left the busy streets of Teheran and came out upon the more quiet highroad. Memories of the preceding eight months crowded fast upon me. One cannot leave forever the scene of a frustrated ambition without a pang at the mere physical realization that it is all over. I had been ambitious to serve the Persian people. When the inhabitants of Teheran learned the day on which we were going they sent several of their deputies to me to say that a great crowd of them wished to come and say farewell. I requested that no such demonstration should be made, and when word of it reached the Cabinet, the police notified the leaders of the different societies that no gathering of the kind would be permitted. The companies of Treasury gendarmes

MR. SHUSTER, MRS. SHUSTER AND THEIR TWO LITTLE DAUGHTERS.
Entering the automobile at Atabak Park to take leave of Persia.

LOADING THE AUTOMOBILE FOR MR. SHUSTER AND HIS FAMILY TO LEAVE
TEHERAN ON JANUARY 11, 1912.

at the Bagh-i-Shah barracks were drilling as our car passed by. They were a body of men not to be despised, and had the organization been allowed to develop many of Persia's most serious problems would have been promptly solved.

Reaching Kasvin at 3 : 30 that afternoon, we passed through the town, which was thronged with Russian troops. As we were leaving the further gate where there was a group of fifty or more Russian soldiers, some stopped and ostentatiously picked up stones, but if they threw them as we passed at a good rate of speed, none hit the machine. Beyond this incident no discourtesy was shown us on the trip.

When we reached Buinak, a little road station fifteen miles beyond Kasvin, we ran into a snow tempest and in ten minutes the road was completely obliterated by the dry snow blowing down in dense clouds from the near-by mountains. We stopped at this little stone hut and passed the night. The following morning the road was reported completely blocked and we were warned that we could not get over the passes. Two hours were necessary to thaw out the engine, the car having been half covered by drifting snow. We got away about 10:30 and on approaching the highest pass found the road packed with four feet of snow. It was only with the assistance of large road gangs, who dug us out several times, and Mons. Varnet's skilful handling of the powerful fifty-horsepower car, that we were enabled to get through and reach the road-station of Menjil at 5 o'clock that evening. A pleasant run of five hours brought us to Enzeli early the following afternoon. We passed several bodies of Russian troops on the road. There was a Russian cruiser in the harbor, and the town was under the control of the Russian Consul there. The next day, January 14, was the Russian New Year, and the cruiser and gunboats engaged in salutes. That afternoon we embarked on the Russian steamer *Teheran* for Baku, and at 5 : 30 o'clock of a raw, blustery day on the Caspian the coast of Persia and the lights of Enzeli had sunk from view. The brief and disappointing chapter of American financial administration in that ancient land had been written.

CHAPTER IX

CHARACTER OF THE REGENT, OF THE DIFFERENT GOVERNMENT
OFFICIALS AND OF THE MEDJLIS.   CHARACTER AND CAPACITY
OF THE PERSIAN PEOPLE.

THE present Regent of Persia, Abu'l Qasim Khan Nasiru'l-Mulk, is a native of the district of Hamadan.   He pursued his advanced studies at Oxford University and was a classmate of Sir Edward Grey, the present Secretary for Foreign Affairs in England.   He is also a personal friend of Lord Curzon. Shortly after the reign of Muzaffaru'd-Din Shah, Nasiru'l-Mulk was appointed Minister of Finance.   He held this portfolio during the Grand Viziership of the late Aminu'd-Dawla for about six months, after which he was appointed Governor of the Province of Kurdistan, an office which he filled for four years.   A year later, and from the time of the proclamation of the first Constitution, he was made President of the Council of Ministers, holding the portfolio of Finance.   He had hardly undertaken certain reforms in his department when he was arrested by the then-reigning Shah, Muhammad Ali, and was under threat of execution when freed through the intervention of the British Legation.   The day that he was set at liberty he left for Europe, where he sojourned until the deposition of Muhammad Ali and the restoration of the Constitution in July, 1909.   Returning to Teheran shortly after this event, he refused all offers of public positions and contented himself with lending his moral assistance to the Nationalists, giving his counsels to the Ministers and Deputies.   Sometime later he again went to Europe, ostensibly on account of his own health and that of his son. Soon after the death of the late Regent, Azudu'l-Mulk, he was elected Regent by the Medjlis, and, on February 8, 1911, returned to Teheran to take up the duties of his position.

From the very first time that I met His Highness, Nasiru'l-Mulk, he showed himself most favorably disposed towards the American finance administrators and towards me personally. During the eight months that I spent in Teheran—with the exception of the month of December, during which I had practically no direct relations with the Persian Government—I had frequent and lengthy interviews with him, usually at his request, and discussed freely with him the various problems, financial and others, which confronted the country. The Regent is a man of most pleasant and dignified appearance; he speaks English perfectly, as well as French, and has sufficiently broad education and experience to realize to the full the difficulties which confronted the Persian people in their endeavor to establish a successful form of constitutional government. He has a most persuasive manner, and could discourse learnedly upon the defects of his countrymen and the needs of the situation. The general feeling which he left with me in our earlier conversations was that I had been talking to an intelligent, broad and well-educated gentleman. After a number of interviews, however, in which I had sought to impress upon him certain financial plans and secure his active personal assistance and the influence and prestige of his name in carrying them out, I found, to my regret, that His Highness was decidedly more fond of describing obstacles and difficulties than of making any practical attempt to overcome them. He left me frequently under the impression that I had been talking with a dying physician diagnosing his own malady. One could not but admire the skill of the diagnosis while regretting the imminent dissolution of the learned diagnostician who was making it. Time and again I went away from

ABU'L-QASIM KHAN, NASIRU'L-MULK, THE PRESENT REGENT OF PERSIA.

a two hours' interview with Nasiru'l-Mulk filled with a vague dissatisfaction, although I was unable to put my finger upon any particular thing that he had said which did not seem to be reasonable and accurate. Many others, both Europeans and Persians, with whom I talked, told me that they had gained the same impression from him.

Perhaps the greatest defect of Nasiru'l-Mulk, after this temperamental one, was the violent obsession, which he had from the very beginning and never lost to the day that I saw him last, that his Regency was being opposed and his life itself endangered by what he described as the " central secret societies " in Teheran. He told me once that when he went to Europe a second time he had not expected to return. He had been offered the Regency before Azudu'l-Mulk had been elected, and had declined it, having made up his mind to retire from public life. At that time the offer was made to him unanimously by the deputies of the Medjlis. After the death of Azudu'l-Mulk, however, in September, 1910, the proposal to elect him Regent came directly from the elements in the Medjlis which were afterwards grouped under the name of the Moderate party, and those more radical elements, who afterwards became known as the Democratic party, did not favor the election of Nasiru'l-Mulk. They had a candidate of their own, a man of high reputation and great ability, named Mustawfi'l-Mamalik. After some discussion, however, the Regent was elected, and his selection subsequently made unanimous by both elements in the Medjlis. It was known that Nasiru'l-Mulk was highly esteemed in Europe, and particularly by Sir Edward Grey, and it was believed that his selection as Regent would do much to win for Persia the friendly support of the European powers. Before the Regent returned to Teheran, however, he received from some unknown and irresponsible parties, several letters threatening his life if he returned, and, in addition to delaying his trip, this event so preyed upon his mind that he was in the gravest doubts as to whether he should go back to Persia at all. From various points along the trip back from London and Paris, he sent long telegrams to the Medjlis laying down certain conditions precedent to his assuming office. Principal among these was the requirement that the Medjlis should divide itself into parties and that the party having the majority should form a cabinet which would be responsible to that party so long as it maintained the majority, and should carry out the program laid down by that majority. There can be no doubt that Nasiru'l-Mulk was correct in theory in bringing about this innovation, which the Medjlis accepted. Representative forms of government do require the rule of the majority and an attitude of mutual consideration for their respective rights between the majority and the minority in the legislative branch of the government. The Persians, however, are a peculiar people, and being totally inexperienced in the technique of democratic forms of government, once the line of political cleavage was established, there quickly developed an intense and bitter rivalry and even personal animosity between the members of the Moderate party—which, upon the count of noses, had the majority—and the Democratic party which was in the minority. Previous to this division the deputies of the Medjlis, while many of them held differing views as to the program and procedure which should be adopted to reorganize the Constitutional Government and produce a stable administration in Persia, had always considered themselves to be Nationalists or Constitutionalists. Their energies were expended directly in the really patriotic endeavor to solve the problems which confronted their country. The strife and bitterness of party rivalry had not entered into their proceedings to any very great extent. Nasiru'l-Mulk was the father of factional hatred in the Persian Parliament. This is said, not as a reproach, but merely as an historical fact. His intentions were undoubtedly of the best, but he failed to take into consideration the defects and weaknesses of his own countrymen when he insisted upon them grouping themselves on the right and on the left as the best means of carrying out a practical plan for the reorganization of the government. I have many times heard him decry party jealousies and the bitter animosities which undoubtedly existed in the Medjlis and point to them as one of the reasons why greater progress was not made. He never seemed to realize the part which he had played in bringing them to an acute stage.

When he reached Kasvin on his journey to Teheran to assume office, so strong was his belief that he was about to be the victim of political assassination that he dismounted from his carriage for a short rest at the road-station there, clasping in both hands a large Mauser automatic pistol, of the use of which he was entirely ignorant.

After assuming office he transmitted to the Medjlis a number of messages, most of which were well thought out and expressed in a scholarly manner. In these he proclaimed in unmistakable terms that while he did not see the wisdom of the extremely limited and, in fact, almost nominal powers of the Regency, he would nevertheless keep strictly within the bounds laid down by the Constitution and not seek to exercise any power which was not granted to him thereunder. I believe that during his entire service as Regent he faithfully kept this pledge. Certainly, a stronger or more ambitious man with his prestige and influence could have easily made himself the absolute dictator of the country on more than one occasion. During the early months of my stay in Teheran the Regent expressed the belief that he should not remain, that his enemies were opposing him so violently that he could accomplish nothing by staying and that he should be allowed to go to Europe upon a leave of absence and present the cause of Persia to the European powers. It was generally recognized that his departure would have had a most disastrous effect upon the situation; and although he was still in Teheran when I left, eight months later, he had never ceased to insist that he should be allowed to go. His insistence became so violent at times that some most lamentable—though ludicrous— scenes took place between him and different members of the Cabinet. He would summon a number of the deputies to his palace and, after haranguing them for hours on their incapacity and failure to solve the problems concerning Persia, he would announce that he intended to depart for Europe.

In the latter part of September, before the defeat of Prince Salaru'd-Dawla by Ephraim Khan and the Bakhtiyaris, the Regent called a number of deputies, principally Democrats, to *Chalharz,* his summer residence outside Teheran, and after one of his dramatic talks, exclaimed, baring his breast: " Why don't you kill me! " and " I will kill myself then! " He made as if to rush from the room to get a pistol, but was seized and prevented from doing so until he had become calmer. On another occasion during the same month, several deputies were called by the Regent to his palace in the *Gulistan* in Teheran at 10 o'clock at night. On their arrival the Regent started to complain bitterly of an article criticizing him which had appeared in the *Ruski Slovo* (a Russian newspaper) and stating that the Democrats had written these fasehoods about him. Sulayman Mirza, the leader of the Democrats in the Medjlis, who was present, took a paper from his pocket, stating that it contained the views of the Democrats as to the Regent and that the article in question was not written by them. The Regent said: " This is not enough; you must state publicly that what the *Ruski Slovo* says is false." Sulayman Mirza replied: " I will never do that, as it is not the business of the Democrats to do such things." At this the Regent jumped up, shouting and beating his breast and crying: " You want to kill me; why don't you kill me? I will leave to-night! " After two hours of incoherencies of this kind, to which the servants and soldiers outside the room were practically witnesses, the Regent called for a scribe and dictated his resignation, adding the statement at the bottom: " I do this because the Democrats are against me and hate me." He then said: " You must all sign this and guarantee me a safe conduct out of the country." When the deputies and ministers present refused, the Regent started to rush from the room, calling for his coachman, but was seized and dragged back. The gathering broke up about 3 o'clock in the morning, after five hours of this hysterical procedure.

Nasiru'l-Mulk was, in my opinion, a most unfortunate choice for Regent. The situation of the Persian people demanded a strong, just hand at the helm, and, however great his intelligence, the Regent was not strong, and, on some subjects, he was not just. A profound egoist, he could look at no question except in its bearing upon him and his dignity. His familiar accusation against the Medjlis and the Ministers was that they were endeavoring to drag him into politics, and that the Regent should be sacrosanct and respected by every one, as is the King of England. The conclusion is inevitable that he was more concerned with his own welfare and peace of mind than with the success of the difficult and complicated task which he had undertaken.

The Cabinet ministers and other high executive officials with whom I came in contact during my stay in Persia, with few exceptions, did not impress me favorably. Many of them were men of good education and great intelligence, but they invariably lacked the ability to regard their power and office purely as a means of serving their country. I am aware that, tested by this standard, many public officials in other countries would leave something to be desired, but the defects of selfishness, of purely personal ambition, of seeking pecuniary profit at the expense of the Government, were more than usually prevalent among the so-called governing classes in Persia. These men were invariably chosen from the aristocracy—and a very degenerate aristocracy —and they were either unwilling or unable to oppose seriously corruption in the Government where it might even faintly affect themselves or their friends.

The deputies of the Persian Medjlis were a very different type of men. Among them were some few of the grandee element, of the wealthy landowners and nobles. But as a rule they were nearer to the people; many had studied law or medicine; some had been clerks and inferior public officials. A number of the deputies were priests or *mullahs,* and, whatever their walk in life, they seemed to feel that the fact of their being chosen by a popular vote, instead of being merely appointed through some form of influence, made them the guardians of the rights of their countrymen. Most of these men sincerely believed that they embodied the dignity and ideals of the Persian people in their struggle to establish a representative form of government.

As to the Medjlis itself, varying opinions have been and doubtless will be expressed. The British and Russian Governments have asserted that it was a most incompetent and unbusinesslike body. Doubtless they had good reason at times to regard it with distaste. Their diplomatic representatives at Teheran found on more than one occasion that it was not quite so easy to give orders or threatening hints to a body of eighty elected representatives as to whisper a word in the ear of a servile and corrupt court favorite in the time of the former Shahs.

I believe that there has never been in the history of the world an instance where a people changed suddenly from an absolute monarchy to a constitutional or representative form of government and at once succeeded in displaying a high standard of political wisdom and knowledge of legislative procedure. Such a thing is inconceivable and not to be expected by any reasonable person. The members of the first Medjlis were compelled to fight for their very existence from the day that the Parliament was constituted. Their unequal struggle against Muhammad Ali Shah and the foreign powers who largely aided him terminated when their Chamber was bombarded by Colonel Liakhoff and his Cossacks. They had no time for serious legislative work, and but little hope that any measures which they might enact would be put into effect.

The second and last Medjlis, practically all of whose members I knew personally, was doubtless incompetent if it were to be judged by the standards of the British Parliament or the American Congress. It would be strange indeed if an absolutely new and untried government in a land filled with the decay of ages should, from the outset, be able to conduct its business as well as governments with generations and even centuries of experience behind them. We should make allowance for lack of technical knowledge; for the important question, of course, is that the Medjlis in the main represented the new and just ideals and aspirations of the Persian people. Its members were men of more than average education; some displayed remarkable talent, character and courage. Nearly all believed that the salvation of their country depended upon their efforts to place the Constitutional Government upon a firm and lasting basis, and that by such means alone would they be able to restore peace, order and prosperity, and check both the sale of their country to foreigners and the future political encroachments of Russia and England. The deputies of the second Medjlis, with comparatively few exceptions, were sincerely devoted to that aim. They responded enthusiastically to any patriotic suggestion which was put before them. They themselves lacked any great knowledge of governmental finances, but they realized the situation and were both willing and anxious to put their full confidence in any foreign advisers who showed themselves capable of resisting political intrigues and bribery and working for the welfare of the Persian people.

No Parliament can be rightly termed incompetent when it has the support of an entire people, when it recognizes its own limitations, and when its members are willing to undergo great sacrifices for their nation's dignity and sovereign rights.

The Medjlis was the only permanent check in the governmental fabric on the reactionary tendencies of numbers of the grandees and cabinet officials, as well as on corruption among many Persian officials of all ranks. So long as the Medjlis existed it was felt that there was a body to which the people could appeal against reaction, gross peculation and the betrayal of their personal and political rights. The Medjlis stood for an honest and progressive administration of Persia's affairs. On the day that this body was destroyed, with the connivance of the foreign powers, the last hope of honest or representative government in Persia disappeared. The Persian people refused to acquiesce in the *coup d'état* which snuffed out the Medjlis, because they recognized that with it went their liberties, their rights, their nationality, and their future as an independent state.

The Medjlis was remarkably expeditious in transacting business. It showed heated partizanship on some occasions, but older legislative institutions have not been free from this defect.

While the Medjlis was not ideally representative in the political sense, that is, only a small proportion of the population had participated in the election of its members, it more truly represented the best aspirations of the Persians than any other body that had ever existed in that country. It was as representative as it could be under the difficult circumstances which surrounded the institution of the Constitutional Government. It was loyally supported by the great mass of the Persians and that alone was sufficient justification for its existence. The Russian and Brit-

MIRZAYANTZ, AN ARMENIAN DEPUTY IN THE MEDJLIS, FROM TEHERAN.

His countrymen fought bravely for the Constitution.

ARBAB KAIKHOSRO, A PARSEE DEPUTY IN THE MEDJLIS.

He was a staunch supporter of the American finance officials.

ish Governments, however, were constantly instructing their Ministers at Teheran to obtain this concession or to block that one, failing utterly to recognize that the days had passed in which the affairs, lives and interests of twelve millions of people were entirely in the hands of an easily intimidated and willingly bribed despot. With a popularly elected parliament in control of railroad, mining and other concessions, the old-time facility for getting certain things done for the time had disappeared. In other words, the Medjlis was inconvenient to the secret purposes, whatever they may have been, of the two powers which were so constantly proclaiming that their " interests " in Persia were in danger.

As to the Persian people themselves, it is difficult to generalize. The great mass of the population is composed of peasants and tribesmen, all densely ignorant. On the other hand, many thousands have been educated abroad, or have traveled after completing their education at home. The Persians are as a rule kind and hospitable. They have an undue respect for foreigners. French, and some English, is spoken among the wealthier classes. They, or at least certain elements among them which had had the support of the masses, proved their capacity to assimilate western civilization and ideas. They changed despotism into democracy in the face of untold obstacles. Opportunities were equalized to such a degree that any man of ability could occupy the highest official posts. As a race they showed during the past five years an unparalleled eagerness for education. Hundreds of schools were established during the Constitutional régime. A remarkable free press sprang up over night, and fearless writers came forward to denounce injustice and tyranny whether from within their country or without. The Persians were anxious to adopt wholesale the political, ethical and business codes of the most modern and progressive nations. They burned with that same spirit of Asiatic unrest which pervades India, which produced the "Young Turk" movement, and which has more recently manifested itself in the establishment of the Chinese Republic. The East has awakened. Persia unfortunately awoke too late. Her futile struggles towards the light were quickly suppressed by a power whose own strength lies only in the path of darkness.

CHAPTER X [1]

THE EUROPEAN DIPLOMATIC FIELD IN 1911. BRITISH AND RUS-
SIAN POLICIES. THE POTSDAM AGREEMENT AND THE SECRET
UNDERSTANDING BETWEEN RUSSIA AND GERMANY. STRATE-
GICAL VALUE OF PERSIA. SIR EDWARD GREY'S CHARGES
AGAINST THE TREASURER-GENERAL. THE ANGLO-RUSSIAN
AGREEMENT.

EVER since the destruction of the Medjlis the old trick of
the ostrich sticking its head in the sand to escape pursuit
has been receiving a new application in Persia. Russia and
England have apparently thought that by maintaining a
" dummy " Persian government at Teheran they could evade
responsibility in the eyes of the world for what is going on in
that stricken country.

As a gentleman styling himself " No Ruz " wrote from Teheran to the *Near East* under date of March 21, 1912:

By leaving a Persian Government in existence the Powers evade all responsibility, while at the same time successfully paralysing the Government
they tolerate.

I would suggest that the Powers (meaning England and Russia) may have thought that they thus escaped all responsibility
for what goes on in Persia, but the world has long since grown
familiar with such methods. Mere cant, however seriously put
forth in official statements, no longer blinds educated public
opinion as to the facts in these acts of international brigandage.
The truth is that England and Russia have been playing a hand
in the game of medieval diplomacy. *Le Prince* is still their text-

---

[1] The views expressed in this Chapter are of the situation on April 30,
1912.

247

book, but they fool no one—not even the Persian tools and Judases who compose the so-called government and take Russian roubles and rulings with equal alacrity.

It is doubtful whether the British public is very much deceived, either. Englishmen have grown a bit tired of Sir Edward Grey's mysterious solemnity whenever a thoughtless M. P. asks an obvious question as to Russia's actions or British policy in Persia. Sir Edward has worn that coat threadbare in the past five years. " Situations " are always " delicate " or " grave " with him; and " negotiations " are always " proceeding." That is about all the inquisitive M. P. gets, be he Liberal or be he Unionist. How long the British people will permit their foreign affairs to be bungled is a question. If there had been no serious internal problems intimately wrapped up with the fortunes of the present Liberal Cabinet, it would probably have been already answered. A referendum on the success of Sir Edward Grey as Secretary for Foreign Affairs or on the diplomatic triumphs obtained under the foreign policy of the Liberal Government during the past two years would show an interesting result. One has only to ask the Liberals themselves about this.

Last summer Persia's fate was definitely sealed by Russia. The long-expected European crisis had arrived, and the Bear had therefore acquired a practically free hand in Asia. What made the tension in Europe so acute as to cause Asia to be forgotten ?

Ask the admiral in command of the German North Sea Fleet which was found cruising off the coast of Scotland in the dawn of a September day. A British cruiser discovered the German dreadnaughts by the merest chance. They were in battle formation, with scouts in advance, and torpedo destroyers steaming actually within English waters.

Ask the two high English naval officers who were put on the retired list because they lost track of this fleet for a few hours.

MUTAMINU'L-MULK, THE PRESIDENT OF THE
PERSIAN MEDJLIS.
This body was destroyed by the "coup d'etat" of December 24,
1911.

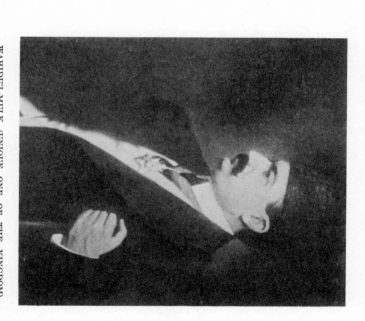

WAHIDU'L-MULK (UNIQUE ONE OF THE KINGDOM).
One of the leaders of the Democrats in the Medjlis. He was a strong
supporter of the Americans.

Ask the Czar of Russia whether he promised at Potsdam that the Anglo-Russian Convention would not be interpreted by Russia as binding herself to any act inimical to Germany in the case of hostilities between the latter country and England.

By the answers to these questions, if they were truthfully given, the sudden onslaught on Persia last autumn by the Russian radical Cabinet would be fully explained. The puerility of talking of Persia having affronted Russian Consular officers and of Persia's Treasurer-general having appointed a British subject to be a tax-collector at Tabriz, as the reasons for Russia's aggressive and brutal policy in Persia, is only too apparent. And this, in spite of the fact that volumes would not contain the bare record of the acts of aggression, deceit and cruelty which Russian agents have committed against Persian sovereignty and the Constitutional Government since the deposition of Muhammad Ali in 1909.

Since when has "lack of tact" by an officer in one government given another nation the right to send 18,000 troops into friendly territory, to massacre peaceful inhabitants, to shoot down, torture, blow from guns and hang non-combatants, and to destroy by force the established forms of a friendly sovereign nation? Would the Hague Tribunal, so ostentatiously promoted and encouraged by His Imperial Majesty the Czar of all the Russias, approve that course as in accord with the law of nations, or with the dictates of justice and humanity? Can any self-respecting nation have a treaty with, or join a peace conference at the invitation of, a government like that of Russia?

The trouble with British foreign policy during the past five years is that there has been no statesman to direct it. Sir Edward Grey is a man of good birth, manners and splendid classical education. He would make an excellent Foreign Minister for Switzerland or Belgium, or even for Anthony Hope's Ruritania. The British Empire, however, is a different affair. Its

12

interests extend beyond Europe, and beyond the grasp of a decidedly provincial gentleman whose longest sea-voyage was across the English channel and whose most tangible accomplishment during a lengthy public career is an authoritative treatise on dry fly-fishing. More than half the British Empire lies in Asia, and Sir Edward Grey is not accused by his most ardent supporters of having any oriental conception or imagination.

Since the Anglo-French *entente* consummated by Lord Lansdowne in 1905, British foreign policy has been greatly modified. It was plainly the belief of that distinguished statesman that England should emerge from what had been termed her splendid isolation in European politics. Germany's remarkable program of naval construction may have had something to do with this.

When the present Liberal Government in England came into power it was confronted abroad by a complicated European and Asiatic diplomatic situation. The Russo-Japanese war had left Russia decidedly weak. She needed money to rebuild her navy, to promote industries, to build railroads. France was just a trifle slow in coming forward. Then appeared the brilliant statesman who suggested that it was good policy for England to strengthen Russia, and to pour London capital into St. Petersburg. Why? Because Germany was growing stronger and the Anglo-French entente was not deemed a sufficient barrier to German ambitions and hostility. To build up the war-spent Russia, therefore, and to make an entente with her which should do for England on the north of Germany what the understanding with the French had done on the south—that was the plan. Some called it " drawing a circle around Germany." The Germans evidently regarded it in that light.

The pretext for carrying out this plan was not lacking. The affairs of England and Russia in Asia needed settling. Behold the Anglo-Russian Convention, published in September, 1907, whereby Sir Edward Grey hoped to establish his fame as a worthy successor to Lansdowne. It was denied, as is customary, that there were any secret clauses to this agreement. Maybe there were not.

Did this Convention settle the questions between Russia and England in this part of Asia? Not for very long, at least.

During the time that the formation of the Triple Entente was going on the Germans had not been entirely asleep. They had a feeling that in some way this startling irruption of England into purely continental politics was connected with themselves. Germany had begun to take a very decided interest in Asiatic Turkey. There has been for years past a very active German diplomat at Constantinople, Baron Marschall von Bieberstein by name.[1] He had something to do with obtaining the Bagdad railway concession for Germany. The world may hear at any time that he had something to do with a change to be announced in the status of the Dardanelles. Admiral Chester and his associates who have been seeking a concession for an American railroad in Turkey have probably come into contact with von Bieberstein. Up to a few years ago, British influence at Constantinople was predominant. Now it is negligible, and German influence reaches throughout the Ottoman Government. The Turks believe that Germany is neither afraid nor decadent.

Germany, however, had only begun her operations in the Middle East. In the autumn of 1910 the Czar and the Kaiser met at Potsdam. From that meeting sprang the so-called "Potsdam Agreement"—a perfectly harmless document as any one can easily see by reading the various versions of it which have been officially given out for publication. Were there any secrets behind it—any undisclosed clauses? None. We know

---

[1] On May 6, the press announcement was made that this eminent diplomat had been assigned to the German Embassy at London.

this, for both the Russian and German foreign offices have said so to the public. Sir Edward Grey likewise informed the British Parliament to this effect.

From the beginning there has been considerable mystery about the scope of this agreement. Its existence was believed to have been prematurely disclosed to the public.

On January 14, 1911, Baron Marschall von Bieberstein declared to the Turkish Government that the Russo-German negotiations *concern exclusively railway construction and railway junctions* in Persian territory.

It is generally understood the agreement contains the following provisions:

Germany and Russia each undertakes to remain aloof from any combination of Powers that has any aggressive [1] *tendency against the other.*

Germany recognizes that Northern Persia is a Russian sphere of influence, and that Russia can claim all the railway concessions granted by the Persian Government in that region. By way of supporting Russian policy in Northern Persia, German capital will be provided to assist in the construction of a railway from Teheran to Khanikin, on the Turco-Persian frontier. This line will thus be financed partly by German and partly by Russian capital, but will remain under the control of the Russian concessionaires.

Russia recognizes Germany's commercial interests in Northern Persia, and guarantees the maintenance of the " open door " policy in that sphere of Russian political influence.

Russia recognizes Germany's rights, granted by concession, in the Bagdad Railway, and undertakes to give diplomatic support to the completion of that enterprise.

[1] The ambiguity contained in the qualification " aggressive " is approved diplomatic style.

EPHRAIM KHAN (WITH FUR-COLLARED OVERCOAT), AMIR MUJAHID (LEANING ON CANE) AND MR. SHUSTER.
Inspecting the Nationalist forces about to be dispatched against Muhammad Ali.

EPHRAIM KHAN.
With his private bodyguard and favorite horse.

A railway will be constructed by German concessionaires from Bagad to Khanikin, on the Persian frontier, to connect the Bagdad line with the Russo-German line from Khanikin to Teheran and with other lines which are to be constructed by the Russian concessionaires in Northern Persia.

Certain tariff questions connected with the transport of goods on the Bagdad Railway and on the projected lines in Northern Persia are regulated by the agreement. The construction of these lines, together with the freight and tariff arrangements, will facilitate the transport of German exports into Northern Persia, while, on the other hand, there will be a route for Russian products to Asia Minor and the Mediterranean. The agreement contains a guarantee of the maintenance of the *status quo* in the Near East, intended to allay any Turkish suspicions regarding the ultimate effect of Russo-German coöperation in those regions.

No one believes, unless it is Sir Edward Grey, that these provisions embody all the points as to which an agreement was reached.

Even the disclosed clauses, however, were sufficient to show that Russia was no longer, if she had ever really been, a member of the Triple Entente, the creation of which was urged in England as the chief justification for the Anglo-Russian Convention of 1907.

We know that Russia is a vast country without a single seaport which is open during the winter. On the one side the Baltic ports are ice-bound; on the other, Vladivostok, on the sea of Japan, is equally useless for the same reason. In the center the Russian ports on the Black Sea are closed to war vessels by the Convention regarding the passage of the Dardanelles. This situation was relieved somewhat when Russia obtained Port Arthur, but its capture by the Japanese again compelled her to seek elsewhere for a port or ports where she could anchor her navy at any time of the year, instead of being compelled to have her ships either cruise in the open sea or be frozen up for an indefinite period.

There are several fairly good ports on the Persian Gulf, some of them in the neutral sphere, and the Gulf is never blocked by ice.

For many years the German nation has been slyly urging Russia to undertake adventures in the Middle East, just as she encouraged Austria to adventures in the Near East, and France to adventures on the Mediterranean, in Africa — the German object always being to occupy these nations, both their forces and their money, in those different directions, while she developed unhampered and became the greatest European power.

Some say that this policy of Bismarck's is still in full force, and that in any forward movement in Asia Russia has and will have the secret support of Germany.

Now suppose that in the conferences at Potsdam a little friendly understanding was reached along the following lines: Despite the general trend and moral effect of the Anglo-Russian Convention of 1907, Russia *will not* do anything to embarrass Germany should the latter become engaged in hostilities with England. In return for this, Germany recognizes Russia's predominant influence *in Persia* (not in Northern Persia), and Germany will support Russia, morally and otherwise, in her measures to exert and increase this control. Lastly, *for the mutual benefit of both nations,* Russia and Germany will see to it that the Bagdad Railway is linked up, at its contemplated terminus at Khanikin, on the Turco-Persian frontier, with another line to be built by Germany from Khanikin to Hamadan (Persia), and thence southward to Khoramabad, through the Karun valley, to Ahwaz and Mohammerah, which means the

Persian Gulf. Russia agrees to *obtain*[1] the necessary " concession " from Persia for this purpose.

Would not these things be very interesting to England, if they were among the undisclosed clauses of the Potsdam Agreement? In a very agreeable interview which I had with Sir Edward Grey at his request in London, last February, I had the pleasure of asking him such a question. Naturally, I cannot give his answer. It occurred to me that Lord Haldane might have been interested in the matter during his visit to Berlin a few days later.

Let us consider, then, the splendid results which have flowed from the Anglo-Russian Convention. The signing of it, following upon the Anglo-French entente, put Germany very much on the *qui vive,* and the Potsdam Agreement was the outcome. That agreement undoes, so far as England is concerned, every moral advantage that Sir Edward Grey ever hoped to obtain by the entente with Russia in 1907, and leaves Russia with the benefits of the notoriously unequal " partition " of Persia into Russian and British spheres of influence. Indeed, Russia almost got the " Lion's share." What is far worse, however, Russia has come to a newer and fresher understanding with Germany (which, by the way, is the only nation in Europe which she fears), whereby Germany — in return, we may be sure, for *something* — has agreed to support the Russian " forward " policy in Asia. Is there any reason why Germany should not do this? It annoys England, not to say frightens her. It means that the Persian Gulf will no longer be *mare clausum* — a status which Lord Curzon was at such pains to emphasize in 1903. In Lord Curzon's own words:

Our [the British] position in the Gulf depends on very much more than on any treaties we may have concluded. It depends upon the unassailable

---

[1] Her ability to do so, since the destruction of the Medjlis on December 24, 1911, can hardly be questioned.

ground of our trade in the Gulf; upon our services for the last hundred years; upon the capital sunk there; upon the naval position we keep up; upon the political predominance we maintain; and most of all, upon the fact that the Gulf is part of the maritime frontier of India in the security of which is involved the security, integrity, and peace of India itself.

Despite this brave show, the Potsdam Agreement means that, with the completion of the Bagdad Railway and its Persian extension, Germany will have a short rail route to the Orient. It shows how Adamzad, "the bear that walks like a man," still clings to the hope of drawing a circle around India and finally pulling the string.

The clever part of this complicated web of intrigue is that Russia picked out the one nation whose alliance with her for the opening up of the Persian Gulf would make it absolutely impossible that England should go to war over the matter. If Russia alone had attacked this watery British sphere by seeking a port on the Gulf there might have been war, but by involving Germany in the plan, through a Persian railroad concession, England is rendered helpless unless she is prepared to fight Russia and the "Teutonic horror" at the same time—a suggestion which would probably give the British public an attack of "nerves." *Par ignobile fratrum,* John Bull might well exclaim.

We read with increased interest, then, the following excerpt from a despatch from the Government of India to the Secretary of State for India in Council, dated September 21, 1899, relating to British policy in Persia:

SIMLA, September 21, 1899.
We desire to address your Lordship, and through your Lordship, Her Majesty's Government, on the subject of the relations of Great Britain with Persia.

. . . .

(Paragraph 5)
The strategical interests of Great Britain in Persia arise from conditions with which India is most intimately concerned. Long before the boundaries

of British India had been extended to their present limits, or before Russia had become a great Central Asian power, approaching or impinging at many points upon the Indian frontiers, the fortunes of Persia, though not at that time a coterminous country, had become a matter of vital concern to the British dominion in India. In the early years of the present century, when the ambitions of France were the main source of apprehension, it was through Persia that a blow at British supremacy was expected to be struck and that an invasion of India was planned. The same idea has reappeared at intervals since. Now that the boundaries of Afghanistan, which have been demarcated and guaranteed by Great Britain, march for many hundreds of miles with those of Persia; that the Persian territory is also coterminous for hundreds of miles with Beluchistan, a State under a British Protectorate, and in large measure actually administered by the officers of the Government of India; and that the sea which washes the southern coast of Persia is one in which, both from its proximity to the Indian Ocean and as a result of the exertions of the past century, Indian interests and influence have become supreme, it is clear that Persia has assumed a strategical importance in relation to British India, which might not be serious were the resources or designs of that country alone to be considered; but which is indisputably great when it is remembered that closely pressing upon Persia and upon Afghanistan is the ever-growing momentum of a power whose interests in Asia *are not always in accord with our own, and that the Persian Gulf is beginning to attract the interests of other and sometimes rival Nations.*

May the officially dead British Indian strategists who so ably formulated this traditional warning not turn too often in their graves at the interpretation of the " spirit of the Anglo-Russian Convention " so debonairly put forth by Sir Edward Grey last August when the Moroccan situation arose and the question of Persia employing Major Stokes was first raised. It became painfully apparent then that the British Foreign Office could not carry more than one idea in its head at a time. " Throw Persia overboard " was the official command that went forth, and *sauve qui peut* on the German sea. Russia was quick to see the opportunities of the situation, and the well-trained bluster of the St. Petersburg semi-official press, followed by a timely diplomatic " feeler " in London, drove the advantage home.

One of the results is that there is no longer a " buffer " state between the Caucasus and the southwestern Indian frontier. The overland route to India is no longer safeguarded against Russia. The British control of the Persian Gulf is seriously threatened.

Another is, that the 72,000,000 Muhammadans in India, who have always been a neutralizing influence between the British Government and the Hindoos, have, as a result of the attacks made with England's acquiescence by Russia and other so-called Christian nations of Europe on the Muhammadan states — Morocco, Tripoli (Turkey) and Persia—lost much of their loyal enthusiasm for the home government. A recent letter from the Muhammadan high priest of India to a former British-Indian official of importance states that after the Persian affair the Muhammadans decided to send representatives to the next Hindoo Congress,—a thing which they had previously declined to do. British political problems in India have not lessened any as a result of the downfall of Persia.

British prestige has suffered all over the world, and the English people are openly dissatisfied because they can no longer appear as the friend of weak and struggling nations.

In Turkey, England had already lost her influence. Through the part recently played by her in Persia British trade and commerce, which had a practical monopoly of the Persian markets as far north as Isfahan, has received a tremendous blow.

From a strategical standpoint the effects are even worse. England's hereditary foe is now marching confidently toward the Persian Gulf. She will be there before many years, and the British-Indian Government will have an opportunity of demonstrating its ability to protect the territory included in the so-called " British sphere "—the limits of which were fixed by Kitchener as being all the Persian soil which could be successfully defended from India. To defend even Southern Persia against the Cossacks will mean a heavy additional burden upon the Indian Government. It may mean keeping half a million British troops in India instead of one-fifth that number. Another feature—perhaps somewhat less important as international affairs go—is that in aiding Russia in her sinister designs on Persia's independence and integrity England has not performed a moral or humane act. She has failed utterly to play the part which history taught us to expect from her, and though the great mass of the British people must be acquitted of the faults and negligence of their Government, the sting will always remain.

Perhaps even Sir Edward Grey will now admit that in diplomacy a given policy must be either moral or successful. His has been neither, to any appreciable extent. Take the attitude of Germany, for instance. If a year ago she had any doubts about the British Government's fear of her, they have now been removed. Germany has been Sir Edward Grey's *bête noire,* but hatred of her in England is the only thing which holds him in power, despite the disastrous effects of his diplomacy.

It may be asked what England could have done to stay Russia's hand in Persia. Great Britain is a naval power, but what could her fleets do against Russia? Where could they attack her, unless and until she came down to the Persian Gulf? England is not able to oppose successfully Russian arms in Northern Persia. She is not a military power, in the sense that several great continental powers are, and the entire British Army could not attack the vast forces which Russia could pour into Persia from the Caucasus.

The answer, however, is not far to seek. Either England is still a first-class power in the world or she is not. Up to the present she has been so considered. Russia has so rated her. When, therefore, it became clear last July that Russia was openly seeking to violate the Anglo-Russian Convention by interfering with Persia's independence, which both England and

Russia had mutually engaged to respect, it was England's obvious right and duty to protest against such a step, and to warn Russia that her actions could be taken only as a repudiation of the Anglo-Russian Convention. This would at least have kept British faith with Persia, and with the world. It might well have prevented Russia from going any further. A nation which voluntarily signs a treaty must be prepared to face a deliberate violation of it by the other party. When such a contingency arises both justice and expediency demand some show of national dignity. Sir Edward Grey preferred to evade his plain responsibility over both the Stokes incident and, later, over the Shuau's-Saltana affair by publicly glossing over Russia's actions and pretending to believe that Persia's sovereignty has not been violated. Subsequently Sir Edward Grey took the remarkable ground that England *had not guaranteed* the integrity and independence of Persia. It is interesting to note, however, that one of England's greatest authorities on Asiatic problems, Lord Curzon, in a debate on Persian Affairs in the House of Lords on March 22, 1911, made the following unchallenged statement:

I am convinced that the integrity and independence of Persia, *which was guaranteed by his Majesty's Government,* in the preamble to the Anglo-Russian Convention of 1907, has no more substantial supporter than his Majesty's Government.

Lord Morley was present, representing the Liberal Government, and never questioned the accuracy of the statement. These pretexts about Russia's actions last summer, so shallow and absurd as to cause any Englishman to blush, served only to show Russia and the rest of the world in what craven dread the Liberal Government stood of Germany.

The remarkable attitude adopted by the British Government leads one to inquire what is the great change which has ap-

PERSIAN NATIONALISTS IN CHAINS AT THE BAGH-I-SHAH.
They were imprisoned by Muhammad Ali in 1909.

parently came over a nation which but a short time ago claimed to possess the deciding vote in most European and Asiatic affairs. Can it be that British ships have lost their efficiency, and British sailors their skill and courage? Was the British Army really "reformed" after the terrible disclosures of the South African war?

The seeds of medieval decay still abound in several plague spots on this earth, and it behooves modern governments to exterminate them, each within its confines. For the sake of humanity and the world's progress England should do her part.

It is clear, therefore, that the unfortunate fate of Persia as an independent nation was not brought about by anything which her Government or her people did or left undone. The destruction of her independence was written down in the book of history at Potsdam in 1910. Secure in the knowledge of Germany's support, Russia could afford to bide her time. The Anglo-Russian Convention was already morally "scrapped," a worn-out and useless instrument, so far as Russia was concerned. Russia proposed to carry out her oft-announced policy of controlling Persia and "the waters which bathe its shores." She awaited only a favorable opportunity to take active steps. The tension in Europe over the Moroccan affair last July gave her the chance, and she was not slow to take advantage of it. Sir Edward Grey flew into a panic, and apparently forgot in an instant everything but the Kaiser's dreadnaughts. Russia realized this, and the trick was turned. The succeeding Russo-Persian incidents leading up to the destruction of the Persian Constitutional Government on December 24, 1911, were the merest pretexts, created and fabricated by Russia herself, possibly "to save Sir Edward Grey's face" before the British public.

Russia is now [1] the sovereign power in Persia. She is the

[1] April 30, 1912.

practical and effective ruler of the country. The whole of Persia is to-day a satrapy. The people, however brutally treated, have no means of protest. Fear, daily sickening fear of the prison, noose and torture, is the force with which Russia governs. A gloomy silence has set in as to what is happening in the land of Cyrus. The American finance administrators at Teheran last year were a mere incident. The Bear has devoured another slice of the Asiatic pasty.

Sir Edward Grey at various times charged me with a number of faults: lack of tact; that I was endeavoring to " Anglicize " the Persian service; and that I was unwilling to recognize the Russian and British spheres of influence.

The best reply which I can make to the first charge is to publish, as I would not otherwise have done, the semi-official correspondence between the Russian and British ministers and myself concerning the Stokes incident, the proposed loan of £4,000,000, and the payments for the arms sold to Persia by Russia, and for the Cossack Brigade.[1]

As to the second charge, it is based on the fact that I employed at different times three British subjects in the Persian Treasury. They were stationed at Teheran, Isfahan and Shiraz. It is true that in seeking for employees on the ground who were familiar with modern accounting methods and possessed a knowledge of the Persian language and customs I found several British subjects available. In the same manner and for the same reasons I employed two Belgians. Had any Russian subjects possessing the necessary qualifications presented themselves, I should have gladly engaged them. Sir Edward Grey's baseless accusation against me of political bias, however, compelled me, in the interests of Persia, to discharge from the Persian Treasury all three British subjects — including Mr.

[1] See Appendix D.

Lecoffre — leaving only Mr. George E. New, who was under contract approved by the Medjlis.

The third charge was even more absurd and unjustified than the others. The Persian Government had formally notified the two powers after the publication of the Anglo-Russian Convention in 1907, that it did not recognize or consider itself in any manner bound thereby. The Medjlis was insistent from the very first that I should do nothing which would either directly or otherwise recognize the existence of so-called spheres of influence within Persia.

This I gave them my promise at the outset not to do. For me to have done so would have been to break faith with the Government which employed me and to betray a trust which had been placed in me. My refusal to do this — a thing which the powers had encountered no difficulty in persuading the Belgians to do — was the real source of Russia's opposition to my work.

Nevertheless, I sought in every way possible to recognize and respect all legitimate foreign interests in Persia, and endeavored to ascertain from the two Legations just what they considered their " special interests " in Persia, to be — that is, what *they* considered the language of the Anglo-Russian Convention to mean.

As that cynical political writer, Dr. E. J. Dillon, so well phrases it in one of his articles on the Potsdam Agreement:

If you want to keep your faith in foreign Governments, be suspicious. For the language of diplomacy was not invented to reveal the thoughts of those that employ it, nor is there any known herb that will enable us to discern them.

This writer must have had a premonition of the bizarre interpretation which was later going to be placed on the perfectly

plain wording of the Anglo-Russian Convention by Sir Edward
Grey, at Russia's behest, in the summer of 1911.

As for myself I neglected no possible means to find out just
what England and Russia *did mean* when they executed and
promulgated that document.

I said in an address under the auspices of the Persia Committee in London on January 29, 1912:

... I would say a word in my own defense which I had not thought of
saying, because after all it does not make much difference whether I personally was right or wrong in any discussions which have taken place over
Persia, but the particular charge which has been laid against me is one
which may or may not be true: that I lacked a certain finesse in recognizing that words do not mean what they say, and that diplomatic agreements sometimes have a secret code by which they must be read. If that
be true, I must plead innocent in this case, on the ground that the governments which expected me to read into their solemn agreements meanings
which did not appear from the words used, should have informed me of the
code by which they translated them. They did not. I was after a very
short time on the best of terms with both the Russian and British Ministers
at Teheran. I esteemed them greatly as men of honor and of high ideals
of justice. I cannot say anything more on this, except that from the time
I arrived to the time I left, I never had an unpleasant word or an unpleasant discussion with them; we never even had a serious disagreement.
They were Ministers Plenipotentiary in Teheran, and if I was tactless in
discussing and arriving at conclusions with Ministers Plenipotentiary, then
I suppose I must plead guilty, but it goes no further than that; and if I
was indiscreet in finally giving publicity to things which were happening
there and which had been happening there, without the world at large or
the people of the governments who were participating in them knowing it,
to that also I plead guilty, but I did what I did, inasmuch as it concerned
an interest far more important than me personally or my staying in or
departing from Persia, after consulting the representatives, the elected representatives, of the Persian people, and asking them whether they preferred
to be slain in a dark alley or to have the crime committed in the public
square; and their verdict was: in the public square.

The London *Times,* the well-known organ of the British
Foreign Office, in several editorial articles, notably in one written two days after my address was delivered, urged as a criti-

cism against me that I had expected England and Russia to
assent to my plans for the reorganization of the finances of
Persia " irrespective of their own interests and as a matter of
course."

The plain implication is that something in the financial plans
initiated by me either did or would have prejudiced some British or Russan interest in Persia. I took the opportunity a day
or so later to ask this distinguished journal to state or specify
what British or Russian interest any financial plan advocated by
me would have injured, in order that the public might examine
the question more intelligently. So far no such interest has
been specified and in view of this silence it seems impossible to
escape the conclusion that, either there was no such interest
subjected to prejudice by my plans, or that if any there was, it
was not of such a nature as could be disclosed. The fact is that
there was no word or act in connection with the Persian finance
law of June 13, 1911, which either did, or could, in any manner
prejudice or injure any legitimate interest of any foreign power
whatsoever in Persia ; quite the contrary, the execution of that
law could not have failed to foster and benefit any legitimate interest of Great Britain or Russia, or of any other foreign nation
having relations with the Persian Empire.

This same journal, however, throws a little more light upon
the thoughts in the mind of its editor in the following sentence,
" It never seems to have crossed his [my] mind, until he had
gained it, that the exercise by him of arbitrary and drastic control of finance might possibly prove inconvenient or undesirable
to the Powers with ' special interests.' " Again the question
leaps to the eye, what were these oft-mentioned but never defined special interests ? Where were they mentioned or indicated except in the terms of the Anglo-Russian Convention of
1907 ? And this brings us to the real point at issue, which is,
whether that law or my execution of it violated the terms or,

13

adopting the vague phraseology of a certain class of diplomacy, the " spirit " of that agreement. Admitting then the existence of a spirit, as distinguished from the plain meaning of the language contained in this document, what light could the Persian Government or any one of its officials, either native or foreign, have been expected to find upon this subject ? Speaking for myself, I can only say that after having read the agreement itself several times with great care, and perused the contemporaneous Blue Books of the British Foreign Office as to the same, I found but one other source of information as to the real meaning of this document which was destined to play so important a part in the future of the Persian people. In Professor Browne's magnificent work, " The Persian Revolution, 1905–1909," at page 190, appears a copy of a communication addressed on September 5, 1907, by Sir Cecil Spring-Rice, the then British Minister at Teheran, to the Persian Minister for Foreign Affairs.

This is a most important and interesting document, which so far as I could learn at that time was and is the only extant detailed official explanation of the interpretation and so-called spirit of the Anglo-Russian Convention.[1] Appearing in so authoritative a work as that of Professor Browne, it was naturally assumed by the public to be authentic, and perhaps even to represent the real views of the two powers in concluding the agreement which they had, a few days before, signed in reference to their " interests " in Persia. It is true that I did not find it in the British Foreign Office Blue Books, but I read this *communique* of Sir Cecil Spring-Rice with the greatest care and, in fact, it went far in convincing me that the real purposes of the two powers in Persia were those which naturally appeared from the language of the Convention itself, and not ulterior and undisclosed ones.

[1] A translation of this communication will be found in the Introductory Chapter.

AZADU'L-MULK, ELECTED REGENT AT THE BEGINNING OF THE REIGN OF
SULTAN AHMAD SHAH.

He died on September 22, 1910, and was succeeded by Nasiru'l-Mulk, the present Regent.

To the best of my ability, therefore, I had carefully acquainted myself in January, 1911, before sailing from the United States for Persia, with the only official detailed explanation of the spirit and purpose of the Anglo-Russian Convention of 1907 and of its distinguished framers, which I was then or have since been able to discover. Despite my efforts in good faith to put myself *au courant* with Persia's general political status, I have been more than once charged with having blundered hastily into a delicate situation which I had been at no pains to study or understand, and with being either ignorant of, or ignoring the spirit of the Anglo-Russian Convention. Statements to this effect have been made from very authoritative sources on the floor of the British House of Commons.

Yet on December 14, 1911, in answer to a question by a Member of the House, the Secretary of State for Foreign Affairs, declared that *he had never seen* the above described *communiqué* of Sir Cecil Spring-Rice to the Persian Government, from which the Member in question had a few minutes before made a quotation.   On the next day, I am informed, a member of Parliament addressed to the Foreign Office a letter enclosing a photograph of the original document sent, in the Persian language, by Sir Cecil Spring-Rice to the Persian Government on September 5, 1907.   To this the Foreign Office replied, in effect, that the British Foreign Office knew nothing of the document.   Six weeks later, on February 1, 1912, the Foreign Office wrote to this same member, stating that the English text of Sir Cecil Spring-Rice's *communiqué* had just then been received at the Foreign Office and that the translation into English made by Professor Browne (published in his book) was substantially correct.[1]

It appears, therefore, that at the time that I was being charged

---

[1] This striking exhibition of official carelessness or ignorance on the part of the British Foreign Office had its counterpart in the Stokes affair.

with having displayed ignorance of the spirit of the Anglo-Russian Convention of 1907, and for months before that date, I was familiar with an important official exposition of the views of the British and of the Russian Governments formulated by the British Minister Plenipotentiary at Teheran. Yet the British Foreign Office Officials who presented these charges of ignorance or negligence against me were themselves at that very time in ignorance even of the existence of this important paper which they have only since come to peruse. Is it at all possible that a department of the Government, so conducted as to permit such a lapse in delicate and important affairs of this nature, may have been equally uninformed as to the real facts or other incidents arising during my administration of the finances of Persia, although this department of the British Government saw no hesitation in promptly endorsing Russia's demand for my removal and dismissal from the post of Treasurer-general?

England and Russia were and are to-day unwilling to *define* what they consider to be the nature and scope of their respective interests in Persia. They claimed the right to pass on any particular act of the Persian Government, or any one of its officials, in the purely internal administration of the country, and to prevent that act by force, if it did not suit their views. It can hardly be claimed that this is not the exercise of sovereignty in Persia, or, at least, of the rights of a protectorate. How then do these facts accord with the preamble of the Anglo-Russian Convention and with Sir Cecil Spring-Rice's official explanation of that document!

Anent the action of the British Government throughout the recent Persian affair there have been no clearer nor more patriotic views expressed than those put forth in a series of articles in *The Nation* — a publication which, if it lacks all the prestige and semi-official authority of the *Times* is none the less a liberal organ of high standing and literary character.[1]

---

[1] Two of these articles may be found in Appendix F.

CHAPTER XI

THE general system of levying taxes in Persia is practically the same to-day as it was in Biblical times. The basis of land taxation is the tithe, or tenth part of the product or crop. The revenues are not all collected in cash, but a large part of them in kind; that is, the Government demands and receives from the landowners and peasants in Persia wheat, barley, straw, cotton, oats, rice, and other agricultural produce. The principal effect of this archaic procedure is to make it extremely difficult for the Government to keep any adequate system of accounts or to know with any reasonable degree of accuracy what its revenues from any given district, town or village *should be* during the year. Furthermore, once in possession—through its hundreds of different tax-collectors and sub-collectors throughout the provinces—of the taxes in kind which are due, the Government is supposed to find the means of transporting this produce, storing it safely, and either converting it into money by sale or paying it out in kind for the expenses of the Government.

There has never been in Persia a tax-register or "Doomsday Book" which would give a complete, even if somewhat inaccurate, survey of the sources of internal revenue upon which the Government could count for its support. Persia is divided for taxation purposes into seventeen or eighteen taxation districts each containing a large city or town as its administrative center. For instance, the province of Azarbayjan, which is the most important and richest province in the Empire, is generally supposed to produce a revenue in money and in kind, for the Central Government at Teheran, amounting to about 1,000,000 tumans, or $900,000 a year. There was, during my service in Persia, a chief tax-collector, or *pishkar,* at Tabriz, the capital of the province and second city of importance in the Empire. The province itself is divided into a number of sub-districts, each in charge of a sub-collector, and these sub-districts are in turn divided up into smaller districts, each in charge of a tax agent. Within the third class of districts the taxes are collected by the local town or village headmen. The chief collector at Tabriz, for example, is called upon to collect and place to the credit of the Central Government at Teheran a given sum in money and a given sum in wheat, straw, and other agricultural products each year. Beyond a very indefinite idea in the heads of some of the chief *mustawfis,* or " government accountants," at Teheran as to what proportion of these amounts should come from the first class of districts within the province, the Central Government knows nothing as to the sources of the revenue which it is supposed to receive. Its sole connecting link with the taxpayers of the province of Azarbayjan is through the chief collector at Tabriz. The latter official, in turn, knows how much money and produce should be furnished by each of the sub-collectors under him within the province, but he has no official knowledge of the sources from which these sub-collectors derive the taxes which they deliver to him. The chief collector has in his possession what is termed the *kitabcha* [little book] of the province, and each of the sub-collectors has the kitabcha of his particular district. These little books are written in a peculiar Persian style, on very small pieces of paper, unbound, and are usually carried in the pocket, or at least kept

EPHRAIM KHAN, SARDAR-I-BAHADUR AND MAJOR HAASE.
On their return from the campaign against the Shahsevens, whom they defeated. Sixty members of the principal families of these tribesmen were brought to Teheran and kept as hostages for the good behavior of the tribe.

in the personal possession, of the tax-collector. They are purposely so written as to make it most difficult, if not impossible, for any ordinary Persian to understand them. There is in Persia, and has been for many generations past, a particular class of men who are known as *mustawfis*. The profession or career of *mustawfi* is, in many cases, hereditary, passing from father to son. These men understand the style in which the *kitabcha* are written, and the complicated and intricate system by which the local taxes are computed and collected. Whether one of them is a chief collector of a province, or the collector of a taxation district, he considers the corresponding *kitabcha* to be his personal property, and not as belonging to the Government. He resents most bitterly any attempt on the part of any one to go into details or to seek to find out whence the taxes are derived or what proportion of them he himself retains. At Teheran, when I arrived, I found in the Ministry of Finance a branch which was called the Bureau of the Chief Mustawfis. There were seven or eight of these gentlemen, each having under his charge two or more provinces or districts. They were supposed to see that the tax-collectors throughout the Empire performed their duties and placed to the credit of the Central Government the sums which it was expected to receive. They came nearer to being permanent employees than any other officials of the Government because of their peculiar training and knowledge of the complicated taxation system of the country. From the first they regarded our advent as a blow to their prestige and as threatening the undisturbed enjoyment of their perquisites. Their salaries were ridiculously small compared to the responsibilities which they were supposed to have. The highest paid *mustawfi* at Teheran received about $135 a month, but it is very safe to say that the fortunes which every one of them was known to have accumulated after a few years' service did not result from the savings from this stipend. Their attitude toward me was one of insolence; and they refused to give out any information about their duties. I took out of their hands, almost from the date of the passage of the law of the 13th of June, their nominal control over the chief tax-collectors throughout the Empire, and announced to the latter, in circular telegrams which I caused to be signed by the Prime Minister and the Cabinet, followed by detailed instructions from myself, that thereafter the chief tax-collectors would communicate with the Treasurer-general direct and would receive all their instructions from the newly created Treasury. The *mustawfis* were thus left to finger their *kitabcha* and reflect upon the error of their ways. I purposely allowed them to remain in the Ministry of Finance, even after a number of other departments had been abolished as useless and unnecessary, because I desired to use them, when they arrived at a proper frame of mind, in a general plan for re-districting and making a rough tax survey of the Empire, with a view to having some definite basis upon which to prepare for the Medjlis a simple internal tax law. Before I could make any serious headway along these lines the arrival of the ex-Shah and the ensuing four months of active military operations, with its consequent confusion in Teheran, and the subsequent political events resulting in my departure from the country, took place.

It is clear, therefore, that in Persia the Central Government has but a most meager knowledge either of the revenues which it could expect to receive, or of the justice or injustice of the apportionment of the taxes among the people of Persia. Nothing is easier than for a chief tax-collector to say, as the agent at Tabriz constantly did during the time that I was in Teheran, that, due to the disturbed condition of the province, it had been impossible to recover the taxes and, having said this, not to send them. The Central Government might well know that these statements were false, and that at least a portion of the taxes were being collected, but it was limited in its remedies either to discharging or imprisoning the collector upon this justifiable but none the less general suspicion, or to accepting his explanation.

It was my intention to establish, gradually, starting with the more important provinces, a sub-treasury in each provincial center, in charge of an American or European assistant who would have under him a European traveling inspector with the necessary Persian employees, and a European officer in command of the body of Treasury gendarmes assigned to assist the sub-treasurer in collecting the taxes in that province. In addition to carrying on the actual work of collection and local disbursements of the Government, under the orders of the Treasurer-general, these sub-treasurers were to make a careful study of the different sources of revenue within their provinces, coupled with a general estimate of the population, crops, industries, etc., and to get possession, if possible, of the *kitabcha* and other data held by the sub-collectors and their various subordinates, as a basis for a general taxation scheme. This work would probably have required between one and two years, but so far as Persia was concerned there was no insurmountable obstacle to its accomplishment.

One of the striking defects in the Persian taxation system is that even the *kitabcha* are out of date and do not afford a just basis for the levying of the duties. Most of them were prepared over a generation ago, and since that time many villages which were prosperous and populous have became practically deserted, the people having moved to other districts. Yet the *kitabcha* are never changed, and a few hundred inhabitants remaining in some village which has before harbored a thousand or more are called upon to pay the same taxes which were assessed on the entire community when it was three or more times as large. In like manner, a village, which, when the *kitabcha* were prepared many years ago, had only a few inhabitants, is still called upon to pay, so far as the Central Government is concerned, only the amount originally fixed in the *kitabcha*, although the agent who collects the taxes in the name of the Government never fails to exact from each man in the community his full quota.

One of the first rules put into force when I established the Persian Treasury was that all transactions in money should be carried on through the Imperial Bank of Persia or some other reputable bank. The Imperial Bank of Persia, which was in reality the Government depository, has branches established in most of the important cities of Persia, and under an arrangement which I concluded with its chief manager, the tax-collectors at these places were required to pay all revenues in money collected by them into the local branch of the Imperial Bank, through which it was immediately credited to the account of the Treasurer-general in Teheran on a telegraphic transfer. In the same manner all payments of every description by the Treasury were made by check. No cash transactions whatever were allowed, and in this manner a full and independent record of both receipts and disbursements was established outside the Persian Treasury. Other administrations of the Central Government, such as the Ministry of Posts and Telegraphs, the Passport Bureau of the Ministry of Foreign Affairs, and the Customs, while under the general control of the Treasury, were required to make their deposits in the bank direct and to send to the Treasury the credit notes instead of the cash.

I soon found that most of the chief tax-collectors, while professing their entire willingness to submit to the rules and regulations laid down by the Treasurer-general, were not depositing their revenues with the branch banks as I had directed. In failing to do this they were simply following the universal rule in Persia, which is to hold on to money through thick and thin

SIPAHDAR-I-AZAM AND SARDAR-I-ASAD (with cane).
The leaders of the Nationalist forces which captured Teheran in the summer of 1909.

until one is absolutely forced to give it up. The prompt dismissal, however, of one or two of the more prominent and influential offenders in this respect, and the news of it which was transmitted to the others with a polite warning as to what they might expect, had a most salutary effect, and the revenues commenced to come in despite the disorder into which the whole country was thrown by the news of the return of the ex-Shah and the local disturbances which in many parts of Persia, particularly in the great province of Fars in the South, had been going on for a year before our arrival. The province of Azarbayjan, duing the entire time that I was in control of the Persian treasury, was in such a state of confusion, due largely to Russian troops which were constantly being sent there, and to the outbreaks of the Shahsevens whose chiefs had found that they could count absolutely upon Russian support and protection, that not a dollar of revenue was ever sent from this province to the Treasury at Teheran. On the contrary, the Central Government transmitted large sums to the local Governor at Tabriz for the police and the military forces in that province, in an endeavor to restore order there.

I found also, on taking charge of the Treasury, that the tax-collectors were paid but nominal salaries in many instances and the fact that they were perfectly contented to receive such insignificant compensation while occupying these responsible positions was pretty clear proof that they were deriving a satisfactory reward in some way other than through the pay-roll. I therefore fixed generous salaries for these men in accordance with the importance of their districts, and informed them that the retention of their posts and future increased compensation would depend directly upon the practical results which they showed in the way of collecting the taxes. While these steps, due to entirely outside causes, were never allowed to produce the results which were anticipated, the Treasury did succeed in collecting, during a period of five months, while the country was in a state of civil war, more of the internal taxes, or *maliat,* than the Government had, so far as the records showed, been able to collect during the entire year preceding our arrival.

The question of getting possession of the wheat, barley, oats, straw, cotton and other agricultural products which the Government received in lieu of cash was a much more difficult one. In the first place, taxes in this form were collected principally in the smaller towns and outlying districts, more or less distant from the provincial centers. The products were compelled to pass through so many hands and to be cared for and transported under such difficult circumstances that, except in those provinces lying within a hundred miles or so of Teheran, it was impossible to make any headway. If a few tons of wheat or straw eventually reached a provincial center, it could not be transported to Teheran by telegraph, like money, and if put up at public auction, the price obtained for it would be but a fraction of its value.

Indeed, in past years, the produce thus collected by the Government in the different districts has constituted one of the principal sources of Government graft. Instances have been reported to me where more than $100,000 profit was cleared in a day or so by a fraudulent sale of the taxes in kind of a single province.

When, in the fall of 1911, I took charge of the work of accumulating a reserve supply of wheat and other grain in Teheran in the Government store-houses, in order that the price of bread might be in a measure controlled during the winter, I found how difficult it was to handle this question, and it was only by the most extraordinary methods that I was able to gather 5000 or 6000 tons of wheat and barley.

Under the term *maliat* are grouped the internal taxes, comprising land taxes, local municipal dues, and revenues derived from various other sources, such as the Crown lands, mines and industrial enterprises. The taxes approximate in many instances our poll or head tax. There are also duties levied upon the manufacture and consumption of opium, upon lambskins and the entrails of the same animal. A considerable revenue is also derived by the Persian Government from the consumption of wines, spirits and other intoxicants. The use of intoxicants is, of course, forbidden by the Muhammadan religion, and duties of this kind cannot, in theory, be imposed by the Medjlis, or by official sanction of the Persian Government. As a matter of fact, however, such duties are both imposed and collected by the central administration, with the double object of restricting the sale of alcoholic beverages and deriving a revenue from them.

Outside the *maliat* the only other definite sources of revenue in Persia are the Customs duties, a small revenue from the Ministry of Posts and Telegraphs, and a small sum from the Passport Bureau of the Ministry of Foreign Affairs.

The Customs administration is in charge of some twenty-seven Belgian employees whose chief, Mons. Mornard, with several assistants, was stationed in Teheran. This administration also collected, through its agents on the frontiers, a certain proportion of the passport fees. The net receipts of the Customs during the Persian year of *It-Il*—which corresponds roughly to the calendar year 1910—were about 3,400,000 tumans.[1] For the two preceding years approximately (1909 and 1908) they were about 3,185,000 tumans and 2,733,000 tumans, respectively. This entire revenue, however, was mortgaged to the Russian and British Governments under a series of loan contracts and agreements which called for a minimum annual payment amounting, at the time of the conclusion of

[1] The tuman, while varying in value according to the exchange, is equal to about 90 cents in American money.

the Imperial Bank Loan of £1,250,000, to about 2,832,000 tumans.

When the Imperial Bank Loan went into effect, as the amortization did not begin for five years, this sum was reduced by about 31,000 tumans a year for the intervening period. Taking, therefore, the maximum Customs revenues collected in recent years as the basis of future collections, the Persian Government can only expect to receive from that important source of taxation about 568,000 tumans annually, and under the loan contract made with the Russian Government in 1910, these surplus Customs revenues are held by the Banque d'Escompte, a branch of the Russian State Bank in Teheran, for a period of six months and only placed to the credit of the Persian Government twice a year.

In addition to this, the interest and amortization upon the Russian loan is payable in roubles, and the Banque d'Escompte has the valuable privilege of fixing each month the rate of exchange at which the Customs revenues collected in Persian tumans shall be applied to the purchase of roubles. It is safe to assert that, in exercising this arbitrary right given it under the loan contract, the Russian Bank takes care not to lose anything on the exchange.

One of the large fixed charges included in the above total secured upon the Customs is the expense of maintaining in Persia the notorious Cossack Brigade. This amounted, during the time that I was in Teheran, to a regular monthly demand of 30,000 tumans, plus an unknown and indefinite sum which the colonel of the brigade or the Russian Legation might demand from the Persian Government on the ground of "extraordinary expenses," "costs of expeditions," etc. In one year these additional demands amounted to more than 70,000 tumans. This famous organization was created in 1882, in the reign of Nasiru'd-Din Shah, under a Russian colonel named Char-

NASIRU'D-DIN SHAH.
He succeeded to the throne on September 17, 1848, and was assassinated on May 1, 1896, by Mirza Muhammad Riza, a fanatic of the town of Kirman.

kovsky, who was appointed by the General Staff of the Caucasus for this work, assisted by a number of commissioned and non-commissioned officers of the Russian army. The idea of Na-siru'd-Din Shah, or of his Russian advisers, in establishing this corps of foreign mercenaries was, of course, to protect him-self against any acts growing out of the just indignation of his cruelly oppressed subjects. The brigade brought into being under such questionable auspices has more than once lived up to its evil standards, and it has constantly been, as it is to-day, the chief weapon of Russian intrigue and oppression in Persia. It is supposed to consist of 1500 or 1600 men, and the payments required to be made by the Persian Government for its up-keep are based upon the enrollment of the maximum number. As a matter of fact, at no time while I was in Teheran, was the brigade within many hundreds of its full strength, yet the amounts demanded and received from the impoverished Per-sian Government never varied, nor was there any accounting had of the large sums which were paid over from time to time to the colonel and other officers of the organization. At one time, during the military operations against Muhammad Ali, I was asked by Samsamu's-Saltana, the Premier, to pay certain amounts which were demanded by the colonel of the brigade as extraordinary expenses. I agreed to do so and wrote a letter to the colonel asking him for a statement of the accounts for the period mentioned in order that I might assure myself that I was not paying a sum for expenses which had already been met by the Government. The colonel of the brigade absolutely refused to furnish any information at all as to how the money was expended, and continued his protests to the Russian Lega-tion against the nonpayment of his demands, alleging that I had refused to pay him.

One of the principal obstacles which we encountered in the endeavor to collect the Government revenues in Persia was the absolute lack of any penal statutes covering fraud or peculation, or similar crimes. A tax-collector, or any Persian Government official having public money or property in his possession, might freely make way with the same with little prospect of ever being brought to justice. The absence of any means of punishing crime of this kind was of course in a large measure responsible for the widespread graft and corruption which pervaded the Persian administrations. It can be readily imagined what the situation would be, even in more modern and civilized countries, if all criminal statutes punishing frauds against the Government were wiped off the books. The tribunals of justice in Persia, where they existed at all, were in an even more disorganized condition than the rest of the Government, and far from being a check upon the criminally inclined, they formed an important part of the Empire-wide organization of grafting public officials who lived and waxed fat upon the products of the toil and suffering of millions of peasants and ignorant tribesmen. Such little attempt as was made by the Persian Government to punish dishonest officials took the form of purely police or administrative measures. If the local political conditions seemed to demand it, or there was enough public sentiment in favor of it, the Government directed the arrest of a dishonest official, gave him a drumhead hearing, and consigned him to jail, which was usually the police headquarters. I speak more particularly of the situation in Teheran. In the provinces the local Governors dispensed their brands of justice with heavy hands, but the net result of the arrest and trial of a man charged with crime is, as a rule, that he or his family and friends are forced to raise a purse sufficiently large to satisfy the demands of the Governor, who is sheriff, prosecutor and judge rolled into one.

This situation and the absolute necessity of exercising some moral influence over the employees of the Government service and over recalcitrant taxpayers who could but would not bear their share of the burden of government, compelled us to establish "private lockups" in Teheran where, after due investigation by a board of Treasury officials, the criminally inclined who ran foul of the tax regulations could be temporarily detained.

On assuming charge of the Treasury I notified the different Persian Ministers to the effect that no funds would be paid out except upon a written requisition, to be made upon a printed form prescribed by me. This form was addressed to the Treasurer-general in French and Persian, and called for detailed explanation of the amount demanded. The plan was received by most of the Cabinet Officers with marked enthusiasm. They evidently believed that on filling out a requisition form their task was done, and that nothing remained but for the Treasurer-general to furnish the amount requested. Demands for requisition forms were immediately made, and for weeks my office was bombarded with requests for money based upon claims and arguments of the most fantastic description. It is needless to say that in time the urgent requisitioners discovered that the Treasurer-general was not convinced of the legality and propriety of making a certain payment merely because a Minister had expressed his desire for it upon a treasury blank. A few of the demands made were so amusing that they will bear mentioning. Two French citizens who were making a tour of the world stopped in the course of their travels at Teheran and called upon His Highness the Regent. On the following day I was surprised to receive a requisition from the Ministry of Foreign Affairs asking me, by direction of His Highness, to pay these enterprising gentlemen a hundred tumans as a token of the royal esteem. Not desiring at that time to raise an international question with the great French Republic, I paid the sum, warning the Minister, however, that under the new Treasury rules there must be some legal justification for the expendi-

14

ture of the public moneys. On another occasion I was visited by the grave and dignified *mustawfi* of the Ministry of the Interior, who, with many salaams, handed me a requisition signed by His Excellency the Minister, a literal translation of which was as follows: " Requisition for 100 tumans to be paid to Sayyid [1] Fathu'llah, who fell from his ass and broke his leg." The unfortunate religious gentleman who had met with this deplorable accident was greatly surprised and grieved at learning that the foreign Treasurer-general was unable to see the justice of his claim.

The Minister of the Court once came forward with two requisitions,—one for the purchase of " oil for the Royal camels," the other for " straw for His Majesty's automobile service." This was too much for my official gravity. Only in Persia would one see the Government furnishing *oil* for camels and *straw* for automobiles. The demands were perfectly serious however, as a certain kind of oil is rubbed on the camels to keep their skin soft, and the employees of the Royal garage received pensions payable in straw. Both requisitions were honored.

As soon as it became clear, in the latter part of September, that Muhammad Ali would not be able to reach Teheran, I laid before the Cabinet an outline of the financial measures which I deemed most important and feasible at that time.

Except for the risk which we would have run, of never being allowed to take up our work at all, if we had not succeeded in obtaining authority from the Medjlis while that body was enthusiastic for financial reforms, we might have pursued either of the two following plans: First, to devote six months or a year to a study of the situation in Persia, and then prepare and present detailed laws covering the collection of taxes, the creation of new revenues, and the expenditure of public moneys.

---

[1] A " Sayyid " is a holy man.

Secondly, to do as we did, and secure the immediate passage of a simple law, in general terms conferring on the Treasurer-general the necessary authority to take practical charge of Persia's finances. This latter course was naturally attended with considerable risk, since we were assuming heavy responsibilities and there was always the chance that we might be "swamped" by jumping into the middle of a number of absolutely disorganized and corrupt administrations, but having had one or two previous experiences of a similar nature, I deemed it wiser to adopt the latter course.

In other words, the sands of Persia's financial life were running out so fast that if something practical was not immediately done to diminish the drain, there would soon have been an utterly hopeless state of bankruptcy, confusion and brigandage, both at Teheran and throughout the Empire.

The first step, therefore, was to secure an honest central control of the funds, and, with that as a *point d'appui,* work outward into the other administrations and departments, seeking to check fraud and negligence, and to bring about a reasonably honest collection and expenditure of the existing revenues,— pending the study of new legislation and the building up of a modern system of accounting and audit.

As soon as the law of June 13 was passed by the Medjlis I endeavored to create a "respect for law" among both foreigners and Persians. There was already a very decent respect for money—for power, influence, prestige and courage—but *absolutely none* for the laws as being the embodiment of the rights of the public. Laws, in Persia, and more especially financial laws, were lightly regarded. I found that the Medjlis, several months before I assumed charge, had adopted a "*Loi de Comptabilité,*" which had been fashioned by throwing together a number of sections taken from the French legislation on this subject. This law had been nominally in force for several months, but I was unable to find a single official who either knew what it meant or had made the slightest effort to apply it. They pointed with pride to its existence, and continued calmly on their predatory ways.

It was for the purpose of educating the Persian people to have a respect for law that, as soon as the excitement and confusion of the civil war last summer began to abate, I demanded the payment of taxes by a number of prominent but notoriously corrupt grandees like Alau'd-Dawla, Prince Farman Farma and the Sipahdar.

With the Alau'd-Dawla incident, readers are already familiar. When Prince Farman Farma at last saw that I was in earnest about his actually paying taxes, he went before the Council of Ministers, recounted his valiant services to the Constitutional Government, both as a general of the army and as Minister of War, and finished by sobbing on the Premier's shoulder. The members of the Council were so overcome that they wrote me a polite letter stating that the Prince would not have to pay any taxes until they could look into the question. Farman Farma brought the letter in person, and I told him that he could take his choice between continuing his valiant services to the Constitution by paying all his overdue taxes the next day, and having me seize his grain warehouses and save him the trouble. I wrote the Council that if they would kindly attend to the rest of the Government, I would endeavor to look after the collection of taxes. The Prince paid most of his taxes the following day, though we had to seize some of his wheat in the case of one estate. He had *saved* several millions of dollars during his official service as provincial governor, general, and cabinet officer.

I found one item of 72,000 tumans of back taxes which the Sipahdar owed the Government. As a set-off he presented a claim for one million tumans for his patriotic services and ex-

A PARTY OF VOLUNTEERS WHO FOUGHT FOR THE CONSTITUTION IN PERSIA.

penses in equipping the " Army of Resht," which formed part of the National force which took Teheran from Muhammad Ali in 1909. He said that he thought a grateful Government should exempt him and his descendants from all taxation for ten generations. As he was worth many millions and claimed title to immense estates in Northern Persia, and as he had at that time a large number of descendants who would probably not let the ancient line die out, it might well happen that the Sipahdar's descendants 250 years from now would own most of the taxable property in Persia. He finally agreed to pay his back taxes, and had actually sent one of his sons to prepare the orders for grain from his estates, when the Russian Government commenced delivering its ultimatums and gave him renewed courage to resist the Treasurer-general.

Without the authority conferred by the law of June 13 absolutely nothing could have been accomplished. It is safe to say that without it the means could not have been found to finance the Bakhtiyari and other military forces which the Government sent against Muhammad Ali and Salaru'd-Dawla during the summer. The control given me by that law enabled me to check, to a certain extent at least, onslaughts on the Treasury which would have emptied it in two weeks. The Regent told me on more than one occasion that he considered that the fight which I had been able to make during the summer months against the reckless and corrupt methods of the Cabinet and the Bakhtiyari Khans had saved the Government more than 2,000,000 tumans, in addition to enabling the Government to keep forces in the field until the rebels were defeated.

The London *Times,* during my visit to England last February, having exhausted nearly every other source of criticism, took the ground that I ought not to have expected the powers to agree to my control of Persian finances under the law of June 13, as it might not be convenient for their " special interests."

This attack was apparently based on the assumption that there was something in that legislation which was, or might have been, prejudicial to some foreign interests, financial or otherwise. This is, of course, the exact opposite of the truth. All foreign loans in Persia are fully guaranteed and protected by formal conventions entered into between the Persian Government and the lenders of the money, and no legislation of any character could avail to weaken or in any manner prejudice those guarantees.

The need for somewhat unusual control of the finances in Persia was not in order to effect any change in the guarantees of the foreign loans, but to enable the Treasurer-general to stamp out the widespread corruption and dishonesty which prevailed among the Persian officials themselves, and, by causing the internal taxes to be paid to the Government, actually to better the position of all foreign creditors whose loans in the last instance, in case the specific guarantees should at any time be insufficient, would have had to be paid out of the general revenues and resources of the Persian Government.

In other words, efficient financial control was necessary for purely internal reasons and had nothing whatever to do with the foreign loans except to increase their security. Had some such legislation not been passed, it would have been utterly impossible for any progress whatsoever to have been made toward practical financial reorganization, and the Treasurer-general and his American associates would have spent their time in fruitless battles against the corrupt cliques of Government officials, whose selfish interests lay in maintaining the *status quo* of chaos and confusion in fiscal matters.

There is absolutely no possible manner in which even drastic control of the finances of Persia, however fully exercised, could have had any effect on foreign creditors except to increase the general security for their loans.

The previous experiences of other foreign finance officials had shown how utterly impossible it was for them to make any progress along the lines of serious, practical work in the absence of authority and control superior to that of the constantly changing bodies of native officials, who from time to time, either as Cabinet officials or other administrative officers, deemed themselves to be in charge of Persian finances.

Although there has never been any modern budgetary system in Persia we were able to ascertain, shortly after assuming charge, that there was a current annual deficit of about 6,000,-000 tumans, assuming that *all the maliat,* or internal taxes, were collected.   As, during the year preceding, there was nothing to indicate that more than one-fifth of the *maliat*—which is supposed to produce about 5,000,000 tumans annually in money and grain—had been received by the Central Government, this minimum annual deficit of 6,000,000 would quickly mount to 11,000,000 tumans, unless we could get in a very much larger share of the *maliat.*

On the other hand, many of the allotments demanded by the different Ministries were absurdly large; not at all too large for the conduct of an efficient government, but exorbitant in view of the purely nominal benefits conferred on the people by the majority of the branches of the public service.   It therefore became necessary to adopt some heroic measures to diminish the immense chasm or gap between the revenues actually received by the Government from all sources and the public expenditures.

To this end I early proposed to the Cabinet and the Medjlis a program of rigid economy in all branches of the Government, central and provincial, to the fullest extent not incompatible with reasonably efficient public service.   For months I labored with the different Ministers to get them to prepare simple budgets of their needs, in order that they might serve as a guide to me in approving or disapproving the requisitions for funds which were being made on the Treasury. They uniformly failed to do so, on one pretext or another, always postponing and explaining, until I gave up in disgust and adopted in my own office an arbitrary total monthly expense for the regular needs of each Ministry, and refused to exceed the amounts so fixed no matter how great the complaint or pressure. I finally prepared a model budget for the Ministry of War, which was the worst offender and loudest in its complaints and threats of mutiny. I demonstrated that with an annual expenditure of about 2,000,000 tumans an efficient army of 15,000 men—infantry, cavalry, and artillery, could be properly equipped and maintained, with better pay for both officers and men than they were even supposed to receive. Yet the annual amount demanded by the Ministry of War, which could not muster 5000 ragged and underfed troops in the entire Empire, was 7,000,000 tumans! The evidences of corruption and waste in the War Ministry which I presented in connection with this proposed budget were so overwhelming that the Council of Ministers were compelled to approve my estimate. The Samsamu's-Saltana, however, who held the portfolio in question, influenced by his mercenary relatives among the Bakhtiyari *Khans,* and by our old friend Amir Azam, who was still Vice-minister of War, refused to give the necessary orders for putting into effect my budget, though he repeatedly promised to do so. The result was that I declined to pay the central administration of the War Ministry at all, and saw that such troops as there were in Teheran, in the barracks, were paid by the Treasury paymasters direct, without the intervention of the Ministry. I scratched off the military rolls the names of about one hundred " general staff officers, military councillors, tactical experts, judge advocates, military instructors, and professors of strategy," forming a *camarilla* of rascals who not only attempted to collect tens of thousands of dollars from the Government by way of salaries, but were the chief manipulators of graft throughout the entire department. They swore many oaths to have my life and attempted to provoke mutinies among the troops, but the fact that the latter had been paid by the Treasury their full wages, without deduction, for the first time in their lives, prevented any serious disturbance.

The second method which I proposed for bridging the chasm between income and even the necessary annual outlay was the adoption of certain new tax laws. I therefore recommended to the Council of Ministers the following changes:

(1) An increase in the tax upon opium. It should be noted that in theory this tax is prohibitive in Persia, but, as a matter of fact, it is by no means prohibitive, and by following out the ostensible intention of the law the tax could be increased and, at the same time, additional revenue be derived therefrom. This would justify to a greater extent the collection of such a tax by means of the rather expensive organization which was necessary to control the opium traffic.

(2) An increase, to be made administratively, in the tax on liquors, as a police measure, since it was not possible, apparently, to depend upon the sanction of the Medjlis [1] for this tax.

(3) A new tax of one *kran* [$0.09] per *batman* [6.2 lbs.] on all tobacco produced in the Empire, with an additional tax on all cigars and all other forms of prepared tobaccos.[2]

(4) The repeal of the tax on entrails [*boyaux*] [3] and the substitution therefor of a tax of one *kran* per carcass for each small animal slaughtered, such as sheep, lambs, etc., with a higher tax upon beef.

---

[1] The official religion of Persia being Muhammadanism, the Medjlis could not by any law take *official* cognizance of a tax on wines and liquors, the use of which is prohibited to Muhammadans.

[2] This new tax would have produced about 1,200,000 tumans per annum.

[3] This tax was collected in kind, with great expense, loss and inconvenience to the Government.

(5) A revision of the law fixing a stamp tax on certain documents, so that the same might cover *all* commercial paper, contracts, receipts, etc.

(6) That steps should be taken to secure the consent of the foreign powers to a revision of the Customs schedule, and to a raising or modification of the existing prohibition contained in the Customs law against the imposition of internal taxes on any imported articles.

(7) A plan for the redemption of the pensions, payable by the Persian Government, amounting to nearly three million (3,-000,000) tumans per year, whereby these pensions should be bought up with Treasury Bonds, running for a period of forty years, and bearing interest at five per centum per annum; the bonds to be payable to bearer, interest to be collectible through coupons, and the amount of the bonds to be issued in favor of each pensioner to be determined in accordance with a sliding scale based upon a classification of the pensions in units of hundreds of tumans per annum.

(8) A loan of four million (£4,000,000) pounds sterling, to be used in part for the redemption of the Russian Bank Loan, amounting to, approximately, one million one hundred thousand (£1,100,000) pounds sterling, and the balance for certain revenue-producing public works only. No portion of this money was to be used for any current expenses of the Government.[1]

---

[1] £4,000,000 worth of bonds, if they netted the Persian Government 87½, as did the bonds issued under the last Imperial Bank Loan of £1,250,000, would have produced £3,500,000, or (at 5.20) 18,200,000 tumans. The conversion of the Banque d'Escompte loan would have required about 5,670,000 tumans, leaving a balance of 12,530,000 tumans, which I proposed to employ as follows: for a cadastre, with a simultaneous rough census, and forestal, mining and crown lands survey, 3,500,000 tumans; irrigation projects and systems, 2,000,000 tumans; repair and construction of roads, 4,000,000 tumans; barracks and equipment for the Treasury Gendarmerie 1,500,000 tumans; total 11,000,000 tumans, leaving a balance for contingencies of 1,530,000 tumans. The execution of these projects in three years would have given the Government, directly and indirectly, an increased revenue of from six to eight million tumans a year.

With the funds derived from this loan there were to be undertaken the following revenue-producing public works, to wit: a *cadastre;* a rough census of the population by cities and districts, for taxation purposes; a survey of the forests and mines; a survey of the public domains *(Khaleseh);* the building of barracks and purchase of equipment for the Treasury Gendarmerie; the repair and improvement of existing roads and the building of certain important new roads; the construction of irrigation systems at various points in Persia. In connection with these plans it is to be noted that one of the gravest criticisms that has been made against the Constitutional Government was the fact that it had done but little practical work for the benefit of the people at large.

I also recommended that the Government should pass a law announcing its intention to build at the proper time the following eight railway lines (or to grant suitable concessions for the building thereof), in whole or in part, from time to time.

First line: Mohammerah to Khoramabad to Hamadan.

Second line: Khanikin to Kirmanshah to Hamadan.

Third line: Hamadan to Kasvin.

Fourth line: Bandar-i-Abbas to Kirman to Yezd to Teheran; branch to Isfahan.

Fifth line: Bushir to Shiraz to Isfahan.

Sixth line: Julfa to Tabriz to Zindjan to Kasvin to Teheran; branch from Kasvin to Caspian ports.

Seventh line: Zindjan to Hamadan.

Eighth line: Bandar-i-Abbas to Shiraz.

I urged the passage of a law prohibiting the cornering by private individuals of grain and other prime necessities of life.

I estimated that a net increased revenue of about 5,000,000

tumans per annum would have been derived from the passage of the tax laws recommended, and no hardship would have resulted.

In addition to this there would have been an annual saving for the Government under my pension redemption plan of nearly 2,000,000 tumans.

The Council of Ministers approved these plans on September 30, 1911, and I was engaged in the preparation of the drafts of the necessary laws for submission to the Medjlis when the Russian ultimatums were presented.

One of the most remarkable examples of Persia's peculiar financial chaos was this system of " pensions." According to the loosely kept records of the different Ministries the Government was expected to pay out each year to nearly 100,000 different people throughout the Empire the sum of about 3,000,-000 tumans, in money and grain.

The greater part of this strange burden had been inherited by the Constitutional Government from the régime of the former Shahs. Some pensions had, however, been decreed by the Medjlis, to priests and others who had served the Nationalist movement, and to the relatives of men who had been killed while fighting for the Constitution.

In former days, if a Shah was feeling in good spirits, or liked the wit, verse, or compliment of some court official, he gave him the revenue of a village, or of a dozen villages, as a token of the royal esteem; or he directed that the name of the favored one be placed on the civil list for a pension of so many hundreds or thousands of tumans per year, or for so many *khavars* [1] of wheat or barley or straw. In a few cases these pensions were granted for public services really rendered. All the Shah's menials received pensions, which passed from father to son. Fully nine tenths of the pensions allotted were pure

[1] A *khavar* is about a third of a ton.

SAMSAMU'S-SALTANA.

Head of the Bakhtiyari tribesmen, and Prime Minister holding the portfolio of War during most of the time Mr. Shuster was at Teheran. The men with the round white hats are his personal bodyguard.

graft. All the grandees enjoyed large pensions. No province failed to have its pension roll. The largest was, of course, at Teheran.

The Constitutional Government had never been able to pay these pensions, nor any great part of them. The system offered a splendid chance for favoritism, and for private speculation by Ministers of Finance and other prominent public officials. As the pension warrants which were issued with considerable regularity during the year could hardly ever be converted into cash at the Treasury, the pensioners discounted them wherever they could, often accepting as little as fifteen per cent of the face value, to get cash. Numbers of small shopkeepers, and, at times, wealthy merchants bought up these warrants for a song and put them into the hands of professional " pension-collectors." These men, having accumulated a number of warrants, would hire crowds of miserable-looking men and women to stand around the Treasury pay-office and shout, moan, beat their breasts, tear their hair, and roll on the grounds in well-feigned fits — all the while waving their pension warrants and calling on Allah to save them and their children from starving. Some women would bring babies and lie groaning on the ground with them, both mother and child apparently starving to death. The actors received a few pennies a day for performances of this kind.

The Finance Ministers, however, had grown rather callous and used to these scenes, and unless a serious disturbance, or *chuluk,* was arranged, they paid little attention.

The payment of the pension warrants for the current year and several preceding years was one of the pleasant prerogatives which fell to me as Treasurer-general.

More than one Finance Minister had found it very convenient to buy up large numbers of pension warrants at about twenty cents on the dollar, and, awaiting a moment when, by accident, there were some thousands of tumans in the Treasury, had cashed the warrants in at their face value. This produced a scandal even in Persia, and loud cries and protests of righteous indignation from public officials who were not in the combination.

There was no hope of there being money to pay those pensions, but there were so many people and interests and the pressure against the abolishment of them was so great that the Medjlis did not dare to take such a step.

I therefore proposed to the Government a " pension redemption plan," and drafted a report and law setting forth my ideas. The project was held up by the Council of Ministers, but I sent it to the individual deputies and it was being favorably discussed when the political storm broke. It was necessary to compile a very complete set of statistics in order to get a working basis for the plan.

In brief, the Government was to buy up the pensions, after an examination into their validity, by issuing Treasury bonds to each pensioner to such amount as, at five per cent interest, would give the owner in the case of small pensions, an annual income equal to one-half his nominal pension, for a period of forty years, with payment of principal at the end of that time. In the case of the larger pensions, the proportion to be received from the interest on the bond diminished, class by class, down to about one quarter of the nominal pensions.

The Government would have issued about 21,500,000 tumans worth of Treasury bonds, on which the annual interest charged would have been 1,075,000 tumans, as against a total annual charge of 3,000,000 tumans under the existing system. The new obligation the Government could have promptly met, thus giving the bonds a value. No injustice would have been done the pensioners, since, with the exception of men who had special influence, and speculators, no pensioner receives from the

Government more than one third or one quarter of the face value of the pension warrants. Any additional amount obtained from the Government goes to the middleman.

Another advantage of the plan would have been the putting into circulation in Persia of a considerable amount of negotiable paper. This is badly needed, as the bank-notes and silver are totally inadequate to the requirements of commerce.

In some instances the cost of transferring Persian money from Teheran to other cities and towns in Persia is as high as eight per cent. It is never less than one per cent. In addition to this the Persian Government is compelled to make good any losses sustained by the foreign banks in sending bank-notes or coin through the mails.

The free circulation of Treasury bonds of this nature, by establishing confidence in the Government among the people, would also have opened the door for the successful flotation within Persia itself of other bond issues, which otherwise would have been necessarily sold in foreign markets and under more or less onerous political conditions.

The existing Customs tariff in Persia is an interesting monument to the insincerity of Persia's neighbor on the North. The rates of duty are fixed under stipulations between the Persian Government and the European Powers, and cannot be changed except by their consent. The schedules of this tariff were established in the time of Mons. Naus, a Belgian official then in the employ of the Persian Government. Mons. Naus was, as his fellow countrymen in the Persian service are now known to be, a notorious protégé and agent of the Russian Government. One result of Mons. Naus' Russophil tendencies is that the Customs tariff in force in Persia to-day is absolutely prejudicial to the interests of Persia, and is so grossly partial to Russian interests and trade as to render it the most conspicuously unsuccessful tariff in the world, from the view-point of the people in whose behalf it is supposed to be framed.

The principal fault of the Persian tariff — and in this it un-duly favors Russian interests to the loss and detriment of Per-sian interests — is that the average rate of duty is too low — so low, in fact, as to make the actual collection of the revenues and the proper safeguarding of the frontiers an unreasonably heavy burden on the Persian Government, when compared with the returns obtained.[1] While the Customs admittedly produce a stable and regular income, the net revenues might easily, in all fairness and perfect justice to all legitimate commercial in-terests, foreign or domestic, amount to double the actual sum through an advance in the rates. The existing tariff, however, was unloaded upon an inexperienced and unsuspecting people as the result of taking the advice of their foreign financial advisers, whose personal interests led them to look elsewhere than to the welfare of the nation which they were employed to serve. The framing of these schedules under Mons. Naus was, in fact, a typical example of the " friendly spirit " which the St. Petersburg Government has been smugly proclaiming for the past fifteen years as the mainspring of Russia's relations with her weaker sister, Persia. Even the British Government, with its usually watchful eye for English commercial interests, was taken unawares when the Persian tariff was manipulated in the interests of Russian trade. Not having a Mons. Naus of its own on the spot and in power, the British Government was compelled to drain to the bitter dregs the tariff decoction pre-pared by Russia. The result is that, despite the admitted in-

---

[1] According to the Customs statistics available, the total value of Persian imports and exports for 1909–1910 was 81,395,470 tumans, upon which the import and export duties collected were 3,634,032 tumans, or slightly less than 4½ per cent. Russia is credited with imports and exports amounting to 48,910,404 — more than half the total. The rates of duty on Russian merchandise are exceptionally low. The principal articles of importation from that country into Persia are sugar, on which the rate of duty is about 3 per cent, and refined petroleum, on which the rate is about ½ per cent.

feriority of Russian goods of every description — with the possible exception of *caviar* — the trade of the entire northern half of Persia is wholly in the hands of Russian merchants. This predominance is strengthened by the medieval policy followed by Russia in refusing transit in bond to goods coming from Europe for consumption in Persia.

This privilege is accorded by nearly every other civilized country in the world, in the case of goods in transit through its territories, and is recognized by modern Governments as both fair and necessary. The absence of such an arrangement in Russia renders it necessary for goods from Europe to be conveyed over long and often impassable or dangerous caravan routes from the ports on the Persian Gulf. The only alternative is for the British or other foreign exporter to suffer the handicap of paying the Russian Customs duties and the delays and annoyances of the Russian Customs officials for the mere privilege of transporting the goods through Russia in order to reach Northern Persia.

It is curious, however, that in carrying out even a high-handed and arbitrary policy of this kind Russia could not avoid making a blunder at some point. A year or so ago the Government suddenly awoke to the fact that it was one of the signatories to the International Postal Convention, under which it is agreed that parcels sent by post should pass through Russian territory unopened and free of Customs duties. Due to this oversight on the part of the Russian Government the amount of foreign merchandise from European countries which is to-day passing into Persia by means of the parcels post, *via* Russia, is increasing rapidly, to the intense disgust and chagrin of the Russian officials and merchants.

Persia has suffered in many ways from the foreigner during the past thirty years. Her hands have been tied by treaties and stipulations, by loan contracts, concessions and agreements, all

15

signed by vicious and selfish rulers or ministers, that they might indulge in debauches abroad at the expense of their people and their national safety. Russia has been a constant panderer to the vices of the Shahs, plying the drunkard with rum that he might sign away his birthright. Concession after concession has been exacted by foreign interests until the resources of the whole country are so tied up that the Government itself cannot develop them to any extent.

Starting with the famous tobacco monopoly of 1891, railroad grants, oil and mining concessions, and loans have followed in swift succession. If Persia seeks to develop herself, some decree of a former Shah is produced to show why she cannot do so. Claims to an unknown number of millions are filed against her. Russian subjects claim anything, and their Government gives to their demands its official support and backing. One of Russia's principal objections to the proposed loan of £4,000,000 was that I would not agree to the Banque d'Escompte at Teheran (a branch of the Russian State Bank) exercising a supervisory control of the expenditures, a thing which would have been tantamount to telling Russia to conduct the Persian Government.

When I assumed charge of the Persian Treasury, in addition to the banking overdraft of 440,000 tumans, the principal central and provincial administrations were unpaid for several months; the diplomatic representatives of Persia abroad had received no pay for years,[1] and I was constantly in receipt of truly

[1] The Government had not a penny in cash at the time I took charge. There was an unknown sum due on outstanding checks, drafts, treasury promises to pay, et cetera, all issued by previous Ministers of Finance. Despite the civil war which commenced in July, 1911, and required for extraordinary military expenditures alone more than 1,500,000 tumans, and despite the dimmution in the revenues caused by the disorders throughout the Empire, the banking overdraft of 440,000 tumans was paid, the necessary funds to conduct the Government were furnished, payments were made to the diplomatic corps and all foreign obligations were promptly met. The only extraordinary receipt during this time was the net proceeds of the Imperial Bank Loan, which after liquidating the converted debt and other

pathetic appeals from officials who were marooned in Europe, unable to get back to Persia because of their debts incurred for living expenses, and protected from arrest only by diplomatic immunity.

The credit of Persia abroad would have required many years to restore, but I was careful throughout the entire time that I was in charge of her finances not to put my name to any order or check unless I had funds to meet it on presentation. No check of the American Treasurer-general was ever refused payment, and the Persians, on learning this, actually kept Treasury checks instead of bank-notes, whereas any former order or obligation of the Persian Government had been cashed or passed off, even at a discount, without an instant's delay. In the Treasury under our charge was the only set of central books which the Persian Government had ever known. These books balanced exactly with the different banks with which the Treasury transacted business, and a permanent record was kept of every receipt or disbursement. Persia never had this before — nor desired it.

Soon after taking charge I organized a Persian secret service, which did yeoman service in reporting frauds and occasional attempts at dishonesty by Treasury employees. This service likewise kept me informed of the secret plans of the different officials of the Government.

The coinage system in Persia is simple. There are no gold coins in circulation. The standard coin is the *kran,* worth about $0.09, or less, according to the rate of exchange. Ten krans make a tuman, but there are no tumans in circulation, the largest coin being the two-kran piece.

advances made on its credit prior to my arrival, amounted to about 2,000,000 tumans. On my relinquishing charge of the Treasury on January 7, 1912, there was standing to the credit of the Government in money and grain a balance of over 600,000 tumans, including the excess Customs revenues up to January 13, 1912.

The Imperial Bank of Persia (a British corporation) issues, under its charter, bank-notes redeemable in krans.

Until a comparatively recent date some of the provincial governments in Persia struck off very crude kran pieces which were little more than flattened balls of silver and alloy. The Imperial Mint at Teheran has antiquated and uneconomical machinery. It coined at the rate of about 700,000 tumans a month when running at full capacity.

The question of railroad development in Persia is a complicated one. Russia and England desire roads which would tend to carry out their strategical purposes, or benefit some particular class of trade, irrespective of the economic development of Persia as a whole. It is generally believed by impartial persons that the first main line which should be built should run approximately from Julfa (Russia) through Tabriz, Zindjan, Kasvin, Hamadan, Khoramabad, to Mohammerah on the Persian Gulf. This would be a North to South trunk line, would tap many of the richest sections of the Empire, and would greatly hasten Persia's economic development. It would have branches, such as from Kasvin to Teheran. It was my intention to have the Persian Government declare its intention of building this line, in sections, and authorize loans for its construction and operation, by a syndicate whose capital should be purely private. There is little question but that such a line would be profitable, if properly managed. The other lines of which mention has been made will be built some day, but they are not so important at present.

CHAPTER XII

THE incidents which marked the departure of my American assistants from Teheran were what might have been expected from a government composed of men who had been willing to sell their country to foreign powers. The very next day after I left the capital Mons. Mornard,[1] the Belgian Customs official who, at the behest of the Russian and British Legations, had been named by the Persian Cabinet Ministers to take charge of the Treasury, presented himself to the acting Treasurer-General, Mr. Cairns, and exhibited an order from the Cabinet threatening the American finance officials with discharge and

[1] Throughout the entire affair, Mons. Mornard lost no opportunity to demonstrate his malice and general unfitness for any responsible position. He had not been named as Treasurer-General, but merely as Acting Treasurer, and although he had at first refused to accept the latter designation, he finally decided to take what he could get as a means of furthering his candidacy for the permanent post. Shortly after taking possession of the offices, in a manifest attempt to curry favor with the St. Petersburg Government, he sent a despatch to Belgium to be given to the press, criticizing the American administration of Persia's finances and insinuating that there was a deficit of 2,000,000 francs in the current account of the Treasury with the different banks at Teheran. He gave similar statements to the Russian newspaper correspondents at the capital informing them that he would have the Americans who were still in Persia detained until this matter was explained. When this charge was brought to my attention in London, I of course promptly denied the statements of Mons. Mornard, adding that he was well known in Persia to be a mere Russian tool and decidedly irregular in his fiscal methods.

As I knew the exact status of the current banking accounts of the Treasury on the day that I left Teheran, I was unable to imagine what could have caused Mons. Mornard to make a charge which was not only absolutely false, but even absurd. It was sometime later that I learned

punishment, if they did not immediately turn over the offices. In view of the fact that I had been trying for weeks to have the Cabinet provide some businesslike method of transfer, and that I had formally notified the Cabinet several days prior to my departure that I had transferred the office to Mr. Cairns, and that he stood ready and was anxious to make a transfer of the Treasury affairs without delay, the threat employed was a gratuitous insult which the Americans promptly resented. When the communication in question was read in the presence of Mons. Mornard, they left the offices in a body and refused to have any further dealings with either Mornard or the Persian Cabinet. Mr. Cairns then sent written protests to both the Russian and British Legations, and to the Persian Ministers who had adopted this impertinent attitude. Seeing that they had gone too far, the two Legations promptly informed the Cabinet that its action was improper, and the latter body, in true Persian style, hastily forged a similar letter which they sent to Mr. Cairns, claiming that it was the original one transmitted through Mornard. The second letter contained no threat or improper language.

In view of this conciliatory attitude, Mr. Cairns took up the question of the status and departure of the Americans with the Russian and British Legations, which were openly controlling the actions of the Persian Cabinet. At the request of the Russian Minister the Americans agreed to remain and assist the Belgians in taking charge of the affairs of the Treasury, provided an equitable adjustment of their own contract rights should be

---

how he came to give out the statement which he did. It seems that in his anxiety to cast discredit upon the Americans in Persia and thereby bolster up his own reputation with the Russian Government and the press at St. Petersburg, he had committed a truly laughable blunder. When he and the Persian Cabinet had dispossessed the Americans from the Treasury offices, the current account of the Persian government with the Imperial Bank of Persia showed a book overdraft of several thousand tumans. Against this nominal overdraft there was more than 300,000 tumans standing to the credit of the Treasury at the Banque d'Escompte.

HEADS OF TURCOMAN CHIEFS, STUFFED WITH STRAW AND BROUGHT TO TEHERAN.

These Turcomans, who are both feared and hated by the Persians, were killed in battle with the Nationalists. They composed Muhammad Ali's principal fighting force in his attempt to regain the throne.

made. The Cabinet Ministers, having made one *faux pas* in their eagerness to do what they thought would please the Legations, were careful thereafter to obey strictly the line of conduct marked out for them by the Russian Minister. Some days later Mr. Cairns and most of the other American Treasury assistants left Teheran. Mr. McCaskey, my second assistant, who had been in charge of the Banking Department of the Treasury, remained and gave the Belgian officials every assistance in taking over the books and accounts. Mr. Dickey agreed to remain in charge of the Imperial Mint until his successor should arrive from Belgium. By March all the Americans had left, except Col. Merrill, who had decided to remain, at the request of the Legations, as an instructor in the Gendarmerie.

This amount was the surplus from the Northern Customs receipts for the six months period which, according to the terms of the loan stipulations with Russia, ended on the last day of the Russian year,— January 13, 1912. The money did not therefore become actually available for expenditure by the Persian Government until two days after I left Teheran, but it was revenue collected during the six months period prior to my departure and against this the Imperial Bank has made the small advances which constituted the book overdraft which has been mentioned. Shortly after taking charge of the office of Treasurer, Mons. Mornard demanded a statement from the Imperial Bank of the accounts of the Treasury with that institution, evidently for the purpose of comparing it with the books of the Treasury. The Imperial Bank, in turn, had certain unliquidated claims against the Persian Government amounting to more than 350,000 tumans. These claims originated long before I assumed charge of Persia's finances. The Chief Manager of the Bank had spoken to me several times regarding their settlement, but on my explaining that the Treasury was at that time in no position to liquidate the obligation, he had consented to let the question rest. As soon, however, as the Americans ceased to be responsible for the Treasury and Mons. Mornard assumed control, the Imperial Bank, having no confidence in him or in his financial methods, promptly charged up the full amount of these claims against the account of the Persian Government. This action, which would be considered somewhat unusual in normal countries, was the only method which the Bank had of collecting its claim. When, therefore, Mons. Mornard called for a statement of the Treasury accounts in the Bank, he was given one which included this 350,000 tumans as an overdraft with the Imperial Bank. It is not difficult to imagine Mons. Mornard and his Belgian associates comparing this statement with the books of the Treasury which showed the overdraft with the Imperial Bank to be a few thousand tumans. The average business man, to say nothing of a finance administrator, would have probably stopped to inquire whether there was

Two days after my departure from Teheran, Major Preuss, one of the American instructors in the Treasury Gendarmerie, was fired on from the window of a house in the city while he was riding from the barracks to Atabak Palace. Rumors had been current that some one of the American officials was to be assassinated. Investigation showed that the shots had been fired by certain "terrorists" belonging to a Russo-Armenian secret society which believed in accomplishing its political ends by that means. The assailants, four in number, had promptly fled from Teheran. Their leader was found to be a former officer of the Gendarmerie. A week after the incident he returned to Teheran and surrendered himself, making a full confession of the plot. He declared that he had not participated personally in the attack on Major Preuss, but that he knew the four members of the society who had been chosen by lot for this purpose. He pointed out the vacant house from which the shots were fired, and described how the two men who actually did the shooting had their legs tied together so that neither could escape in case of pursuit. He made the interesting statement that the secret society in question had no enmity whatever against Major Preuss, or the other Americans, but had decided to sacrifice some one of them *in order to create an incident which might cause the American Government to interfere in Persian affairs in some manner favorable to that country.* The informant was promptly imprisoned by the Persian Cabinet and his fate was undetermined when the Americans left. It

any explanation of this surface discrepancy. Not so Mornard; the difference shown on the face of the statement was sufficient for his purposes and he immediately decided to proclaim that the American Treasury officials had made off with the sum of 2,000,000 francs. It probably was not long before he discovered his absurd and foolish mistake. He apparently has not been heard from on this subject since. Some time after the original statement was published in the European press, the Belgian Finance Minister denied, in an interview, that he had ever received such a despatch as Mons. Mornard was alleged to have sent.

was fortunate for Major Preuss that this truly remarkable plan did not succeed.

Not long after the destruction of the Medjlis, Russia commenced to agitate the question of building the long-discussed " Trans-Persian Railway." That Russia should bring forward this proposal again was not surprising, but that the British Government should for an instant give countenance to the scheme was indeed remarkable. Yet a number of British capitalists actually went to St. Petersburg, among other purposes to discuss ways and means for financing such a road, and in this they had the apparent approval and support of the British Foreign Office. This road, as planned, would traverse Persia from northwest to southeast, connecting with the Russian lines at Julfa and stopping only at the Indian frontier. It was a truly sinister proposal in every respect. Ordinary decency should have prevented talk of " obtaining a concession from the Persian Government " for such a purpose, at least while Russian and British troops were overrunning the entire country, while Russian flags were flying over the largest and richest provinces in Northern Persia, and while the sword and the noose in Russian hands were being put to their grim use in the stricken city of Tabriz. Even the Government of India, whose traditional policy for the defense of the Empire has apparently been tempered in recent years with the advent of Lord Hardinge as Viceroy,[1] must have balked at the prospect of a line of steel running down from the barracks and storehouses of the Russian army in the Caucasus, directly to the very borders of the Indian Empire. The Indian Government was moved, in giving its approval to the plan for the construction of this road to demand, with great show of prudence, a

[1] Lord Hardinge obtained his finishing touches as a British diplomat at St. Petersburg, where as British Ambassador, he became an ardent Russophile.

change of gauge at the Indo-Persian frontier, but modern military strategy is believed to have now reached the point where it can successfully accomplish the transfer of troops and supplies from one train to another with considerable alacrity, and Russian troops, once transported to the Indian frontier on a hostile mission, might not be unwilling to continue their journey even over a road of a different gauge.

One of the principal objects which the Russian and British Governments apparently sought to obtain by this scheme was the permanent and complete crippling and mortgaging of all Persia's financial resources. It was suggested at the time by Mons. Mornard,— doubtless not of his own initiative,— that this road should be built *under a guarantee to be given by the Persian Government.* For sheer impudence and audacity this proposal is unique. Persia has no need whatever for such a railroad. It would be purely strategic in character and, commercially speaking, impossible. If Persia should be forced to guarantee the bonds for the construction of this road, her whole financial resources for the next century would be absorbed to meet this charge alone. In addition to this, if we may judge by what has occurred in other somewhat similar cases, Russian railroad construction materials would be forced on the helpless Persians at greatly inflated prices, at least for the portion of the line between Julfa and Isfahan. Were the road to be constructed only as far as the latter point, the advantages to Russia's influence and purely selfish interests would be enormous, and if it should be built to the Indian frontier, the strategical advantages for Russia would be incalculable. This type of Trans-Persian Railway would not pay as an investment for many generations to come. Its *raison d'être* would be purely political and it could have no economic advantage to Persia at all comparable with its cost.

Of much the same ilk has been the " great constructive pro-

FRONT VIEW OF ATABAK PALACE TAKEN FROM ACROSS THE LAKE.
Mr. Shuster, his family and the American Treasury assistants resided here during their stay in Teheran.

A CORNER OF THE LARGE SALON AT ATABAK PALACE.

gram " so frequently referred to by the British Government during the last three months as being about to be launched in Persia under the friendly auspices of the two Powers. Despite this latest attempt by Sir Edward Grey to gull the British public, this product of statesmanship is found, on examination, to be nothing more than turning over to the puppets who now compose the " Imperial Government of Persia " the sum of £200,000 recently advanced by the two Legations at Teheran at the generous interest rate of 7 per cent. per annum. *Parturiunt montes, nascetur ridiculus mus.* The loan in question is coupled with a number of vaguely worded but none the less ominous political conditions, which the Persian Cabinet has already " accepted." As an example of shallow pretense, this Joint Note which was presented by the two Legations on March 18, 1912, is well worth perusal. Let us see by it how far since the Anglo-Russian Convention of 1907, Persia has traveled along the path of independence, progress and prosperity:

Animated by the desire to place upon a solid basis of friendship and confidence the relations between the Government of His Britannic Majesty, the Imperial Government of Russia, and the Imperial Government of Persia, and desirous of assisting the Persian Government as far as possible in their task of re-establishing and maintaining order and tranquillity in the country, the Russian and British Legations have the honour, by instruction of their Governments, to make to the Persian Government the following proposals:—

1. The two Governments are prepared, in order to meet urgent expenditure, to advance to the Persian Government a sum of 100,000*l*. each. The Imperial Bank and the Banque d'Escompte will each open an account for this sum as soon as the two legations have received a favourable reply to the present note, and it is understood that the sum paid into the account by the Banque d'Escompte will be placed at the disposal of the Persian Government in roubles, amounting to the sum of 945,750 roubles.

2. The above-mentioned sums will be lent at a rate of interest of 7 per cent. per annum, and will be repayable out of the first proceeds of the forthcoming loan of the Persian Government, and until then the surpluses of the northern and southern customs revenues, which have hitherto been

placed by the two banks at the disposal of the Persian Government, will be wholly and respectively assigned to the amortisation of and to the payment of interest on the Russian and British portions of the present advance.

3. The advance will be expended under the control of the treasurer-general, in accordance with a programme prepared by him in agreement with the Cabinet and approved by the two legations. It is understood that a considerable part will be assigned to the organisation of the Government gendarmerie with the assistance of the Swedish officers. In making this proposal, and in order to attain the ends indicated at the beginning of this note, the two legations *hope* [1] that the Persian Government will undertake (1) to conform their policy henceforth with the principles of the Anglo-Russian Convention of 1907; (2) as soon as Mohamed Ali Shah and Salar-ed-Dowleh have left Persia, to dismiss the fedais and irregular forces now in the Persian service; (3) to discuss with the two legations a scheme for the organisation of a small regular and effective army; (4) to come to an agreement with Mohamed Ali Shah on the subject of his departure from Persia, of his pension, and of a general amnesty to his followers. [2]

Hoping [1] to receive a favourable reply, we avail, &c.

G. BARCLAY.
POKLEWSKY-KOZIELL.

The "hopes" of the two Legations *were* fulfilled, and on March 20, 1912, two days after the receipt of the Joint Note, the tried and true Minister of Foreign Affairs, our old acquaintance Wuthuqu'd-Dawla, "being deeply sensible of the good intentions of the two neighboring Powers," accepts. One

[1] The italics are the author's.

[2] In August, 1911, the two Powers formally declared to the Persian Government that by entering Persia in an attempt to regain the throne, the ex-Shah, Muhammad Ali, had forfeited all right to the pension of 100,000 tumans which he had been receiving from the Persian Government under the stipulation signed by the Powers with Persia in September, 1909. Despite this declaration made in August, we find the two Governments on February 18, 1912, forcing the so-called Persian Government to restore to Muhammad Ali his pension and to grant his plundering followers a general amnesty. This unjustifiable action casts a strange light on the oft-repeated protestations of the Russian Government and the frequent declarations made by Sir Edward Grey in the House of Commons to the effect that the Russian Government had no sympathy with, or participation in, the ex-Shah's attempt to overthrow the constitutional government of Persia and seat himself upon the throne. The plain truth is that his filibustering expedition was initiated, executed and financed with the full connivance of the St. Petersburg Cabinet.

more link is forged in the chain which shall bind Persia forever to at least one of her two kind neighbors.

The fact that the recent destruction of Persian nationality by Russia and England is no novelty in history takes nothing from the sadness of the story. In some cases where the independence of a people has been wiped out there has been at least a quasi-justification for the act,— such as the advancement of civilization or the creation of better political institutions. In Persia's case no such excuse existed. No serious claim can be made that Russia will further the cause of civilization and progress in Persia.

Throughout the entire controversy between the Persian Government and the two Powers there has never been more than a weak pretense that what was being done was to benefit the Persian people. Every utterance and claim has been based on a cynical selfishness that shocks all sense of justice. It is in the pursuit of " Russian interests " or " British trade " that innocent people have been slaughtered wholesale. Never a word about the millions of beings whose lives have been jeopardized, whose rights have been trampled under foot and whose property has been confiscated.

The very recent publications of two British Blue Books on Persia,[1] despite the official editing and the expurgation of anything which it was thought might discredit the two Powers, will enable the public to realize the cold-blooded attacks which were made on Persia's sovereignty. Not a single line in these smug documents would ever lead one to believe that Persia was a friendly nation whose sovereignty had been actually proclaimed and guaranteed by the two Powers who destroyed it in December, 1911.[2]

[1] " Further Correspondence Respecting the Affairs of Persia," Nos. 3 and 4 (1912), presented to Parliament in March, 1912.
[2] In this connection the following official version (Persia No. 1, 1912) of a Joint Note sent by Russia and England to the Persian Government on Sept. 11, 1907, is of interest: (See next page.)

The Anglo-Russian *condominium* in Persia has arrived. True, it is decidedly more Russian than English in its character, but that is due merely to England's weakness and the effect on the Persians will be the same. They are doomed to political annihilation and economic servitude. The world cannot heed their moral appeal, because they are weak and Asiatic, and under the shadow of the Caucasus. Morroco, Tripoli and Persia, three Moslem states, have been destroyed in one year by their enlightened Christian neighbors. It is not a pretty spectacle. Can one blame the hundreds of millions of Muhammadans in the world for being deeply resentful? Can they help regarding the events of the year 1911 as part of

" The Governments of Great Britain and Russia, desiring to avoid any cause of conflict between their respective interests in certain regions in Persia contiguous to, or in the immediate neighbourhood of, the frontiers of Afghanistan and Baluchistan on the one hand, and the Russian frontier on the other hand, have signed a friendly agreement on the subject.

In that agreement the two Governments mutually agree to the strict integrity and independence of Persia, and testify that they sincerely desire the pacific development of that country as well as the permanent establishment of equal advantages for the commerce and industry of all other nations.   Each of the two States further engages, in case the Persian Government grants concessions to foreigners, not to seek concessions adjoining, or in the neighbourhood of, the frontiers of the other.   In order to prevent misunderstandings in future, and to avoid creating an order of things which might place the Persian Government in an embarrassing situation in any respect whatever, the above-mentioned regions are clearly defined in the arrangement.   In mentioning the revenues which are affected to the loans concluded by the Persian Government with the Discount and Loan Bank and the Imperial Bank of Persia, the Russian and British Governments recognise that these revenues will be in future affected to the same purpose as in the past, and the two Governments equally engage, in the case of irregularities in the amortisation of or in the payment of interest on the above-mentioned loans, to enter on a friendly exchange of views in order to determine by common agreement the measures which, in conformity with the law of nations, it would be necessary to take in order to safeguard the interests of the creditors and to avoid all interference which would not be in conformity with the principles of that arrangement.

In signing that arrangement the two States have not for a moment lost sight of the fundamental principle of absolute respect of the integrity and independence of Persia.   The arrangement has no other object than that of avoiding any cause of misunderstanding between the contracting parties on the ground of Persian affairs.   The Government of the Shah will convince itself that the agreement arrived at between Russia and Great Britain can but contribute in the most efficacious manner to the security of the prosperity and the ultimate development of Persia."

a concerted plan on the part of the Christian Powers of Europe to leave not a single Muhammadan nation?

The Muhammadans, in Persia at least, were beginning to have a very real respect for Christianity and its teachings. They had begun to accept Western ethical codes, and to seek to imitate both our commercial systems and our political institutions. They knew the general trend of the Decalogue. But what answer can the Christian world make to Muhammadanism to-day, if a question is put as to the value of the Ten Commandments, when the doctrine of " Thou shalt not steal " is interpreted, as it has been in the cases of Morocco, Tripoli and Persia?

The writer has no illusions about altruism in international affairs. There is, of course, no excuse for self-deception. But one of the lessons to be learned from the overthrow of Persia is that the civilized world has far to travel before it may rise up and call itself blessed. The Persian people, fighting for a chance to live and govern themselves instead of remaining the serfs of wholly heartless and corrupt rulers, deserved better of fate than to be forced, as now, either to sink back into an even worse serfdom or to be hunted down and murdered as " revolutionary dregs." British and Russian statesmen may be proud of their work in Persia; it is doubtful whether any one else is.

Kipling has intimated that you cannot hustle the East. This includes a warning and a reflection. Western men and Western ideals *can* hustle the East, provided the Orientals realize that they are being carried along lines reasonably beneficial to themselves. As a matter of fact, the moral appeal and the appeal of race-pride and patriotism, are as strong in the East as in the West, though it does not lie so near the surface; and naturally the Oriental displays no great desire to be hustled when it is along lines beneficial only to the Westerner.

Persia's sole chance for self-redemption lay with the reform of her broken finances. It might have been possible in the past to create a strong central government, without sound financial operations — indeed, several of the old Shahs succeeded in maintaining a strong control throughout the Empire — but in recent years the time had gone by when Persia could be put in order except through an efficient handling of her taxation and other financial problems. The Persians themselves realized this, and with the exception of the corrupt grandees and dishonest public servants, all desired that we should succeed. Russia became aware of this feeling, and unwittingly *paid us the compliment of fearing that we would succeed in our task.* That she never intended to allow; the rest of the controversy was detail.

APPENDIX

A.[1]

(I) THE FUNDAMENTAL LAWS OF DECEMBER 30, 1906.

The Fundamental Law of Persia, promulgated in the reign of the late Muzaffaru'd-Din Shah, and ratified by him on Dhu'l-Quada 14, A.H. 1324 (= December 30, 1906).

In the Name of God the Merciful, the Forgiving.

WHEREAS in accordance with the Imperial *Farman* dated the fourteenth of Jumada the Second, A.H. 1324 (= August 5, 1906), a command was issued for the establishment of a National Council, to promote the progress and happiness of our Kingdom and people, strengthen the foundations of our Government, and give effect to the enactments of the Sacred Law of His Holiness the Prophet,

AND WHEREAS, by virtue of the fundamental principle [therein laid down], we have conferred on each individual of the people of our realm, for the amending and superintending of the affairs of the commonwealth, according to their degrees, the right to participate in choosing and appointing the Members of this Assembly by popular election,

THEREFORE the National Consultative Assembly is now opened, in accordance with our Sacred Command; and we do define as follows the principles and articles of the Fundamental Law regulating the aforesaid National Council, which Law comprises the duties and functions of the above-mentioned Assembly, its limitations, and its relations with the various departments of the State.

On the Constitution of the Assembly.

Article 1. The National Consultative Assembly is founded and established in conformity with the Farman, founded on justice, dated the fourteenth of the Second Jumada, A.H. 1324 (= Aug. 5, 1906).

Art. 2. The National Consultative Assembly represents the whole of the people of Persia, who [thus] participate in the economic and political affairs of the country.

Art. 3. The National Consultative Assembly shall consist of the Members elected in Teheran and the provinces, and shall be held in Teheran.

Art. 4. The number of elected Members has been fixed, in accordance

---

[1] Translation made by Professor E. G. Browne, of Cambridge University, England. See " The Persian Revolution, 1905–1909."

with the Electoral Law separately promulgated, at one hundred and sixty-two, but in case of necessity the number above mentioned may be increased to two hundred.

Art. 5. The Members shall be elected for two whole years. This period shall begin on the day when all the representatives from the provinces shall have arrived in Teheran. On the conclusion of this period of two years, fresh representatives shall be elected, but the people shall have the option of reëlecting any of their former representatives whom they wish and with whom they are satisfied.

Art. 6. The Members elected to represent Teheran shall, so soon as they meet, have the right to constitute the Assembly, and to begin their discussions and deliberations. During the period preceding the arrival of the provincial delegates, their decisions shall depend for their validity and due execution on the majority [by which they are carried].

Art. 7. On the opening of the debates, at least two-thirds of the Members of the Assembly shall be present, and, when the vote is taken, at least three-quarters. A majority shall be obtained only when more than half of those present in the Assembly record their votes.

Art. 8. The periods of session and recess of the National Consultative Assembly shall be determined by the Assembly itself, in accordance with such internal regulations as itself shall formulate. After the summer recess, the Assembly must continue open and in session from the fourteenth day of the Balance (October 7), which corresponds with the festival of the opening of the First Assembly.

Art. 9. The National Consultative Assembly can sit on occasions of extraordinary public holidays.

Art. 10. On the opening of the Assembly, an Address shall be presented by it to His Imperial Majesty, and it shall afterwards have the honor of receiving an answer from that Royal and August quarter.

Art. 11. Members of the Assembly, on taking their seats, shall take and subscribe to the following form of oath:

(Form of the Oath)

" We the undersigned take God to witness, and swear on the Qur'an, that, so long as the rights of the Assembly and its Members are observed and respected, in conformity with these Regulations, we will, so far as possible, discharge, with the utmost truth, uprightness, diligence and endeavor, the duties confided to us; that we will act loyally and truthfully towards our just and honored Sovereign, commit no treason in respect of either the foundations of the Throne or the Rights of the People, and will consider only the advantage and well-being of Persia."

Art. 12. No one, on any pretext or excuse, shall have any right, without the knowledge and approval of the National Consultative Assembly, to molest its Members. Even in case of a Member committing some crime or misdemeanor, and being arrested *flagrante delicto*, any punishment inflicted upon him must be with the cognizance of the Assembly.

Art. 13. The deliberations of the National Consultative Assembly, in order that effect may be given to their results, must be public. According to the Internal Regulations of the Assembly, journalists and spectators have the right to be present and listen, but not to speak. Newspapers may print and publish all the debates of the Assembly, provided they do not change or pervert their meaning, so that the public may be informed of the subjects of discussion and the detail of what takes place. Every one, subject to his paying due regard to the public good, may discuss them in the public Press, so that no matter may be veiled or hidden from any person. Therefore all newspapers, provided that their contents be not injurious to any one of the fundamental principles of the Government or the Nation, are authorized and allowed to print and publish all matters advantageous to the public interest, such as the debates of the Assembly, and the opinions of the people on these debates. But if any one, actuated by interested motives, shall print in the newspapers or in other publications anything contrary to what has been mentioned, or inspired by slander or calumny, he will render himself liable to cross-examination, judgment and punishment, according to law.

Art. 14. The National Consultative Assembly shall organize and arrange, in accordance with separate and distinct Regulations called "the Internal Code of Rules," its own affairs, such as the election of a President, Vice-presidents, Secretaries, and other officers, the arrangements of the debates and divisions, etc.

On the Duties of the Assembly and its Limitations and Rights.

Art. 15. The National Consultative Assembly has the right in all questions to propose any measure which it regards as conducive to the well-being of the Government and the People, after due discussion and deliberation thereof in all sincerity and truth; and, having due regard to the majority of votes, to submit such measure, in complete confidence and security, after it has received the approval of the Senate, by means of the First Minister of the State, so that it may receive the Royal Approval and be duly carried out.

Art. 16. All laws necessary to strengthen the foundations of the State and Throne and to set in order the affairs of the Realm and the establishment of the Ministries, must be submitted for approval to the National Consultative Assembly.

Art. 17. The National Consultative Assembly shall, when occasion arises, bring forward such measures as shall be necessary for the creation, modification, completion or abrogation of any Law, and, subject to the approval of the Senate, shall submit it for the Royal Sanction, so that due effect may thereafter be given to it.

Art. 18. The regulation of all financial matters, the construction and regulation of the Budget, all changes in fiscal arrangements, the acceptance or rejection of all incidental and subordinate expenditure, as also the new Inspectorships [of Finance] which will be founded by the Government, shall be subject to the approval of the Assembly.

Art. 19. The Assembly has the right, after the Senate has given its approval, to demand from the Ministers of State that effect shall be given to the measures thus approved for the reform of the finances and the facilitation of coöperation between the different departments of the Government by division of the departments and provinces of Persia and their governments.

Art. 20. The Budget of each Ministry shall be concluded during the latter half of each year for the following year, and shall be ready fifteen days before the Festival of the Nawruz.[1]

Art. 21. Should it at any time be necessary to introduce, modify or abrogate any Fundamental Law regulating the [functions of the] Ministries, such change shall be made only with the approval of the Assembly, irrespective of whether the necessity for such action has been declared by the Assembly or enunciated by the responsible Ministers.

Art. 22. Any proposal to transfer or sell any portion of the [National] resources, or of the control exercised by the Government or the Throne, or to effect any change in the boundaries and frontiers of the Kingdom, shall be subject to the approval of the National Consultative Assembly.

Art. 23. Without the approval of the National Council, no concession for the formation of any public Company of any sort shall, under any plea soever, be granted by the State.

Art. 24. The conclusion of treaties and covenants, the granting of commercial, industrial, agricultural and other concessions, irrespective of whether they be to Persian or foreign subjects, shall be subject to the approval of the National Consultative Assembly, with the exception of treaties which, for reasons of State and the public advantage, must be kept secret.

Art. 25. State loans, under whatever title, whether internal or external, must be contracted only with the cognizance and approval of the National Consultative Assembly.

Art. 26. The construction of railroads or *chaussees*, at the expense of the Government, or of any Company, whether Persian or foreign, depends on the approval of the National Consultative Assembly.

Art. 27. Wherever the Assembly observes any defect in the laws, or any

---

[1] The *Nawruz*, or Persian New Year's Day, falls about March 21 in each year.

neglect in giving effect to them, it shall notify the same to the Minister responsible for that department, who shall furnish all necessary explanations.

Art. 28.   Should any Minister, acting under misapprehension, issue on the Royal Authority, whether in writing or by word of mouth, orders conflicting with one or the laws which have been enacted and have received the Royal Sanction, he shall admit his negligence and lack of attention, and shall, according to the Law, be personally responsible to His Imperial and Most Sacred Majesty.

·Art. 29.   Should a Minister fail to give a satisfactory account of any affair conformably to the laws which have received the Royal Sanction, and should it appear in his case that a violation of such law has been committed, or that he has transgressed the limits imposed [on him], the Assembly shall demand his dismissal from the Royal Presence, and should his treason be clearly established in the Court of Cassation, he shall not again be employed in the service of the State.

Art. 30.   The Assembly shall, at any time when it considers it necessary, have the right to make direct representations to the Royal Presence by means of a Committee consisting of the President and six of its Members chosen by the Six Classes. This Committee must ask permission, and the appointment of a time for approaching the Royal Presence through the Master of the Ceremonies (*Wazir-i-Darbar*).

Art. 31.   Ministers have the right to be present at the Sessions of the National Consultative Assembly, to sit in the places appointed for them, and to listen to the debates of the Assembly. If they consider it necessary, they may ask the President of the Assembly for permission to speak, and may give such explanations as may be necessary for purposes of discussion and investigation.

On the representation of affairs to the National Consultative Assembly.

Art. 32.   Any individual may submit in writing to the Petition Department of the Archives of the Assembly a statement of his own case, or of any criticisms or complaints. If the matter concerns the Assembly itself, it will give him a satisfactory answer; but if it concerns one of the Ministries, it will refer it to that Ministry, which will inquire into the matter and return a sufficient answer.

Art. 33.   New laws which are needed shall be drafted and revised in the Ministries which are respectively responsible, and shall then be laid before the Assembly by the responsible Ministers, or by the Prime Minister. After being approved by the Assembly, and ratified by the Royal Signature, they shall be duly put into force.

Art. 34.   The President of the Assembly can, in case of necessity, either personally, or on the demand of ten Members of the Assembly, hold a private conference, consisting of a selected number of Members of the Assembly, with any Minister, from which private meeting newspaper correspondents and spectators shall be excluded, and at which other Members of the Assembly shall not have the right to be present. The result of the deliberations of such secret conference shall, however, only be confirmed when it has been deliberated in the said conference in presence of three quarters of those selected [to serve on it], and carried by a majority of votes. Should the proposition [in question] not be accepted in the private conference, it shall not be brought forward in the Assembly, but shall be passed over in silence.

Art. 35. If such private conference shall have been held at the demand of the President of the Assembly, he has the right to inform the public of so much of the deliberations as he shall deem expedient; but if the private conference has been held at the demand of a Minister, the disclosure of the deliberations depends on the permission of that Minister.

Art. 36. Any Minister can withdraw any matter which he has proposed to the Assembly at any point in the discussion, unless his statement has been made at the instance of the Assembly, in which case the withdrawal of the matter depends on the consent of the Assembly.

Art. 37. If a measure introduced by any Minister is not accepted by the Assembly, it shall be returned supplemented by the observations of the Assembly; and the responsible Minister, after rejecting or accepting the criticisms of the Assembly, can propose the aforesaid measure a second time to the Assembly.

Art. 38. The Members of the National Consultative Assembly must clearly and plainly signify their rejection or acceptance of measures, and no one has the right to persuade or threaten them in recording their votes. The signification by the Members of the Assembly of such rejection or acceptance must be effected in such manner that newspaper correspondents and spectators also may perceive it, that is to say their intention must be signified by some outward sign such as [the employment of] blue and white voting-papers, or the like.

The proposal of measures on the part of the Assembly.

Art. 39. Whenever any measure is proposed on the part of one of the Members of the Assembly, it can only be discussed when at least fifteen Members of the Assembly shall approve the discussion of that measure. In such case the proposal in question shall be forwarded in writing to the President of the Assembly, who has the right to arrange that it shall be subjected to a preliminary investigation in a Committee of Inquiry.

Art. 40. On the occasion of the discussion and investigation of such measure as is mentioned in Article 39, whether in the Assembly or in the Committee of Inquiry, notice shall be given by the Assembly to the responsible Minister, if any, concerned in the measure, that if possible he himself, or, if not, his Assistant Minister, shall be present in the Assembly, so that the debate may take place in the presence of one or other of them.

The draft of the [proposed] measure, with its additions, must be sent from ten days to a month before the time (with the exception of matters added at the last moment) to the responsible Minister; and so likewise the day of its discussion must be determined beforehand. After the measure has been discussed in the presence of the responsible Minister, and in case it should, by a majority of votes, receive the approval of the Assembly, it shall be officially transmitted in writing to the responsible Minister, so that he may take the necessary steps [to put it in force].

Art. 41. If the responsible Minister cannot, for any reason, agree with the Assembly about a measure proposed by it, he must offer his excuses to it and give it satisfaction.

Art. 42. Should the National Consultative Assembly demand explanations on any matter from the responsible Minister, the Minister in question must give an answer, which answer must not be postponed unnecessarily or without plausible reason, save in the case of secret measures, the secrecy of which for some definite period is to the advantage of the State and the People. In such cases, on the lapse of the definite period the responsible Minister is bound to disclose this measure in the Assembly.

On the Conditions regulating the formation of the Senate.

Art. 43. There shall be constituted another Assembly, entitled the Senate, consisting of sixty Members, the sessions of which, after its constitution, shall be complementary to the sessions of the National Consultative Assembly.

Art. 44. The Regulations of the Senate must be approved by the National Consultative Assembly.

Art. 45. The Members of this Assembly shall be chosen from amongst the well-informed, discerning, pious and respected persons of the Realm. Thirty of them shall be nominated on the part of His Imperial Majesty (fifteen of the people of Teheran, and fifteen of the people of the Provinces), and thirty by the Nation (fifteen elected by the people of Teheran, and fifteen by the people of the Provinces).

Art. 46. After the constitution of the Senate, all proposals must be approved by both Assemblies. If those proposals shall have been originated in the Senate, or by the Cabinet of Ministers, they must first be amended and corrected in the Senate and accepted by a majority of votes, and must then be approved by the National Consultative Assembly. But proposals brought forward by the National Consultative Assembly must, on the contrary, go from this Assembly to the Senate, except in the case of financial matters, which belong exclusively to the National Consultative Assembly. The decision of the Assembly, in respect to the above-mentioned proposals, shall be made known to the Senate, so that it in turn may communicate its observations to the National Assembly, but the latter, after due discussion, is free to accept or reject these observations of the Senate.

Art. 47. So long as the Senate has not been convoked, proposals shall, after being approved by the National Consultative Assembly, receive the Royal assent, and shall then have the force of Law.

Art. 48. If any proposal, after undergoing criticism and revision in the Senate, be referred by a Minister to the National Consultative Assembly, and be not accepted, such disputed proposal shall, in case of its being of importance, be reconsidered by a third Assembly composed of Members of the Senate and Members of the National Consultative Assembly elected in equal moieties by Members of the two Assemblies. The decision of this [third] Assembly shall be read out in the National Council. If it be then accepted, well and good. If not, a full account of the matter shall be submitted to the Royal Presence, and should the Royal judgment support the view of the National Consultative Assembly, it shall become effective; but if not, orders will be issued for a fresh discussion and investigation. If again no agreement of opinion results, and the Senate, by a majority of two-thirds, approves the dissolution of the National Consultative Assembly, this approval being separately affirmed by the Cabinet of Ministers, then the Imperial Command will be issued for the dissolution of the National Consultative Assembly, and at the same time orders shall be given for the holding of fresh elections, the people, however, having the right to reëlect their former representatives.

Art. 49. The new representatives of Teheran must present themselves within the space of one month, and the representatives of the provinces within the space of three months. When the representatives of the Capital are present, the Assembly shall be opened, and shall begin its labors, but they shall not discuss disputed proposals until the provincial representatives shall arrive. If, after the arrival of all its Members, the new Assembly shall by a clear majority confirm the first decision, His Most Sacred and Imperial Majesty shall approve that decision of the National Consultative Assembly, and shall order it to be carried into effect.

Art. 50. In each electoral period, which consists of two years, orders for the renewal of representatives shall not be given more than once.

Art. 51. It is agreed that the kings of our successors and posterity shall regard as a duty of their sovereign state and an obligation incumbent upon them the maintenance of these laws and principles, which we have established and put into force for the strengthening of the edifice of the State, the consolidation of the foundations of the Throne, the superintendence of the machinery of Justice, and the tranquillity of the Nation.

Dhu'l-Qada 14, A.H. 1324
(= December 30, 1906).

These Fundamental Laws of the National Consultative Assembly and the Senate, containing fifty-one Articles, are correct.

" Dhu'l-Qada 14, A.H. 1324 "
(= December 30, 1906).

[Underneath the concluding words is the signature of the late Shah, Muzaffaru'd-Din, and on the back of the page are the seals of the then Crown Prince or *Wali-ahd* (the deposed Shah, Muhammad Ali) and of the late *Mushiru'd-Dawla*.]

(II) THE SUPPLEMENTARY FUNDAMENTAL LAWS OF OCTOBER 7, 1907.

The original Fundamental Law, containing Fifty-one Articles, was promulgated on Dhu'l-Qada 14, A.H. 1324 (= December 30, 1906) by the late Muzaffaru'd-Din Shah. The following supplementary laws were ratified by his successor, the now deposed Shah, Muhammad Ali, on Shaban 29, A.H. 1325 (= October 7, 1907).

In the Name of God the Merciful, the Forgiving.

The Articles added to complete the Fundamental Laws of the Persian Constitution ratified by the late Shahinshah of blessed memory, Muzaffaru'd-Din Shah Qajar (may God illuminate his resting-place!) are as follows:

GENERAL DISPOSITIONS.

Article 1. The official religion of Persia is Islam, according to the orthodox Jafari doctrine of the *Ithna Ashariyya* (Church of the Twelve Imams), which faith [1] the Shah of Persia must profess and promote.

Art. 2. At no time must any legal enactment of the Sacred National Consultative Assembly, established by the favor and assistance of His Holiness the Imam of the Age (may God hasten his glad Advent!),[2] the

---

[1] The Shitite form of Islam includes the "Church of the Twelve" (*Ithna ashariyya*) and the "Church of the Seven" (*Sabiyya*). Both agree as to the sequence of their Imams down to the sixth, Jafar as-Sadiq (from whom the epithet "*Jafari*" is derived), but diverge from this point. Both are regarded as heterodox by the Sunnis, but the "Church of the Twelve" is orthodox in Persia.

[2] I.e., the Twelfth Imam, or Imam-Mahdi, who is believed to have disappeared in the year A.H. 260 (= A.D. 873–4) and who is expected to return at the end of time, "to fill the earth with justice after it has been filled with iniquity."

favor of His Majesty the Shahinshah of Islam (may God immortalize his reign!), the care of the Proofs of Islam [1] (may God multiply the like of them!), and the whole people of the Persian nation, be at variance with the sacred principles of Islam or the laws established by His Holiness the Best of Mankind [2] (on whom and on whose household be the Blessings of God and His Peace!).

It is hereby declared that it is for the learned doctors of theology (the *ulama*)—may God prolong the blessing of their existence!—to determine whether such laws as may be proposed are or are not conformable to the principles of Islam; and it is therefore officially enacted that there shall at all times exist a Committee composed of not less than five *mujtahids* or other devout theologians, cognizant also of the requirements of the age, [which committee shall be elected] in this manner. The ulama and Proofs of Islam shall present to the National Consultative Assembly the names of twenty of the ulama possessing the attributes mentioned above; and the Members of the National Consultative Assembly shall, either by unanimous acclamation, or by vote, designate five or more of these, according to the exigencies of the time, and recognize these as Members, so that they may carefully discuss and consider all matters proposed in the Assembly, and reject and repudiate, wholly or in part, any such proposal which is at variance with the Sacred Laws of Islam, so that it shall not obtain the title of legality. In such matters the decision of this Ecclesiastical Committee shall be followed and obeyed, and this article shall continue unchanged until the appearance of His Holiness the Proof of the Age (may God hasten his glad Advent!).[3]

Art. 3.   The frontiers, provinces, departments and districts of the Persian Empire cannot be altered save in accordance with the Law.

Art. 4.   The capital of Persia is Teheran.

Art. 5.   The official colors of the Persian flag are green, white and red, with the emblem of the Lion and the Sun.

Art. 6.   The lives and property of foreign subjects residing on Persian soil are guaranteed and protected, save in such contingencies as the laws of the land shall except.

Art. 7.   The principles of the Constitution cannot be suspended either wholly or in part.

RIGHTS OF THE PERSIAN NATION.

Art. 8.   The people of the Persian Empire are to enjoy equal rights before the Law.

---

[1] I.e., the *ulama*, or doctors of theology, especially the *mujtahids*.

[2] I.e., the Prophet Muhammad.

[3] I.e., until the Imam Mahdi shall return and establish the reign of perfect Justice.

Art. 9. All individuals are protected and safeguarded in respect to their lives, property, homes, and honor, from every kind of interference, and none shall molest them save in such case and in such way as the laws of the land shall determine.

Art. 10. No one can be summarily arrested, save *flagrante delicto* in the commission of some crime or misdemeanor, except on the written authority of the President of the Tribunal of Justice, given in conformity with the Law. Even in such case the accused must immediately, or at latest in the course of the next twenty-four hours, be informed and notified of the nature of his offense.

Art. 11. No one can be forcibly removed from the tribunal which is entitled to give judgment on his case to another tribunal.

Art. 12. No punishment can be decreed or executed save in conformity with the Law.

Art. 13. Every person's house and dwelling is protected and safeguarded, and no dwelling-place may be entered, save in such case and in such way as the Law has decreed.

Art. 14. No Persian can be exiled from the country, or prevented from residing in any part thereof, or compelled to reside in any specified part thereof, save in such cases as the Law may explicitly determine.

Art. 15. No property shall be removed from the control of its owner save by legal sanction, and then only after its fair value has been determined and paid.

Art. 16. The confiscation of the property or possessions of any person under the title of punishment or retribution is forbidden, save in conformity with the Law.

Art. 17. To deprive owners or possessors of the properties or possessions controlled by them on any pretext whatever is forbidden, save in conformity with the Law.

Art. 18. The acquisition and study of all sciences, arts and crafts is free, save in the case of such as may be forbidden by the ecclesiastical law.

Art. 19. The foundation of schools at the expense of the Government and the Nation, and compulsory instruction, must be regulated by the Ministry of Sciences and Arts, and all schools and colleges must be under the supreme control and supervision of that Ministry.

Art. 20. All publications, except heretical books and matters hurtful to the perspicuous religion [of Islam] are free, and are exempt from the censorship. If, however, anything should be discovered in them contrary to the Press law, the publisher or writer is liable to punishment according to that law. If the writer be known, and be resident in Persia, then the publisher, printer and distributor shall not be liable to prosecution.

Art. 21. Societies (*anjumans*) and associations (*ijtimaat*) which are not productive of mischief to Religion or the State, and are not injurious to good order, are free throughout the whole Empire, but members of such associations must not carry arms, and must obey the regulations laid down by the Law on this matter. Assemblies in the public thoroughfares and open spaces must likewise obey the police regulations.

Art. 22. Correspondence passing through the post is safeguarded and exempt from seizure or examination, save in such exceptional cases as the Law lays down.

Art. 23. It is forbidden to disclose or detain telegraphic correspondence without the express permission of the owner, save in such cases as the Law lays down.

Art. 24. Foreign subjects may become naturalized as Persian subjects, but their acceptance or continuance as such, or their deprivation of this status, is in accordance with a separate law.

Art. 25. No special authorization is required to proceed against government officials in respect of shortcomings connected with the discharge of their public functions, save in the case of Ministers, in whose case the special laws on this subject must be observed.

POWERS OF THE REALM.

Art. 26. The powers of the realm are all derived from the people; and the Fundamental Law regulates the employment of those powers.

Art. 27. The powers of the Realm are divided into three categories:

First, the legislative power, which is specially concerned with the making or amelioration of laws. This power is derived from His Imperial Majesty, the National Consultative Assembly, and the Senate, of which three sources each has the right to introduce laws, provided that the continuance thereof be dependent on their not being at variance with the standards of the ecclesiastical law, and on their approval by the Members of the two Assemblies, and the Royal ratification. The enacting and approval of laws connected with the revenue and expenditure of the kingdom are, however, specially assigned to the National Consultative Assembly. The explanation and interpretation of the laws are, moreover, amongst the special functions of the above-mentioned Assembly.

Second, the judicial power, by which is meant the determining of rights. This power belongs exclusively to the ecclesiastical tribunals in matters connected with the ecclesiastical law, and to the civil tribunals in matters connected with ordinary law.

Third, the executive power, which appertains to the King — that is to say, the laws and ordinances — is carried out by the Ministers and State officials in the august name of His Imperial Majesty in such manner as the Law defines.

Art. 28. The three powers above mentioned shall ever remain distinct and separate from one another.

Art. 29. The special interests of each province, department and district shall be arranged and regulated, in accordance with special laws on this subject, by provincial and departmental councils (*anjumans*).

RIGHTS OF MEMBERS OF THE ASSEMBLY.

Art. 30. The deputies of the National Consultative Assembly and of the Senate represent the whole nation, and not only the particular classes, provinces, departments or districts which have elected them.

Art. 31. One person cannot at one and the same time enjoy membership of both Assemblies.

Art. 32. As soon as any deputy accepts any lucrative employment in the service of one of the departments of the Government, he ceases to be a member of the Assembly, and his reacceptance as a member of the Assembly depends on his resigning such government appointment, and being reëlected by the people.

Art. 33. Each of the two Assemblies has the right to investigate and examine every affair of state.

Art. 34. The deliberations of the Senate are ineffective when the National Consultative Assembly is not in session.

RIGHTS OF THE PERSIAN THRONE.

Art. 35. The sovereignty is a trust confided (as a Divine gift) by the people to the person of the King.

Art. 36. The constitutional Monarchy of Persia is vested in the person of His Imperial Majesty Sultan Muhammad Ali Shah Qajar (may God prolong his sovereignty!) and in his heirs, generation after generation.

Art. 37. The succession to the Throne, in case of there being more than one son, passes to the eldest son of the King whose mother is a Princess and of Persian race. In case the King should have no male issue, the eldest male of the Royal Family who is next of kin shall rank next in succession to the Throne. If, however, in the case supposed above, male heirs should subsequently be born to the King, the succession will *de jure* revert to such heir.

Art. 38. In case of the decease of the Sovereign, the Crown Prince can only undertake in person the functions of the Throne, provided that he has attained the age of eighteen years. If he has not reached this age, a Regent shall be chosen with the sanction and approval of the National Consultative Assembly and the Senate, until such time as the Crown Prince shall attain this age.

Art. 39. No King can ascend the Throne unless, before his coronation, he appears before the National Consultative Assembly, in presence of the Members of this Assembly and of the Senate, and of the Cabinet of Ministers, and repeat the following oath:

"I take to witness the Almighty and Most High God, on the glorious Word of God, and by all that is most honored in God's sight, and do hereby swear that I will exert all my efforts to preserve the independence of Persia, safeguard and protect the frontiers of my Kingdom and the rights of my People, observe the Fundamental Laws of the Persian Constitution, rule in accordance with the established laws of Sovereignty, endeavor to promote the Jafari doctrine of the Church of the Twelve Imams, and will in all my deeds and actions consider God Most Glorious as present and watching me. I further ask aid from God, from Whom alone aid is derived, and seek help from the holy spirits of the Saints of Islam to render service to the advancement of Persia."

Art. 40. So in like manner no one who is chosen as Regent can enter upon his functions unless and until he repeats the above oath.

Art. 41. In the event of the King's decease, the National Consultative Assembly and the Senate must of necessity meet, and such meeting must not be postponed later than ten days after the date of the King's decease.

Art. 42. If the mandate of the deputies of either or both of the Assemblies shall have expired during the period of the late King's life, and the new deputies shall not yet have been elected at the time of his decease, the deputies of the late Parliament shall reassemble, and the two Assemblies shall be reconstituted.

Art. 43. The King cannot, without the consent and approval of the National Consultative Assembly and the Senate, undertake the government of any other kingdom.

Art. 44. The person of the King is exempted from responsibility. The Ministers of State are responsible to both Chambers in all matters.

Art. 45. The decrees and rescripts of the King relating to affairs of State can only be carried out when they are countersigned by the responsible Minister, who is also responsible for the authenticity of such decree or rescript.

Art. 46. The appointment and dismissal of Ministers is effected by virtue of the Royal Decree of the King.

Art. 47. The granting of military rank, decorations and other honorary distinctions shall be effected with due regard to the special law referring to the person of the King.

Art. 48. The choice of officials as heads of the various government departments, whether internal or foreign, subject to the approval of the responsible Minister, is the King's right, save in such cases as are specifically excepted by the Law; but the appointment of other officials does not lie with the King, save in such cases as are explicitly provided for by the Law.

Art. 49. The issue of decrees and orders for giving effect to the laws is the King's right, provided that under no circumstances shall he postpone or suspend the carrying out of such laws.

Art. 50. The supreme command of all the forces, military and naval, is vested in the person of the King.

Art. 51. The declaration of war and the conclusion of peace are vested in the King.

Art. 52. The treaties which, conformably to article 24 of the Fundamental Law promulgated on Dhu'l-Quada 14, A.H. 1324 (= December 30, 1906), must remain secret, shall be communicated by the King, with the necessary explanations, to the National Consultative Assembly and the Senate after the disappearance of the reasons which necessitated such secrecy, as soon as the public interests and security shall require it.

Art. 53. The secret clauses of a treaty cannot in any case annul the public clauses of the same.

Art. 54. The King can convoke in extraordinary session the National Consultative Assembly and the Senate.

Art. 55. The minting of coin, subject to conformity with the Law, is in the name of the King.

Art. 56. The expenses and disbursements of the Court shall be determined by law.

Art. 57. The Royal prerogatives and powers are only those explicitly mentioned in the present Constitutional Law.

CONCERNING THE MINISTERS.

Art. 58. No one can attain the rank of Minister unless he be a Mussulman by religion, a Persian by birth, and a Persian subject.

Art. 59. Princes in the first degree — that is to say the sons, brothers and paternal uncles of the reigning King — cannot be chosen as Ministers.

Art. 60. Ministers are responsible to the two Chambers, and must, in case of their presence being required by either Chamber, appear before it, and must observe the limitations of their responsibility in all such matters as are committed to their charge.

Art. 61. Ministers, besides being individually responsible for the affairs specially appertaining to their own Ministry, are also collectively responsible to the two Chambers for one another's actions in affairs of a more general character.

Art. 62. The number of Ministers shall be defined by law, according to the requirements of the time.

Art. 63. The honorary title of Minister is entirely abolished.

17

Art. 64. Ministers cannot divest themselves of their responsibility by pleading verbal or written orders from the King.

Art. 65. The National Consultative Assembly, or the Senate, can call Ministers to account or bring them to trial.

Art. 66. The Law shall determine the responsibility of Ministers and the punishments to which they are liable.

Art. 67. If the National Consultative Assembly or the Senate shall, by an absolute majority, declare itself dissatisfied with the Cabinet or with one particular Minister, that Cabinet or Minister shall resign their or his ministerial functions.

Art. 68. Ministers may not accept a salaried office other than their own.

Art. 69. The National Consultative Assembly or the Senate shall declare the delinquencies of Ministers in the presence of the Court of Cassation, and the said Court, all the members of the tribunals comprised in it being present, will pronounce judgment, save in cases when the accusation and prosecution refer to the Minister in his private capacity, and are outside the scope of the functions of government entrusted to him in his ministerial capacity.

(N.B. So long as the Court of Cassation is not established, a Commission chosen from the Members of the two Chambers in equal moieties shall discharge the function of that Court.)

Art. 70. The determination of the delinquencies of Ministers, and of the punishments to which they are liable, in case they incur the suspicion of the National Consultative Assembly or of the Senate, or expose themselves to personal accusations on the part of their opponents in the affairs of their department, will be regulated by a special law.

POWERS OF THE TRIBUNALS OF JUSTICE.

Art. 71. The Supreme Ministry of Justice and the judicial tribunals are the places officially destined for the redress of public grievances, while judgment in all matters falling within the scope of the Ecclesiastical Law is vested in just *mujtahids* possessing the necessary qualifications.

Art. 72. Disputes connected with political rights belong to the judicial tribunals, save in such cases as the Law shall except.

Art. 73. The establishment of civil tribunals depends on the authority of the Law, and no one, on any title or pretext, may establish any tribunal contrary to its provisions.

Art. 74. No tribunal can be constituted save by the authority of the Law.

Art. 75. In the whole Kingdom there shall be only one Court of Cassation for civil cases, and that in the capital; and this Court shall not deal with any case of first instance, except in cases in which Ministers are concerned.

Art. 76. All proceedings of tribunals shall be public, save in cases where such publicity would be injurious to public order or contrary to public morality. In such cases, the tribunal must declare the necessity of sitting *clausis foribus*.

Art. 77. In cases of political or press offenses, where it is desirable that the proceedings should be private, this must be agreed to by all the members of the tribunal.

Art. 78. The decisions and sentences emanating from the tribunals must be reasoned and supported by proof, and must contain the articles of the Law in accordance with which judgment has been given, and they must be read publicly.

Art. 79. In cases of political and press offenses, a jury must be present in the tribunals.

Art. 80. The presidents and members of the judicial tribunals shall be chosen in such manner as the laws of justice determine, and shall be appointed by Royal Decree.

Art. 81. No judge of a judicial tribunal can be temporarily or permanently transferred from his office unless he be brought to judgment and his offense be proved, save in the case of his voluntary resignation.

Art. 82. The functions of a judge of a judicial tribunal cannot be changed save by his own consent.

Art. 83. The appointment of the Public Prosecutor is within the competence of the King, supported by the approval of the ecclesiastical judge.

Art. 84. The appointment of the members of the judicial tribunals shall be determined in accordance with the Law.

Art. 85. The presidents of the judicial tribunals cannot accept salaried posts under government, unless they undertake such service without recompense, always provided that [in this case also] there be no contravention of the Law.

Art. 86. In every provincial capital there shall be established a Court of Appeal for dealing with judicial matters in such wise as is explicitly set forth in the laws concerning the administration of justice.

Art. 87. Military tribunals shall be established throughout the whole Kingdom according to special laws.

Art. 88. Arbitration in cases of dispute as to the limitations of the function and duties of the different departments of government shall, agreeably to the provisions of the Law, be referred to the Court of Cassation.

Art. 89. The Court of Cassation and other tribunals will only give effect to public, provincial, departmental and municipal orders and by-laws when these are in conformity with the Law.

Provincial and Departmental Councils (Anjumans).

Art. 90. Throughout the whole empire provincial and departmental councils (*anjumans*) shall be established in accordance with special regulations. The fundamental laws regulating such assemblies are as follows:

Art. 91. The members of the provincial and departmental councils shall be elected immediately by the people, according to the regulations governing provincial and departmental councils.

Art. 92. The provincial and departmental councils are free to exercise complete supervision over all reforms connected with the public interest, always provided that they observe the limitations prescribed by the Law.

Art. 93. An account of the expenditure and income of every kind of the provinces and departments shall be printed and published by the instrumentality of the provincial and departmental councils.

Concerning the Finances.

Art. 94. No tax shall be established save in accordance with the Law.

Art. 95. The Law will specify the cases in which exemption from the payment of taxes can be claimed.

Art. 96. The National Consultative Assembly shall each year by a majority of votes fix and approve the Budget.

Art. 97. In the matter of taxes there shall be no distinction or difference amongst the individuals who compose the nation.

Art. 98. Reduction of or exemption from taxes is regulated by a special law.

Art. 99. Save in such cases as are explicitly excepted by Law, nothing can on any pretext be demanded from the people save under the categories of state, provincial, departmental and municipal taxes.

Art. 100. No order for the payment of any allowance or gratuity can be made on the Treasury save in accordance with the Law.

Art. 101. The National Consultative Assembly shall appoint the members of the Financial Commission for such period as may be determined by the Law.

Art. 102. The Financial Commission is appointed to inspect and analyze the accounts of the Department of Finance and to liquidate the accounts of all debtors and creditors of the Treasury. It is especially deputed to see that no item of expenditure fixed in the Budget exceeds the amount specified, or is changed or altered, and that each item is expended in the proper manner. It shall likewise inspect and analyze the different accounts of all the departments of State, collect the documentary proofs of the expenditure indicated in such accounts, and submit to the National Consultative Assembly a complete statement of the accounts of the Kingdom, accompanied by its own observations.

Art. 103. The institution and organization of this commission shall be in accordance with the Law.

THE ARMY.

Art. 104. The Law determines the manner of recruiting the troops, and the duties and rights of the military, as well as their promotion, are regulated by the Law.

Art. 105. The military expenditure shall be approved every year by the National Consultative Assembly.

Art. 106. No foreign troops may be employed in the service of the State, nor may they remain in or pass through any part of the Kingdom save in accordance with the Law.

Art. 107. The military cannot be deprived of their rights, ranks or functions save in accordance with the Law.

(Copy of the august Imperial Rescript.)
" In the Name of God, blessed and exalted is He.

" The complementary provisions of the Fundamental Code of Laws have been perused and are correct. Please God, our Royal Person will observe and regard all of them. Our sons and successors also will, please God, confirm these sacred laws and principles.

" 29 *Shaban,* A.H. 1325, *in the Year of the Sheep* (= October 7, 1907),

" In the Royal Palace of Teheran."

B.[1]

(Translations.)

(1) Law passed by the Medjlis on May 30, 1911, for the control by the Treasurer-general of the money derived from the Imperial Bank Loan of 1911.

(2) Law of June 13, 1911, passed by the Medjlis " to organize the financial system of the Persian Empire."

A LAW RELATING TO THE CONTROL OF THE LOAN.

Dated 30 May, 1911.   1st Jemadi ul sani, 1329.

WITH REGARD to the project for the control of the amount of the loan,

---

[1] These laws were originally prepared in French, from which an accurate translation was made into Persian, the official language of the Medjlis.

the Parliament voted and passed by a majority on Wednesday, the 1st *Jemadi us sani,* the following articles:

Article I. The High and efficient control of the transactions concerning the £1,250,000 loan which, in accordance with the terms of the Law of 5th *Rabi us sani,* 1329 (5th April), was done with the Imperial Bank of Persia and the control of the expenditure which in agreement with Arts. 1, 2, 3, 4 and 5 of the law of 19 *Jemadi-ul-avval* (18th May) has been specified therewith, is entrusted to the Ministry of Finance under the supervision of the Treasurer-general.

Art. II. Until the new Institutions at the Ministry of Finance are created, the control of the transactions and expenses aforesaid shall be temporarily delegated to a section to be specially formed, such action being under the control of the Treasurer-general.

Art. III. At the end of each month, the Ministry of Finance will prepare a statement on the financial affairs concerning the Loan, which, with a covering report, he will submit to the Parliament.

Art. IV. The section referred to in clause 2 of this project shall take the place of and substitute the Commission mentioned in the law of *Jemadi-ul-avval,* 1329.

REPORT OF THE PARLIAMENTARY FINANCE REGULATIONS COMMISSION.

Dated 14 Jemadi II, 1329 — 12th June, 1911.

On Saturday the 10th June, Sunday the 11th, and Monday the 12th, the Finance Regulations Commission sat, and duly discussed the project of Law regarding the establishment of financial organization of the Empire of Persia which had been submitted to it. At Sunday's séance, their Excellencies the Ministers of Finance and of Justice, and the Assistant Minister of Finance, were present; at the sitting on Monday, the Assistant Minister of Finance and Mr. Shuster, the Treasurer-general, attended; and the aforesaid project of Law was amended and is hereby submitted to the National Assembly, as follows:

(1) The Treasurer-general of the Empire of Persia is charged with the direct and effective control of all financial and fiscal operations of the Persian Government, including the collection of all receipts of every description and the control and accounts of all Government expenditures.

(2) The Treasurer-general shall establish the following organizations in the Ministry of Finance:

(a) Chief Office for the collection of the *maliat,* taxes and Government revenues of every description — whether such *maliat* and taxes as actually exist, or shall hereafter be established.

(b) Chief Office for the inspection and control of all receipts and approved expenditures and the keeping of accounts in connection therewith.

(c) Chief Office for fiscal operations. All transactions of the Government with the Bank and operations respecting the minting of bullion, and questions of exchange, loans, interest, amortization, conversion, concessions and financial agreements, whether any such Agreement yield a revenue to the Government or whether it imply a financial obligation of the Government, shall, the provisions of the laws established being duly observed, be effected by this office.

(3) In each of the three offices referred to in Article 2, the Treasurer-general shall establish such sections and subsections as he may deem necessary.

(4) Whenever the central organization shall have been effected, the Treasurer-general shall, whenever expedient, establish the services he may consider essential for the organization of each of the different Provinces.

(5) The Treasurer-general shall be charged with the custody of the Treasury of the Empire, and no Government expenditure shall, without his signature — in the case of direct mandates,— or without his authorization — in the case of credit orders,— be made.

(6) The Treasurer-general shall prepare such regulations as he thinks fit for the proper execution of the reforms referred to in the preceding Articles, which regulations shall, after being viséed by the Minister of Finance and published, have the form of law.

(7) A credit of *Tumans* Sixty thousand (Ts. 60,000) shall be granted to the Treasurer-general for the purpose of establishing a special *Corps d'Inspection.* In the event of new employees under contract for the establishment of such Corps d'Inspection being required, the contracts shall, as customary, be submitted to Parliament for approval.

(8) The preparation of the Budget of the Empire which is to be submitted to Parliament on behalf of the Government is one of the functions of the Treasurer-general, and all the Ministers and Government employees are bound to furnish and submit without delay such information as the Treasurer-general may require.

(9) The Treasurer-general shall make any such economies in the Government expenditure and transactions as are proper and expedient — this being one of his specific functions.

(10) The Treasurer-General shall prepare and submit to the Government every quarter a report on the situation of the finances of the Empire.

(11) The Treasurer-general shall make the necessary investigations as to reforms in existing financial laws and the creation of new sources of

revenue which shall be at the same time expedient, profitable and favorable to the Empire, so that such may be submitted by the Government
to Parliament.

(12) The Treasurer-general shall have authority over the personnel
of the services which, by virtue of the above articles, shall be established under his control.

(s) Muazziz-ul-Mulk
(Hon. Sec. to the Commission.)

The above Project of Law was passed by a majority of sixty-one votes
in Parliamentary session on the 13th of June, 1911.

C.

MR. SHUSTER'S OPEN LETTER TO THE LONDON "TIMES."

TEHERAN, October 21, 1911.

To the Editor of the Times.

SIR:—According to a Reuter's despatch, dated London, October 18, the
Times states editorially that my recently expressed opinions of Russia's
hostility to Persia's financial regeneration and of Britain's acquiescence in
Russia's attitude are unjust and unfounded.

Much as I dislike this class of controversy, still, the importance of the
subject, my belief in the fair-mindedness of the British public and in
the desire of your journal to be entirely just, and a slight regard for
my own reputation, lead me to address you this letter, with the request
that you give it due publicity in your columns. It is but a relation of
certain facts and incidents which have either come under my personal
observation or are of official record during the past five months of my
stay in Teheran. My opinion was reached after a calm and impartial
consideration of those facts, in addition to the corroborative impressions
received in a great number of transactions in which I personally participated but which are not susceptible of legal proof. I am, of course,
willing to abide by the judgment of the thinking public for whatever
justification may seem necessary.

I arrived here on May 12, last, with three American assistants and
with but one object in view — to do a fairly creditable piece of constructive work in behalf of Persia's finances.

On June 13 the Medjlis passed a law, drafted by me, conferring on
the Treasurer-general plenary powers in matters fiscal. The law was a
public one, voted after full and open discussion, and was manifestly
designed to bring some order out of the pitiable state of chaos into

which Persia's finances had fallen. The Persian Cabinet and Medjlis had almost unanimously approved it. One might expect that the foreign powers in interest here would gladly have done likewise. Unfortunately they did not. Direct legal proof, of course, being lacking, I nevertheless assert that there is ample documentary evidence of a circumstantial nature to show that there was a deliberate agreement between a number of foreign legations here, headed by the Russian Legation, to defeat my execution of that law, and to thwart the general system of centralization of collections, payments and accounting prescribed thereunder. The pretexts urged against the system were flimsy and untenable in the extreme and their manifest purpose was to prevent any material change in the old style of conducting Persia's fiscal affairs. This campaign of threats, nagging and general opposition, which even descended into vulgar personalities against me, and into crude attempts to frighten the Persian Government, failed utterly, though it did entail a period of delay and confusion in initiating certain financial reforms. Among the threats made was that of one legation to seize the Northern Customs and put in their own officials to collect the revenues.

Last July, in defiance of Article II of the Protocol of September 7, 1909, Russia and Britain, and particularly the former, permitted Muhammad Ali, ex-Shah, to escape from Russia; that is, Russia failed utterly "to take efficacious measures" to prevent political agitation against Persia on his part. In fact, he passed through Russia with a suite, a false beard and a consignment of guns and cannon marked "mineral water," if we may believe the ante-mortem statement of his late lieutenant, Arshadu'd-Dawla. He embarked with his party from a Russian port on the Russian steamer *Christoforos* and landed, about July 18, at Gumesh-Teppeh on Persian soil — a filibusterer in full swing.

Assuming that this escape was accidental and that the Russian passport authorities were off their guard for once, was Russia's attitude one of real regret? On the contrary, it is notorious here that her official representatives in Persia received the news of the landing with unconcealed joy. Later, I shall prove that they did not even scruple to show that feeling in official communications addressed to Persian Government officers.

On July 23 the Persian Government addressed a note to all the legations here, informing them of a law which had just been passed declaring a state of siege. Most of the legations replied in the usual manner, merely calling attention to certain provisions in the Treaty of Turkmanchay, but the Russian Legation adopted from the very outset a far different and most unfriendly tone, claiming among other things the right to arrest directly the so-called "illegal Russian subjects" (who were defined in the Legation's note), "who might take part in the events actually going on in the country." The patent object of this claim put forward at this time was to give the Russian Legation and Consuls throughout Persia the excuse to arrest, on the mere allegation that they were a kind of Russian subject, any Persian fighting men of known reputation who might take the side of the Government against Muhammad Ali. If this threat to arrest all Russian subjects "who might take part in events" had been literally executed, it would have been necessary, as we shall see shortly, to arrest most of the Russian Consuls and consular employees themselves.

At Resht, the Russian Consul went further and actually informed the Persian Government of his intention to arrest any one on suspicion of his being a Russian subject, to investigate the matter at his leisure and to hold them until the end of the trouble.

On July 31, when Muhammad Ali had barely put foot on Persian soil, and had made no appreciable advance towards subjugating the country, Britain and Russia addressed to the Persian Government the following *identique de facto* recognition of the ex-Shah's belligerency:

> "Seeing that the ex-Shah, contrary to the advice frequently given him by the Governments of England and Russia, in effect that he should forbear from any agitation whatever in Persia, has now landed in Persia, the British (Russian) Government declares that the ex-Shah has now forfeited his right to the pension fixed by the Protocol. But, on the other hand, the British (Russian) Government believes that, as the ex-Shah is now in Persian territory, the British (Russian) Government cannot intervene. Therefore, the British (Russian) Government states that, in the conflict that has unfortunately arisen in Persia, *they will in no way interfere.*"

Scant comfort from friends of a government plunged into the throes of civil strife through the negligence or worse of those who had solemnly pledged themselves to prevent exactly this contingency! But even this declaration of "neutrality" (though the word itself was omitted on the demand of the British Legation) might have passed had it been observed. And here let us examine what nature of advice was given to the ex-Shah by the Government of Russia through its Ambassador at Vienna, according to the ante-mortem statement of Arshadu'd-Dawla. I quote from the account given by the *Times'* correspondent at Teheran, who speaks Persian and heard the statement a few hours before Arshadu'd-Dawla died. (See *Times* of October 11.)

"Then Muhammad Ali and I met in Vienna. The Russian Ambassador came to see us, and we asked for help. He told us that Russia could not help us. Russia and England had an agreement with regard to Persia, from which neither would depart. They had resolved not to interfere in any way, internally. 'But, on the other hand,' he said, 'the field is clear. If we can do nothing for you, we equally will do nothing against you. It is for you to decide what are your chances of success. If you think you can reach the throne of Persia, then go. Only remember we cannot help you, and, if you fail, we have no responsibility.' 'Well, there is something you can do for us,' we answered. 'Lend us some money.' 'No, it is quite impossible,' he replied. And, though we begged much and had a second interview, he rejected our proposal. Only he suggested that, if Muhammad Ali had a receipt for some jewels which were in the keeping of the Russian Bank at Teheran, money could be raised on that receipt. But Muhammad Ali had not got the document, and so nothing came of that."

Perhaps this is " advising the ex-Shah to forbear from any agitation whatever in Persia," and perhaps it is not. Perhaps, also, the Russian Ambassador (who has never denied the interview) did not advise his Government of Khalil's projected journey through Russia, and of his purpose, but the unbiased public will probably continue to hold its own opinion.

We shall now see how well Russian officials in Persia observed neutrality in the internal struggle thus precipitated.

On July 29 the Russian Acting Consul at Isfahan, proceeding upon his conception of neutrality, wrote to the Persian Foreign Office representative there in a plain attempt to stifle a public expression of the people in favor of the Constitutional Government. He said: " According to information received by this Consulate, the Government of Isfahan intends to hold a meeting of the clergy, nobles, prominent citizens and merchants for the purpose of framing a telegram to the representatives of foreign powers to the effect that they, the people, do not desire Muhammad Ali, and to protest against his arrival in Persian territory. I request you in advance to inform the proper quarters that, as this matter concerns Persia and the Persians (delightful sarcasm), it would be useless to give trouble (*sic*) to the Imperial Legation and the Consulates of Russia."

Later he wrote:

" You must not uselessly give trouble in the matter of Muhammad Ali Shah (*sic*) to the Imperial Russian Legation and the Consulates. It is the duty of the Persian Foreign Office representative and of the Government to restrain and prevent any such incidents and they must fulfil it."

Comment seems unnecessary.

Rashidu'l-Mulk, Persian subject, former Governor of Ardebil, having been in command of Government forces, had treacherously fled before an inferior number of Shahsevens, tribesmen who had always remained supporters of the ex-Shah. He was accused of high treason, arrested and confined at Tabriz. On July 27, the Russian Consul-General at Tabriz, having demanded his release of the Acting Governor, and having been informed that Rashidu'l-Mulk was held by orders of the central Government, sent three hundred Russian soldiers, fully armed, to the Governor's palace, beat off the Persian guards, insulted the Acting Governor, liberated Rashidu'l-Mulk and took him away. Shortly afterwards he joined the rebel forces of Shujaju'd-Dawla, which were threatening Tabriz.

To the formal protest lodged by the Persian Government over this affair, the Russian Legation replied, officially admitting responsibility for the orders given to the Russian Consul-General at Tabriz to "take the necessary steps" to prevent certain punishment, which was alleged to be threatened, from being inflicted on Rashidu'l-Mulk. We have seen what steps the Russian Consul-General took — steps which, in the case of two equal powers, would have meant immediate war.

The sole justification attempted by the Russian Legation for this outrage was that "the representatives of the Government of Russia have accorded a certain protection (*sic*) to Rashidu'l-Mulk." As a matter of fact, no sentence at all had been passed on Rashidu'l-Mulk, though, even if it had, the outrage would have been none the less.

After a full examination of the record, I unhesitatingly assert that a clearer and more flagrant case of violation of sovereignty could with difficulty be found.

At the moment when Shujaju'd-Dawla was preparing to attack Tabriz and the garrison of the city was preparing for defense, the local Government received a note from the Russian Consul-General there, stating that no defensive measures should be taken and that under no circumstances should there be any fighting within the city. At the same time, a Russian subject was in charge of the advance guard of Shujaju'd-Dawla.

Shuja-Nizam, likewise accused of high treason, had been arrested by the Governor of Marand. The Russian authorities took him from prison.

Shuja-Nizam afterwards succeeded in establishing himself at Marand and in capturing the Governor. The Russian authorities, alleging that he is in the service of the Russian road company of Djulfa-Tabriz, continue to protect him.

The citizens of Tabriz having inflicted serious losses on the forces of the rebel Shujaju'd-Dawla, the commander of the Russian troops at Tabriz sent a detachment of Cossacks to the field, and there, on the pretext that the director of a road station had been slightly wounded in the forehead by a bullet (he having voluntarily gone to the neighborhood of a skirmish), arrested seven Persian gendarmes and took them prisoners to the Russian barracks.

When the rebel leader, Mujallalu's-Sultan, was about to enter the town of Ardebil, the inhabitants prepared to resist him. The Russian Vice-Consul thereupon sent his agent, Esmail Bey, to the Vice-Governor and chief of police to give them the following false information: That Muhammad Ali had arrived at one day's journey from Teheran with an army of twelve thousand men and had announced a general amnesty; that he had charged His Highness the Sipahdar with the control of the city and that the latter had accepted; that the prohibition ordered by the police of Ardebil about speaking of Muhammad Ali Mirza was wrong; " I announce these facts to you privately and for your personal information. The Consulate has received instructions, in effect, telling them to watch over the security of the town." Similar announcements were made by public criers, the inhabitants were advised to illuminate the town in honor of Muhammad Ali's victory and to prepare to receive the Governor whom he was sending to them. Later, Mujallalu's-Sultan, protected by Russian Cossacks, entered Ardebil in triumph and committed the usual acts of barbarism.

After a stay at Ardebil, Mujallalu's-Sultan joined Shujaju'd-Dawla, leaving behind Ghavamu's-Sultan as Governor of the town. The tribe of Khameslous having refused to submit to Muhammad Ali's rule, the Russian Vice-Consul sent Cossacks to reduce them.

A Russian cruiser having been stationed for some time at the port of Enzeli, the commander, with the Russian Consular agent, visited all merchant vessels entering the port, searched passengers, arrested some and forced them to return to Russia.

When the force of Muhammad Ali was defeated and dispersed, many of the leaders demanded refuge at the Russian Consulate at Astarabad. The Consul received them and refused absolutely to deliver them up to the Persian Government for punishment.

The Russian Commissioner for Gonbad-Ghabous came to Gumesh-Teppeh to concert with Muhammad Ali. Later he returned to his post, whence he continued to force Turcoman-Persian subjects, by threats, to take part with Muhammad Ali. He has since come to Astarabad and made himself virtual governor of that place, while the forces of Muhammad Ali remain outside the town.

At Bender, Djez, the Russian Consular agent, with a party of Russian Cossacks, arrested the Persian frontier official and sent him a prisoner to Astarabad, treating him in a thoroughly brutal manner.

At Resht, a number of Russian subjects, armed and led by the son of an employee of the Russian Consulate there, arrested a Persian subject and beat him to the point of death. They announced at the same time that those who might come to the aid of a certain Persian officer there would be shot.

An employee of the Russian Consulate at Resht called a great number of Russian subjects to his house and discoursed to them on the lack of security in the town. Failing to arouse sufficient response and his plan being discovered, he sent Russian deserters to make trouble in the streets — all for the manifest purpose of creating disorder as a pretext for calling in Russian troops to quell it.

After the departure of Muhammad Ali from Savad Kuh, a Russian officer came to Barfrush to visit Muhammad Ali's camp, where he remained six hours, returning to Sari with six thousand tumans in notes.

When the Teheran Government arrested the well-known reactionary, Majdu'd-Dawla, on July 23, the British Minister immediately interfered in his behalf; as a result, he was released and immediately took *bast* in the Russian Legation. The effect produced on the excited minds of the Persians at this time was that both Britain and Russia were siding with Muhammad Ali and the reactionaries, thus making the task of the Constitutional Government vastly more difficult.

About July 31, the Consular agent of Russia at Enzeli arrested several persons as deserters, while the Russian Consul at Resht sent Russian Cossacks to police headquarters to release a Persian subject who had been arrested, pretending that the latter was the " lamplighter " of the Cossack barracks.

According to the Convention of 1907 between Russia and Britain, which both parties are so fond of quoting to Persia, the latter's complete independence and sovereignty are fully recognized, although the need for such avowal is not apparent. Yet in the face of that document Russia has put forward and still maintains, under the name of " Protégé-ship," the most novel and remarkable theory ever heard of in international relations. The Russian Legation and Consulates not only claim absolute rights in Persia over all Russian subjects, " legal or illegal," but they claim a species of protectorate over another class of persons, chiefly well-known reactionaries and traitors, who are admittedly Persian subjects, yet against whom Russia will not permit the simplest governmental step to be taken, under penalty of incurring her anger and her vengeance. This protégé-ship is likewise used to shield these persons from paying their taxes to the Persian Government, and, as most of them are rich through methods well known in the former régime, there is not only a decided financial loss, but the loss of prestige to the Government and the encouragement thus given others to rebel against the payment of their just dues are even worse. In many instances the Russian authorities do not even claim that the protégé is anything but a Persian subject; in others, some of the pretexts alleged for claiming for them Russian nationality are bizarre beyond the wildest dreams. Ask the Russian Legation to explain seriously, for instance, why the Princess Banou Uzma, of Isfahan, should not pay the Persian Government the thousands of tumans of taxes which she has been owing for the past few years, and you will be unable to restrain a smile at the answer. Or the famous Kamran Mirza, uncle of the ex-Shah. Or why the Russian Legation interfered recently when the tax collector of Teheran seized the horse of Prince Ezted Dawla for failure to pay his contributions to the Government under which he lives. Beyond all this, of course, is the trifling fact that even foreign subjects in Persia are not exempt from paying their local taxes, despite the truly absurd claims as to the meaning of Article IV of the Customs Convention between Persia and Russia.

The Persian law of naturalization is based on the consent of the sovereign, given in a formal manner through prescribed channels, yet we have such claims put forth and maintained as that a certain Persian subject, having once taken *bast* in a Russian Consulate, he was a Russian, or that he claimed Russian nationality under a decree (unproduced) from the Emperor of Russia. Naturalization laws and regulations are generally esteemed to be the subject of friendly negotiation and arrangement between nations at peace, not as the pretext for abuses of the grossest description by the stronger power.

A better example of Russia's open hostility to the Persian Government could hardly be found than the very recent actions of the Russian Consul-General at Teheran, Pokhitanof, with all the details of which I am personally familiar. The facts are still fresh in the public mind, but it may be noted that the arrest and brutal treatment of a few Treasury gendarmes by a superior force of Russian Cossacks, led by two Russian Consular officers in full uniform, and the subsequent incarceration of the Persian gendarmes in the Russian Consulate General, is but a fair sample of Russia's real attitude. When it is remembered that this was done in the face of the Convention of 1907, whereby Britain and Russia mutually engaged to respect the integrity and independence of Persia, and that Russia has completely ignored the Persian protest over this incident, and that Britain, the other signatory, has quietly looked on, the real value to Persia of the famous Convention in question becomes immediately apparent.

To Persia's protest demanding the removal of these three Consular officers, the Russian Legation returned the ludicrous answer that in certain instances in Mazandaran and Veramin the Russian sovereignty had been insulted, in that certain insurgents in arms in the field against the Government having hoisted a Russian flag over themselves, they should not have been touched. Presumably, they should have been allowed to attack the Government forces in peace.

I could go further and cite the attempts made by Russia to prevent any arrangements by which Persia might emerge from her present state of financial bondage to Russia, and the claims of Britain that, under the rescript of Nasiru'd-Din-Shah of 1888, the Persian Government itself has no right to build railroads in the south, that right being reserved to Britain, but the list grows too long.

I do want to mention the Stokes case, not because it is transcendentally important in itself, but because of the noxious principle which both Britain and Russia have labored to have established with Persia's acquiescence. The British Minister here wrote me on July 22 that he was authorized by his Government to tell me " that Major Stokes, before accepting the command of the gendarmerie (Treasury), will have to resign his commission in the Indian Army."

As the original tender made by me to Major Stokes did not mention that he would be required to resign from the British service, and as the situation would have been equally well met from Persia's standpoint by his being seconded for three years, I naturally assumed that on his tendering his resignation, which he immediately did, by cable, it would be accepted. To my intense surprise, I learned that the reply of the British Government was the presentation of a *note verbale* on August 8 to the Persian Foreign Office, " warning the Persian Government that they ought not to persist in the appointment of Major Stokes, 'unless he is ·not to be employed in Northern Persia. If the Persian Government do persist, His Majesty's Government will recognize Russia's right (*sic*) to take such steps as she thinks are necessary in order that her interests in Northern Persia may be safeguarded."

A mere trifling threat between friends, this.

This was followed on August 19 by another note, repeating " the warning given on the 8th instant to the effect that, unless Major Stokes is not to be employed in North Persia, the Persian Government ought not to persist in the appointment, and, if they do persist, His Majesty's Government will recognize the right of Russia to take what steps she thinks necessary (*sic*) to safeguard her interests in North Persia."

Is it at all pertinent to inquire here just what are those undefined "interests" in Northern Persia on which so much stress is thus laid? Certainly they are not defined in the Convention of 1907; and it is equally clear that the Persian Government does not know them; nor did the British Government know of them as late as July 22. Otherwise, how could she have contemplated accepting Major Stokes' resignation from the Indian Army in order that he might sign the contract offered him?

To complete the record, it should be mentioned that the Russian Legation, on August 19, addressed a memorandum to the Persian Foreign Office, stating that "the Imperial Government of Russia, for reasons explained at the time to the Persian Government, considers the engagement by the latter of Major Stokes as chief of the armed forces — called gendarmerie — for the collection of taxes as incompatible with its interests, and I am charged to protest against that appointment. Failing satisfaction, the Imperial Government would reserve to itself the right to take such measures as it might judge to be necessary for the safeguarding of its interests in the North of Persia."

On learning of the first note presented to the Persian Government by the British Legation, I expressed the following views to the British Minister here:

"I beg leave to address you, unofficially, on a subject of great importance to my work here. I have been intensely surprised to learn this evening that your Government has conveyed to the Persian Foreign Minister a note of warning or protest against my proposed employment of Major Stokes in the Treasury Gendarmerie. You are doubtless aware of the course of this matter up to the present. Need I say that, in view of the tone of the communication which your Government authorized you to address to me on July 22 last, in effect that Major Stokes could accept the position upon resigning from the Indian Army, the apparent *volte face* indicated by their note of to-day is almost incomprehensible?

". . . Does your Government quite realize the position in which it is placing me before the Persian people and their Government in now suddenly joining with another Power to prevent the exercise of the most elementary act of sovereignty by this country, whose independence and integrity both of those foreign Powers have solemnly pledged themselves, jointly and severally, to respect?

"My personal feelings are of no importance, but the success or failure of my mission here is of moment both to Persia which entrusted her financial affairs to my care and to my countrymen

18

who are not unnaturally interested in the creditable accomplishment of my task.

" Before accepting this work I was given clearly to understand that neither of the two principal powers having interests here offered any objection to my undertaking it, and surely such a statement was something more than an empty pledge.

" No one, I am assured, knows better than yourself that the choice of Major Stokes was actuated by no political motive in the faintest degree, and no thinking person could suspect me of any intention to engage in political jobbery here — a thing which would only make me ridiculous and spell absolute ruin for my work.

" What, then, am I to think when I see the first vital step which I undertake in the task of bringing order out of chaos here obstructed and relentlessly opposed by the very two nations who have time and again professed their sincere desire to see the progress and prosperity of the stricken country which I am seeking to serve?

" Does your Foreign Office fully realize that, in adopting its most recent attitude in this affair, it is inevitably producing the impression on the Persian people that it is in reality opposed to the successful accomplishment of my work, in addition to forcing me to assume that I can count on no friendly moral assistance from your Government in a vital matter of this kind?

" If this were a normal place, where well-trained, capable and experienced men could be had in comparative abundance, the result (though not the principle) of your Government's objections might not be so bad, but here, where, as you know, good men are extremely scarce, the attitude adopted amounts to a virtual veto of my efforts and a nullification of my chances of success.

" I hope and trust that in some manner your Government may be brought to see the matter in this light, apart from what I am frank to say seems to me a totally uncalled-for interference in the purely routine and internal affairs of the financial organization which I am endeavoring to build up.

" Personally, I feel so strongly on the subject that I am forced to contemplate the necessity of setting right my own countrymen, at least with a formal public statement of all my experiences in this connection since arriving at Teheran. Needless to say, such a course would be much to my regret, but there is such a thing as just dealing even between Government and individuals, and certainly in this case I feel that my own record is sufficiently clear to bear the light of the most thorough inspection."

From a review of this incident it is manifest that, unless the Convention of 1907 is a farce or a deception, by its own terms it has no bearing whatever on the proposed appointment of Major Stokes as a financial aide to the Treasurer-general.

First, because the preamble of that document, as published to the world, avows that Britain and Russia mutually engage to respect the integrity and independence of Persia, and declares the sincere desire of the two signatories for the preservation of order throughout that country and its peaceful development. Yet one of the primary elements of sovereignty is the right to manage internal affairs, at least within the limitations of the law of nations, and surely the appointment of its own officials by any country can be considered as nothing else.

Secondly, the plain purpose of the Convention was that neither signatory power should seek for herself, or support in favor of her subjects, any concessions of a political or commercial nature — such as concessions for railways, banks, telegraphs, roads, transport, insurance, etc.,— within the so-called " sphere of influence " of the other power.

But this is no case of a " concession." Major Stokes is not a bank, or a railroad, or a political or a commercial concession of any kind, and the voluntary tender to him of a post in the Persian service can, by no stretch of the imagination, be converted into a " seeking " or " supporting " by Britain of such a concession.

The second fallacy in the position of the two powers lies in the fact that the British Foreign Office itself never thought of construing Major Stokes' appointment into a violation of even the so-called " spirit of the Convention " until Russia raised the point. The proof of this has been cited above.

Without in any manner recognizing the application or validity of the Convention as relating to herself, Persia might point out that, where the language of a document is plain and clear, there is no room for interpretation of the spirit.

Now that the forces of Muhammad Ali and Salaru'd-Dawla have just been routed and dispersed, and before the Persian Government can get a breathing-space after all the anxiety, expense and difficulty from which it might have been spared by a due observance of the Protocol regarding efficacious measures against the agitations of Muhammad Ali, the announcement is made that Britain proposes to send two regiments of Indian cavalry to Southern Persia to strengthen various Consular guards. The reason stated is the unsafe condition of the southern roads and the disorders at Shiraz. Regarding the latter, it might be mentioned that the prolonged asylum granted up to a short time ago by the British Consulate at Shiraz to Ghavamu'l-Mulk, the sworn foe of the *Kashghais*, has tended in no small degree to render the task of the

Persian central Government in restoring order there more difficult, especially in view of the continued efforts of the son of Ghavamu'l-Mulk to stir up the Arab tribes against the late Governor, Nizamu's-Saltana.

The generally expected effect of this incursion of the Indian troops into Southern Persia at this time will be the despatch of even larger forces of foreign troops into Northern Persia on even smaller pretexts.

I have so far confined myself to incidents occurring during the five months of my stay here, but this account by no means exhausts the evidence of the unfriendly attitude of Russia and Britain toward Persia. The spectacle given to the world last winter, when the British and Russian Legations stooped to personal insults and had the footsteps of the Persian Minister of Foreign Affairs dogged by their uniformed Legation servants, on the ground that the pension of the ex-Shah was in arrears, was sufficiently indicative of the disposition of the two powers and their representatives at Teheran towards the Persian Government.

In all the cases cited above the Persian Foreign Office has lodged formal protests against the evident violation of her sovereignty and her dignity, and in but few, if any, instances has even a pretense of reparation or satisfaction been made.

Perhaps many of these incidents do not constitute absolute acts of war — perhaps some of them may be accounted for as the unauthorized acts of subordinate agents, even though they have rarely, if ever, been disavowed by the guilty Government,— but that they indicate a " genuine friendly feeling " on the part of Russia and Britain toward Persia, I do not believe any fair-minded person will maintain.

Some one may here be tempted to ask what all this has to do with finance, and with the financial regeneration of Persia. If so, let the answer be that no one who has been in Persia a week can fail to realize that all possibility of reforming Persia's finances is absolutely dependent upon the prompt restoration of order throughout the Empire and the creation and maintenance of a strong central Government, powerful enough to make itself felt and its decree respected to the furthermost parts of the country. So long as the present policy of thwarting the upbuilding of such a government continues — so long as it is the manifest attitude of the powers to nullify all serious efforts on one pretext or another, but always selfish — and to ruin the Government's prestige in the eyes of the Persian people themselves, meanwhile keeping the country in a state of financial collapse,— just that long will any efforts at financial regeneration be as unavailing as certain documents written on the sands of temporary advantage or as promises of a neutrality which does not neutralize.

The internal difficulties of Persia are great enough to tax her resources to the uttermost limit; they alone will retard her progress for many years. If to them we are to add flagrant bullying by outsiders, varied by "finger-on-the-nose" diplomacy, the situation is very bad.

If money is to be obtained for permanent improvements, it must be taken on impossible political terms; if railroads are to be built, they must be coterminous with our old friends, the "spheres of influence"; if rifles are to be bought, they must be paid for to a rich and friendly foreign government at just three times their market price; if officers of experience are to be taken into the Persian service to hasten progress, they must come from a minor power, or prove themselves to have been of the spineless, nerveless type of which the tools of foreign interests are produced; even if they are from a minor power, there must not be so many of them taken as to indicate a serious attempt at reform.

Surely in these days of humanitarian principles and international comity the land of Cyrus has fallen upon evil times.

However, even the ragged misery of the beggar and his indifference to fate does not justify us in giving him a gratuitous kick.

The incidents and facts cited in this letter do not constitute one-third of those with which I am familiar; they are merely typical, and, if any one doubts the facts, the documentary evidence is available to substantiate them and many more of the same style.

I therefore venture to hope that, with the knowledge of these cases before it, the *Times*, with that spirit of fairness for which it is noted, will withdraw the opinion expressed in its leading article of October 18, to the effect that my statements as to the attitude of certain powers toward Persia were unjust and unfounded.

I am,

Your obedient servant,

(Signed) W. MORGAN SHUSTER,
Treasurer-general of Persia.

D.

CORRESPONDENCE BETWEEN SIR GEORGE BARCLAY, K.C.M.G., BRITISH MINISTER AT TEHERAN, AND MR. W. MORGAN SHUSTER, TREASURER-GENERAL OF PERSIA.

TREASURY GENERAL
OF THE
EMPIRE OF PERSIA.

TEHERAN, July 6, 1911.

Major C. B. Stokes,
  Military Attaché,
    British Legation, Teheran.

Dear Sir:

Having heard that you will shortly be giving up your present post in the British Legation and leaving Teheran, it has occurred to me that your thorough knowledge of Persia and her general conditions, coupled with your military training and acquaintance with the Persian language, would render you exceedingly valuable to the Imperial Government in connection with one most necessary branch of the financial reorganization with which I have recently been charged. I refer to the proposed formation of a small but efficient Treasury gendarmerie, whose duty it will be to give the necessary aid and support, especially in the provinces of the South, to the financial agents engaged in the collection of the maliat, opium, boyaux and other direct taxes.

The Medjlis has authorized me to enter into a contract [1] with a suitable person to serve as a financial aide in charge of this particular work. I, therefore, take pleasure in tendering you a three years' contract for this work on the terms set forth in the accompanying draft.

I should be glad to know as soon as possible whether you are willing to accept this offer, in order that in such case I may at once take steps to have a formal application made to the British Government for your services.

With kind regards, I am

Sincerely yours,
(Signed) W. MORGAN SHUSTER,
Treasurer-general of Persia.

(Note: The above letter was the original tender of appointment to Major C. B. Stokes, from which the subsequent correspondence arose.)

---

[1] See draft of contract at end of this Appendix.

BRITISH LEGATION,
    TEHERAN.

July 14, 1911.

Dear Mr. Shuster:

My Government, to whom I have referred the question of the proposed appointment of Major Stokes as organizer of the " Treasury gendarmerie," evidently thinks that the appointment might cause some international jealousy, and they ask me whether the appointment of a Swedish officer or of a subject of some other Minor Power would not be a way out of the difficulty.

I should like to have your views as to the willingness of the Persian Government to accept this alternative before I reply to my Government.

Believe me, dear Mr. Shuster,

Yours sincerely,

(Signed) G. BARCLAY.

TREASURY GENERAL
    OF THE
EMPIRE OF PERSIA.

TEHERAN, July 14, 1911.

Dear Sir George:

I am in receipt of your note of to-day's date, in which you state that your Government evidently thinks that the appointment of Major Stokes to organize the Treasury gendarmerie might cause some international jealousy. You ask me whether the appointment of a Swedish officer or of a subject of some other minor Power might not be a way out of the difficulty.

In reply, I beg to state that the Medjlis having recently authorized me to appoint a suitable person to organize, under my direct supervision and control, a force of Treasury gendarmerie, I tendered the position to Major Stokes for the sole reason that I consider him to be the best fitted man for the work whom I could possibly obtain. I am personally aware of Major Stokes' peculiar qualifications for this task — such as his military training, his four years' sojourn in Persia, his knowledge of the country, of the Persian language and of French (which is widely spoken here) — and, in general, of the high esteem in which he is held in this community as an officer and a man.

I have no hesitancy in assuring you that, in seeking the most efficient financial aide whom I could find for this particular branch of my work, the question of nationality played no part whatsoever in making up my opinion. Had this been so, it is but natural to presume that, the matter being left entirely to my discretion, I would have sought such an assistant from my own country.

I may take this occasion to repeat that the work of financial reform here, which I have undertaken in the midst of many grave difficulties, and on which I have in a manner risked my professional reputation, is in no sense political in its character. No act of mine has been guided by political considerations, either local or international, and I naturally feel that I could not in any manner accept any suggestion which would cast upon my perfectly frank and disinterested tender of a post to Major Stokes the light of political bias.

With all due respect to the subjects of minor Powers, and without any disrespect to several of my own countrymen whom I have appointed to serve with Major Stokes in the Treasury gendarmerie, I believe that Major Stokes is the best qualified to give efficient service to this country in connection with my own financial mission, and I would be unwilling, under any circumstances, to appoint any one, from any power whatsoever, for this or any other branch of my work unless I, personally, was aware of and satisfied with the appointee's special qualifications.

We know, of course, that one of the greatest handicaps from which any foreigner suffers here is, as in my own case, a lack of knowledge of the language, habits and modes of thought of the Persian people. This defect becomes even more serious in the case of one called upon to deal directly with a large number of such men as would go to make up an armed force. A Swedish officer, be he ever so competent, would have to spend at least a year or more before he could possibly be of any real assistance in this line of work, whereas the necessity of getting my gendarmerie force organized and at work at once is urgent in the extreme.

In conclusion, permit me to say that, as the fact of my tender of this post to Major Stokes is now generally known here, any withdrawal of that offer by me could not fail to be interpreted as being dictated by purely political considerations, which I could by no means permit.

Trusting that this statement will enable you to reassure your Government upon this subject, and that I may receive an early and favorable consideration by your Government of Major Stokes' acceptance, I am, dear Sir George,

Very sincerely yours,

(Signed) W. MORGAN SHUSTER.

TREASURY GENERAL
    OF THE
EMPIRE OF PERSIA.

TEHERAN, July 16, 1911.

Dear Sir George:

The Minister of Foreign Affairs has transmitted to me the enclosed receipts (2), which I understand are for the sum of Fcs. 12,500, which the

Imperial Government is accustomed to receive from your Legation on behalf of the Indo-European Telegraph Baluchistan line. The Minister requests me to have these payments made to me direct, if entirely agreeable to your Legation, in return for my official receipts. I suggested that he should indicate this change to you, but he requested me to take the matter up.

If, therefore, there is no objection on your part, I will be very glad to receive the payment (and future payments) and to give my official receipt as Treasurer-general,— in which case I would request that the enclosed receipts of the Ministry of Foreign Affairs be returned.

With kindest regards, I beg to remain, dear Sir George,

Sincerely yours,

(Signed) W. MORGAN SHUSTER,
Treasurer-general of Persia.

2 *Enclosures.*

His Excellency,
Sir George Barclay,
etc., etc., etc.,
Ghulhak.

BRITISH LEGATION,
TEHERAN.

GHULHAK, July 18, 1911.

Dear Mr. Shuster:

I regret to say in reply to your letter of the 16th instant that a draft for the 12,500 francs drawn as usual in favour of the Minister of Finance had been already purchased for the payment of this half-year. I therefore inclose the Foreign Office receipts for the favour of return to me with the addition of whatever countersignature legally represents that Minister. On their receipt I will despatch the draft which on future occasions will be made payable to the Treasurer-general.

I cannot, however, I fear, do otherwise than continue to transmit the drafts and receive discharge through the channel of the Ministry of Foreign Affairs, with which department alone I am authorized to communicate officially.

Trusting that this arrangement will suit your convenience, I am

Yours sincerely,

(Signed) G. BARCLAY.

W. Morgan Shuster, Esq.,
etc., etc., etc.

P.S. May I take this opportunity of drawing your attention to the fact that I have an accumulated balance of some 25,000 francs on account of the rental of the Central Persia line at the disposal of the Persian Government as soon as they have signified their acceptance of our capital account for the construction of the line (see our notes of March 20 and July 1, 1911).

G. B.

TREASURY GENERAL
OF THE
EMPIRE OF PERSIA.

TEHERAN, July 20, 1911.

Dear Sir George:

May I trouble you by asking whether you can suggest any manner in which the signing of Major Stokes' contract with the Persian Government may be hastened.

The fact is that the entire matter of the Treasury Gendarmerie is necessarily being held up, pending the settlement of this question, and I have no hesitancy in saying that the formation of this force is most urgently and vitally necessary to the financial reorganization of Persia.

Without this gendarmerie, I am practically helpless, and without Major Stokes I am at a loss where to turn for a man possessing anything like his qualifications.

I therefore beg of you to do what you can to expedite this matter. May I suggest that you cable your Government, asking for a prompt and favorable reply.

With kindest regards, I am, dear Sir George,
Very sincerely yours,
(Signed) W. MORGAN SHUSTER,
Treasurer-general of Persia.

Sir George Barclay, K.C.M.G.,
etc., etc., etc.,
Ghulhak.

BRITISH LEGATION,
TEHERAN.

July 21, 1911.

Dear Mr. Shuster:

I yesterday telegraphed to the Foreign Office privately to hasten their decision about Stokes, and now that I have had your letter of yesterday I have telegraphed officially.

Yours very sincerely,
(Signed) G. BARCLAY.

BRITISH LEGATION,
TEHERAN.

July 22, 1911.

Dear Mr. Shuster:

I am authorized by my Government to tell you that Major Stokes, before accepting the command of the gendarmerie, will have to resign his commission in the Indian Army.[1]

I am, dear Mr. Shuster,

Yours very sincerely,

(Signed) G. BARCLAY.

TREASURY GENERAL
OF THE
EMPIRE OF PERSIA.

TEHERAN, July 22, 1911.

Dear Sir George:

I have just received your note of to-day informing me that your Government holds that Major Stokes, before accepting the command of the Treasury Gendarmerie, will have to resign his commission in the Indian Army.

I still feel that the Imperial Government should have Major Stokes' service at any cost, and I trust that the matter may be speedily arranged.

Permit me to thank you for the friendly efforts which you have made to expedite the decision in this case, and to express the belief that the kindly attitude thus displayed towards the financial regeneration of this nation will be duly appreciated by all well-wishers of Persia.

With kindest regards, I am, dear Sir George,

Very sincerely yours,

(Signed) W. MORGAN SHUSTER.

Sir George Barclay, K.C.M.G.,
etc., etc., etc.,
Ghulhak.

TREASURY GENERAL
OF THE
EMPIRE OF PERSIA.

TEHERAN, August 8, 1911.

Dear Sir George:

I beg leave to address you, unofficially, on a subject of great importance to my work here.[2] I have been intensely surprised to learn this evening

---

[1] This condition, laid down by the British Government itself, was promptly complied with by Major Stokes, who cabled the resignation of his commission in the British-Indian army.

[2] In the interval between this letter and the preceding one Major Stokes

that your Government has conveyed to the Persian Foreign Minister a note of warning or protest against my proposed employment of Major Stokes in the Treasury gendarmerie. You are doubtless aware of the course of this matter up to the present. Need I say that, in view of the tone of the communication which your Government authorized you to address to me on July 22 last, in effect that Major Stokes could accept the position upon resigning from the Indian army, the apparent *volte face* indicated by their note of to-day is almost incomprehensible?

I recognize that I would have no right to say such things to you in an official communication, and nothing is further from my thoughts than to give offense to any one, but does your Government quite realize the position in which it is placing me before the Persian people and their Government in now suddenly joining with another power to prevent the exercise of the most elementary act of sovereignty by this country, whose independence and integrity both of those foreign powers have solemnly pledged themselves, jointly and severally, to respect?

My personal feelings are of no importance, but the success or failure of my mission here is of moment both to Persia, which entrusted financial affairs to my care, and to my countrymen, who are not unnaturally interested in the creditable accomplishment of my task.

Before accepting this work, I was given clearly to understand that neither of the two principal powers having interests here offered any objection to my undertaking it, and surely such a statement was something more than an empty pledge.

No one, I am assured, knows better than yourself that the choice of Major Stokes was actuated by no political motive in the faintest degree, and no thinking person could suspect me of any intention to engage in political jobbery here,— a thing which would only make me ridiculous and spell absolute ruin for my work.

What, then, am I to think when I see the first vital step which I undertake in the task of bringing order out of chaos here obstructed and relentlessly opposed by the very two nations who have time and again professed their sincere desire to see the progress and prosperity of the stricken country which I am seeking to serve?

Does your Foreign Office fully realize that, in adopting its most recent attitude in this affair, it is inevitably producing the impression on the Persian people that it is in reality opposed to the successful accomplishment of my work, in addition to forcing me to assume that I can count on no friendly moral assistance from your Government in a vital matter of this kind?

---

had cabled his resignation and the British and Russian Governments had made a joint protest to the Persian Government against his proposed employment.

If this were a normal place, where well-trained, capable and experienced men could be had in comparative abundance, the result (though not the principle) of your Government's objections might not be so bad, but here, where, as you know, good men are extremely scarce, the attitude adopted amounts to a virtual veto of my efforts and a nullification of my chances of success.

I hope and trust that in some manner your Government may be brought to see the matter in this light, apart from what I am frank to say seems to me a totally uncalled-for interference in the purely routine and internal affairs of the financial organization which I am endeavoring to build up.

Personally, I feel so strongly on the subject that I am forced to contemplate the necessity of setting right my own countrymen, at least with a formal public statement of all my experiences in this connection since arriving at Teheran. Needless to say, such a course would be much to my regret, but there is such a thing as just dealing even between Governments and individuals, and certainly in this case I feel that my own record is sufficiently clear to bear the light of the most thorough inspection.

Please pardon me for writing you thus freely, but I know you will acquit me of any desire to offend or to increase the perplexities of your situation. Unfortunately, we all appear to have our own peculiar difficulties in this strange land, and the Stokes case happens likewise to be one of mine.

With kindest regards and best wishes for what you may yet be able to do, I am, dear Sir George,

> Very sincerely yours,
> (Signed) W. MORGAN SHUSTER,
> Treasurer-general of Persia.

Sir George Barclay, K.C.M.G.,
   etc., etc., etc.,
     Ghulhak.

BRITISH LEGATION,
  TEHERAN.

GHULHAK, August 12, 1911.

Dear Mr. Shuster:

I did not fail to communicate to my Government the substance of your letter to me of the 8th instant, drawing attention to its purely personal nature.

His Majesty's Government desire me to assure you in reply that they appreciate your work and the singlemindedness of your motives and they express their regret that there should be any wish of yours with which they are unable to conform. But, His Majesty's Government point out, they might themselves have had occasion to object to the appointment of a Russian officer to organize an administration, say, on the Indian frontier, and that, as soon as they found that Russia would make objections to the appointment of Major Stokes, they could not deprecate such objection and were bound to warn the Persian Government of the difficulties that would arise.

An understanding with the Persian Government has existed for some time past that only subjects of minor Powers should be selected for their service.[1] The only exception made was in favour of the United States, and the Russian agreement to this exception was influenced by the opinion of His Majesty's Government that no political motives in Persia could be imputed to the United States. If a departure from this understanding was to be made, my Government think it a pity that the Persian Government did not sound the Russian Government in advance.

Sir Edward Grey fears that the appointment of some subject of a minor Power in the place of Major Stokes is the only way out of the difficulty that has now arisen.

In communicating this purely private message, permit me to add the assurance of my kindest regards towards yourself and believe me to remain,

Yours very sincerely,

(Signed) G. BARCLAY.

W. Morgan Shuster, Esq.,
Treasurer-general of the Empire of Persia, Teheran.

BRITISH LEGATION,
TEHERAN.

August 21, 1911.

My dear Shuster:

Would it suit you if I visited you at five o'clock on Friday? If not, please fix another hour on that or any other day except Wednesday.

Also, should I come to the Treasury General or to your private residence?

Yours sincerely

(Signed) G. BARCLAY.

---

[1] The Persian Government had no knowledge of this alleged understanding, and sometime later a British subject was engaged by me under contract to serve in the Ministry of Posts and Telegraphs with the full official approval of the British Government (which was necessary as he was in the Indo-European Telegraph Department of the Indian Government), and without objection, special or general, by Russia.

P.S. I should like particularly to talk to you about railways, and I am very keen to hear something of Hart's proposals before the Persian Government in any way commits itself to his group.

TREASURY GENERAL
OF THE
EMPIRE OF PERSIA.

TEHERAN, September 13, 1911.

His Excellency,
Sir George Barclay, K.C.M.G.,
Minister of Great Britain, Teheran.

My dear Mr. Minister:

I take pleasure in informing you that on the 15th ultimo I applied to Colonel H. R. Beddoes, the representative of Messrs. Seligman Bros. of London, for a loan of £4,000,000 sterling. I enclose herewith copy of my letter to him.

I now request the good offices of Your Excellency's Government and Your Excellency's great personal influence to the end that this loan may be successfully and satisfactorily negotiated.

I am, Mr. Minister, with great respect,
Sincerely yours,
(Signed) W. MORGAN SHUSTER,
Treasurer-general of Persia.

TREASURY GENERAL
OF THE
EMPIRE OF PERSIA.

TEHERAN, September 18, 1911.

Dear Sir George:

The delay which has occurred in getting any intimation of the attitude of your Government and of that of the Russian Government towards the proposed loan contract with Seligman Brothers of London is proving somewhat embarrassing to my work. Even after the matter is under way there will inevitably be a number of delays, and if, for any reason, there is going to be opposition to the proposed contract, I should like to know about it as soon as possible, since it will then be necessary for me to take up immediately certain other similar propositions which I have had presented.

I should like very much to know the views of your Government on this matter without further delay, and should likewise appreciate anything you could do to secure an expression of opinion from the Russian Government in this same affair.

It certainly seems to me that the frank manner in which we have laid this proposed loan before the two Legations should entitle us to a reasonably prompt and clear expression of opinion from the respective governments upon this, to us, important and urgent matter.

With kindest regards, I remain, dear Sir George,

Very sincerely yours,

(Signed) W. Morgan Shuster,

Treasurer-general of Persia.

His Excellency,
   Sir George Barclay, K.C.M.G.,
    H. B. M. Legation, Teheran.

British Legation,
   Teheran.
                                 September 23, 1911.

My dear Shuster:
   I am doing my best to hasten an expression of views as to the Seligman proposals.

Yours sincerely,

(Signed) G. Barclay.

British Legation,
   Teheran.
                                 October 3, 1911.

My dear Shuster:
   It has been suggested to me that there might be no objection, if the organization of your gendarmerie by Swedish officers is impossible, to Stokes' organizing a force at or near Isfahan, provided, of course, any portion of it employed in Northern Persia would be commanded by Persians or by officers of a minor Power.

Could you let me know what you think of the idea?

Yours very sincerely,

G. Barclay.

Treasury General
    of the
Empire of Persia.
                          Teheran, October 5, 1911.

Dear Sir George:
   Regarding your note of the 3d, to which I was about to reply, let me say that the suggestion as to localizing Stokes at Isfahan is, of course, out of the question, both on principle and as a matter of practicability.

   I hope that some day the British and Russian Foreign Offices will come to believe that when I said I wanted Stokes *here in Teheran* to *assist me,* by his advice and peculiar knowledge, in the formation 'of a Treasury gendarmerie, I meant just that and nothing more: no *arrière pensée*, no military expeditions, no intrigues, nothing but what I said.

It seems impossible at times for one to gain any credence for a frank, open statement of facts or intentions, but it is equally true that it was neither within the letter nor the spirit of my statement to go through the truly absurd performance of marooning him at Isfahan or anywhere else in order that he might *advise and assist me here*.

Is it not about time, dear Sir George, that two big Governments stop playing at this matter, and state plainly whether they intend to continue to oppose the employment of Stokes along the lines which I have mentioned, or not?

With kindest regards, I am, dear Sir George,

Sincerely yours,

(Signed) W. MORGAN SHUSTER,

Treasurer-general of Persia.

Sir George Barclay, K.C.M.G.,
British Minister,
Ghulhak.

BRITISH LEGATION,
TEHERAN.

October 5, 1911.

My dear Shuster:

The suggestion as regards the localization of Stokes' functions to Isfahan came to me through the Foreign Office and I ought to reply to-day.

I remembered what you had said about the impossibility of giving any expression to any localization of his work, but I did not like to reply to the Foreign Office without having submitted to you the particular suggestion in regard to Isfahan, which does not come so near to a recognition of the hated spheres of influence as would any undertaking regarding Stokes' employment at Shiraz.

Yours very sincerely

(Signed) G. BARCLAY.

BRITISH LEGATION,
TEHERAN.

October 10, 1911.

My dear Shuster:

Many thanks for your letter. I will await you this afternoon.

I don't think you will have any further difficulty about Shuau's-

19

Saltana's garden, but I am sure that your men have been told to avoid all unnecessary activity. A conflict would be quite disastrous.

Yours sincerely,

(Signed) G. BARCLAY.

TREASURY GENERAL
OF THE
EMPIRE OF PERSIA.

TEHERAN, November 2, 1911.

Purely Personal.

Dear Sir George:

Mrs. Shuster and I have received yours and Lady Barclay's very kind invitation to dine with you on Monday, the 13th of this month. Needless to say that it would give us great pleasure to do so. I feel, however, that under all the circumstances I should not accept the hospitality of the British Legation without acquainting you with the fact that I have felt impelled, in an open letter to the *Times*, to criticise in no uncertain terms the general attitude of your Government towards my work and the nation which I am serving. While there is nothing personal in my statements, and though, as I think you know, I entertain the highest respect and warmest regard for you, it occurs to me that it would relieve you of any possible embarrassment if Mrs. Shuster and I did not attend a formal dinner at the Legation. It is solely from this standpoint that I write. I feel sure that you will realize that nothing but some such reason would keep us from partaking of your hospitality.

May I even suggest, to avoid all possible misunderstanding on your part, that Mrs. Shuster and I would be very happy, should you so desire it, to dine with you and Lady Barclay informally some time, or something of the sort.

Personally, I do not believe in mixing business or political differences with purely social matters, but others may not share my view, and it is sometimes difficult to draw the line. In doubtful cases, it is probably safe to err on the side of caution.

If, however, in spite of what I say above, you still desire that we should accept your kind invitation, we will do so, but only after having from you that you considered that it could be in no manner used as a source of criticism of you by either your Government or your colleagues here in Teheran.

With kindest regards and best wishes, believe me, dear Sir George,

Sincerely yours,

(Signed) W. MORGAN SHUSTER.

Sir George Barclay, K.C.M.G.,
British Legation, Teheran.

BRITISH LEGATION,
TEHERAN.

November 2, 1911.

Many thanks, my dear Shuster, for your friendly note of to-day, the spirit of which I warmly appreciate.

In all the circumstances, I think perhaps it would be better that we should postpone our dinner till times are better.

It is most kind of you to have been so open with me.

Please give my kindest regards to Mrs. Shuster, and believe me

Yours sincerely,

(Signed) G. BARCLAY.

BRITISH LEGATION,
TEHERAN.

November 7, 1911.

My dear Shuster:

Could I see you for a moment to-morrow?

I have to read you a telegram I have from my Government about Lecoffre's appointment which tells me that I am to " point out " certain considerations to you in regard to this appointment; no doubt you can guess what these are.

So far as I know, any time to-morrow will suit me, but I have asked for an audience of the Regent and I can't tell what hour he will fix.

Yours very sincerely,

(Signed) G. BARCLAY.

BRITISH LEGATION,
TEHERAN.

November 10, 1911.

My dear Shuster:

I see that your open letter has been published. I should be very much obliged if you would let me have a look at it.

Yours very sincerely,

G. BARCLAY.

BRITISH LEGATION,
TEHERAN.

November 14, 1911.

My dear Shuster:

You once said that you would let me see your contract. I wonder whether this still holds good, and, if so, whether I could have a copy.

I have read your open letter with the greatest interest, but I think you are too hard on the two Powers.

Yours sincerely,

(Signed) G. BARCLAY.

BRITISH LEGATION,
TEHERAN.

November 15, 1911.

My dear Shuster:

Could you let me know whether I am right in telegraphing that the Prime Minister requested you to withdraw the gendarmes from Shuau's-Saltana's house in town and that you replied that the order to seize the property had been signed by all the Ministers in the Cabinet, and you would only withdraw the gendarmes on a similar order?

Yours very sincerely,

(Signed) G. BARCLAY.

TREASURY GENERAL
OF THE
EMPIRE OF PERSIA.

TEHERAN, November 15, 1911.

Dear Sir George:

I have your note about the rumor of a letter from the Samsamu's-Saltana to me and my reply. Personally, I should be most happy to give you any facts, but, as you apparently request them for transmission to your Government, I feel somewhat doubtful, in the present difficult situation, as to whether I should say anything.

Let me illustrate: Suppose I should ask you to confirm the story that the Indian Government had accepted Stokes' resignation, would you feel at liberty to do so, not knowing the final outcome of the affair? If you wish to know personally, as a friend, the exact situation re the Shuau's-Saltana matter, I will be glad to run over and tell you, unofficially.

I may add that, to the best of my knowledge, there has been no Prime Minister or Cabinet for two days.

With kindest regards, I remain,

Sincerely yours,

(Signed) W. MORGAN SHUSTER.

Sir George Barclay, K.C.M.G.,
En Ville.

BRITISH LEGATION,
TEHERAN.

November 15, 1911.

My dear Shuster:

I quite understand and shall not telegraph.

In a letter which I wrote yesterday, but which I omitted to send till now, I ask for something else. You will, of course, feel perfectly free to decline. For I see that what you might have been ready to let me know some weeks ago may be impossible now.

Yours very sincerely,

(Signed) G. BARCLAY.

TREASURY GENERAL
OF THE
EMPIRE OF PERSIA.

November 17, 1911.

Dear Sir George:

I have your two notes of the 14th, and thank you very much for the friendly view-point which you took of my last note to you.

I have not the slightest objection to having you see a copy of my contract, nor even to having your Government see a copy of it, if I could be assured that it would not go further. But as it is not a matter that, strictly speaking, concerns any one but myself and the Persian Government (and my friends), I could not see that any government could desire to see it for any good purpose. If you would like to examine it, I should be very glad to send you a copy.

With kindest regards, believe me, dear Sir George,

Very sincerely yours,

(Signed) W. MORGAN SHUSTER.

Sir George Barclay, K.C.M.G.,
    British Legation,
    Teheran.

TREASURY GENERAL
OF THE
EMPIRE OF PERSIA.

November 19, 1911.

Dear Sir George:

Colonel Beddoes is leaving to-morrow for home, and expects to go via St. Petersburg.

I think that it would be a great advantage, certainly from the Persian point of view, and I think, possibly, from that of England and Russia, if he could secure a personal interview with Mons. Kokovtsoff. I have fully explained to Colonel Beddoes my own views upon the financial problems of Persia and the lines upon which a durable working arrangement, satisfactory to these Governments, Persia, Great Britain and Russia, might be reached. If you also think that this end is desirable, I should be very gratified if you would give to Colonel Beddoes such a letter of introduction to the British Ambassador at St. Petersburg as would secure Colonel Beddoes a talk with the Russian Premier. If you should wish to state in your note that it is given at my request, I should see no objection.

With kindest regards, I am, dear Sir George,

Sincerely yours,

(Signed) W. MORGAN SHUSTER.

Sir George Barclay, K.C.M.G.,
British Minister,
Teheran.

BRITISH LEGATION,
TEHERAN.

January 10, 1912.

My dear Mr. Shuster:

Many thanks for your kind thought in writing and also for the kind words of your letter.

I also have very much regretted that we have not seen more of each other during your time here and I hope that we may meet again one day in happier and less constrained circumstances.

Wishing you a pleasant journey and really agreeable recreation in Paris, where I believe you will be staying, I remain

Very sincerely yours,

(Signed) G. BARCLAY.

CORRESPONDENCE BETWEEN HIS EXCELLENCY, S. POKLEWSKI-KOZIELL, RUSSIAN MINISTER AT TEHERAN, AND MR. W. MORGAN SHUSTER, TREASURER-GENERAL OF PERSIA.

TREASURY GENERAL
OF THE
EMPIRE OF PERSIA.

TEHERAN, August 10, 1911.

His Excellency
S. Poklewski-Koziell,
Russian Minister, Teheran.

(Through the Minister of Foreign Affairs of Persia.)

Excellency:

Pursuant to Requisition No. 205 of the Minister of War of the Imperial Government, I have the honor to transmit to Your Excellency herewith an order of payment on the Imperial Bank of Persia for Roubles Three hundred and sixty thousand, three hundred and ninety-five (360,-395), the same being in settlement of some seven thousand (7,000) rifles and three million five hundred thousand (3,500,000) cartridges purchased in accordance with the authority of the Medjlis heretofore granted.

Enclosed herewith please find receipt for this amount, which I request that Your Excellency sign and return at your convenience.

With the assurances of my highest esteem, I remain, Excellency,

Sincerely yours,

(Signed) W. MORGAN SHUSTER,

Treasurer-general of Persia.

LEGATION IMPERIALE DE RUSSIE

TEHERAN.

August 12, 1911.

W. Morgan Shuster, Esq.,

Treasurer-general of Persia,

Teheran.

(Through the Minister of Foreign Affairs of Persia.)

Dear Mr. Morgan Shuster:

I beg to acknowledge, with many thanks, the receipt of your letter of August 10 and of an order of payment on the Imperial Bank of Persia for Roubles 360,395, the same being in settlement of rifles and cartridges purchased in Russia by the Persians.

Enclosed please find receipt for the above-mentioned amount.

I remain, dear Mr. Morgan Shuster.

Yours sincerely,

(Signed) S. POKLEWSKI-KOZIELL.

TREASURY GENERAL

OF THE

EMPIRE OF PERSIA.

TEHERAN, August 19, 1911.

My dear Mr. Minister:

I have just received word from the Ministry of Foreign Affairs to the effect that there has been a delay in the payment of the Cossack Brigade, and requesting me to take the matter up directly with Your Excellency. This I am very happy to do.

I may say that up to the present time I had supposed that the Banque d'Escompte would promptly inform me when any further payment to the Cossack Brigade fell due, in the same manner as the Banque did on July

18, 1911, in the case of a payment for Tumans 16,304.90 for certain expenses, for which I immediately sent my check.

It appears now that, without my knowledge, there has been some delay in the matter of paying the Brigade. I regret this exceedingly, but I must state that I cannot hold myself responsible for it. I have been at any and all times entirely ready to pay the sums due the Cossack Brigade, and to in every manner maintain the guarantees given by the Persian Government in the Convention of December, 1910.

In order to prevent any further delay, I suggest to Your Excellency that the Banque d'Escompte, or the Colonel of the Brigade, immediately inform me of the amount now due, in order that I may give the Banque an order to transfer this sum on the books of the Banque to the credit of the Colonel or any other officer whom he may designate,— in the same manner as the transfers are made for the annuities of the loans. It seems to me that this procedure is in entire compliance with both the letter and the spirit of the Convention, and effectually assures *for all time* the payment of these expenses *from the Customs revenues of the North.*

Under any circumstances, in order to avoid any further delay in this matter, I suggest to Your Excellency that the sum now in arrear be paid at once in this way, with the understanding (if Your Excellency so desire to have it) that this particular payment *shall not be regarded as a precedent,* but is only adopted at this time to prevent further loss of time.

I may say that I will be lunching in Ghulhak to-morrow (Sunday), and hope to run over and shake hands with Your Excellency during the afternoon,— when we may have a chance to chat for a few moments on this subject.

With kindest regards, I remain, Mr. Minister,

Very sincerely yours,

(Signed)   W. MORGAN SHUSTER.

His Excellency
S. Poklewski-Koziell,
Minister of Russia, Zargundeh.

LEGATION IMPERIALE DE RUSSIE,
TEHERAN.

ZARGUNDEH, August 20, 1911.

Dear Mr. Morgan Shuster:

Many thanks for your letter and your desire to promptly settle the payment of the Cossack Brigade.

I regret, however, to say that I have very precise instructions on this subject from my Government and am unable to change them. My Government has always thought it necessary, in dealing with Oriental coun-

tries, to hold them to the strict execution of the very letter of their en-
gagements, as otherwise the respect of the treaties themselves would be
easily shaken.

The Convention of December, 1910, provides that certain fixed charges
of the Persian Government be paid by our Bank " à l'intervention de
l'Administration des Douanes " and I am told by my Government to see
that this procedure shall not be changed while the Convention remains in
force. I therefore earnestly hope that you will see your way to giving
Mr. Mornard the necessary powers,— once for all, or every year,— to
send to our Bank his " mandats " for all the payments mentioned in the
above-named Convention.

The payment to the Brigade on July 18 last was an extra one, quite
outside of its yearly budget and the scope of the Convention, and for
these reasons it naturally could not be effected without your direct
intervention.

I am most pleased at the prospect of seeing you this afternoon and
hope that our personal intercourse will make in future any misunderstandings between us impossible and will facilitate that cordial coöperation which I sincerely desire.

With kindest regards, I remain, dear Mr. Morgan Shuster,

Yours sincerely,

(Signed)   S. POKLEWSKI-KOZIELL.

LEGATION IMPERIALE DE RUSSIE,
  TEHERAN.

September 2, 1911.

Dear Mr. Morgan Shuster:

I have just received a telegram from my Government which took nine
days to reach Teheran.

Before giving a final answer to the points raised in the conversation
we had here two weeks ago, my Government would like to have detailed
information about the numbers and composition of the future Treasury
Gendarmerie, about its functions, and also where and how it will perform
its duties. Will there be another Gendarmerie for other purposes, or
will the Treasury Gendarmerie be the only force of this sort performing
ordinary gendarmerie duties besides collecting taxes?

There is also another point which I personally should like elucidated.
If, after six months' work at Teheran, Major Stokes is going to be
removed to the South of Persia, is he to retain the command of the
Gendarmerie also in the North? Would it be possible to arrange that,
after six months, one of the Swedish officers should be put in command
of the whole Gendarmerie and that Major ·Stokes should work then
nominally under him and outside the so-called Russian zone and that

both these last conditions should be clearly expressed in Major Stokes' contràct?

Or would it not be simplest to appoint at once the senior Swedish officer to the chief command of the Treasury Gendarmerie while retaining Major Stokes for six months in the town of Teheran to assist him and with the explicit undertaking that Major Stokes should, at the expiry of that time, be sent to the British or neutral zone?

No doubt the assurances about the character and territorial limits of Major Stokes' activities ought to be given to us in writing by the Persian Government. Do you think the latter is prepared to do so?

I should be most grateful to you if you would enable me to give to my Government clear and comprehensive data about the points raised above and I feel sure that our decision will largely depend on the character of your reply.

Believe me, dear Mr. Morgan Shuster,
Yours sincerely,
(Signed) S. POKLEWSKI-KOZIELL.

TREASURY GENERAL, EMPIRE OF PERSIA.

TEHERAN, September 3, 1911.

Dear Mr. Minister:

I am in receipt of your note of the 2d instant, stating that your Government, before giving a final answer to the points discussed in our friendly conversation some two weeks ago, would like to have certain information concerning the proposed Treasury Gendarmerie.

In reply, I take pleasure in laying before you all the data which I possess along these lines.

As to the numbers and composition of the Treasury Gendarmerie, and its functions: As the name implies, the main purpose of the proposed organization is to collect the taxes, both by direct intervention under the orders of the different representatives of the Treasurer-general, and by producing that feeling of public security and order without which, in this county at least, the collection of the internal taxes becomes impossible; the composition will be Persian, with the exception of a few European or American supervising officers: as to the number, I estimate that from 12,000 to 15,000 will eventually be necessary to perform the work properly throughout the Empire, though probably we will be unable to reach that strength for eighteen months or more.

As to whether there will be another gendarmerie, my own view is, very positively, that two gendarmerie forces would be both unnecessary and uneconomic in view of the existence of a regular army. This, however, is only my personal opinion. The mere presence, in most instances, of a well-organized and disciplined force will be sufficient to maintain public order; such attempts at local disturbances as might arise from time to time could well be repressed by a force having general police powers, unless the disorder became serious enough to demand the attention of the regular army.

With regard to your personal question, I would say that I have selected Major Stokes as chief of the entire Treasury Gendarmerie, and have tendered him a three-year contract for that post. I could, therefore, have no intention of putting any other officer over Major Stokes during the period of the satisfactory performance of his duties. The same reasons which led me to select him would of course lead me to retain him, so long as his duties were satisfactorily fulfilled.

The expression of any conditions concerning Major Stokes working outside the so-called Russian zone either in his contract or otherwise is, for reasons which I have already stated and which I am sure your Government fully recognizes, impossible of consideration.

I have no intention of appointing any one but Major Stokes to be my principal assistant in my task of organizing the Treasury Gendarmerie, for a number of valid reasons touching upon his qualifications which are too well known to require repetition here. Major Stokes will, of course, be under my personal orders and he will pursue no other policy in any respect than that which I may direct.

Regarding the next-to-last paragraph of your note, my clear understanding and belief is that the Persian Government is not prepared to give any assurances whatsoever as to the territorial limits of Major Stokes' activities. Certainly I am not, and it is my intention to utilize his services throughout the Empire in such manner as to me, during my period of responsibility for the financial reorganization, might seem best calculated to accomplish my task.

I have sought, dear Mr. Minister, to give you with entire frankness my views on this matter, and I trust that your Government will see by this statement that what is contemplated is but a necessary and proper organization for the accomplishment of the difficult task which I have undertaken. It seems unnecessary to add that, with the reorganization of the finances and internal taxation system of Persia on a modern basis, nothing but benefit can accrue to all legitimate commercial interests, both foreign and domestic, which are connected with the Persian Empire.

With kindest regards, I remain, dear Mr. Minister,

Sincerely yours,
(Signed) W. MORGAN SHUSTER,
Treasurer-general of Persia.

His Excellency
S. Poklewski-Koziell,

TREASURY GENERAL, EMPIRE OF PERSIA.

TEHERAN, September 5, 1911.

Dear Mr. Minister:

It has come to my knowledge that in some manner my note to you of yesterday has been misconstrued by you and that it is regarded as an intentional termination of the discussion of the Stokes affair. If such is the fact, please permit me to say that nothing of course could be further from my wishes. I did not understand your note of the 2d inst. as written in a spirit of negotiation, but that it was, as it appears on its face to be, a categorical request for certain detailed, clear and comprehensive data, which you and your Government desired to have in order to enable you to formulate future action. It was in this light that I endeavored to reply to your note by giving to you a full, frank and unevasive statement of such information on the questions propounded as I possess.

I should sorely regret that you should have found anything in either the tone or the contents of my written reply which would lead you to presume on my part any change in the ardent hope which I have felt ever since our original conversation that your Government might be brought to see the difficulties of this Government and of myself in this particular instance over this affair and thereby be inclined to perform a gracious and friendly act in withdrawing certain objections which up to the present have been maintained against the proposed contract with Major Stokes.

It was my original intention to see you yesterday and endeavor to learn more of the recent view which your Government may be taking of this matter, but I afterwards felt that perhaps you were not prepared to discuss the probable future action of your Government in any more detail than has already been done, until you had conveyed to it the precise and detailed information which your letter alone appeared to call for and which I had hoped my reply conveyed.

I should like very much to see you soon, especially if there has been any misconception on your part of the purport of my note, and if agreeable will endeavor to get up to Zargundeh some time to-morrow afternoon, say about three o'clock. I will ask you to be good enough to let Colonel Beddoes know whether this hour is agreeable to you, and he will find the means to convey the news to me.

With kindest regards, dear Mr. Minister, I remain

Very sincerely yours,

(Signed) W. MORGAN SHUSTER,

Treasurer-general of Persia.

His Excellency
  S. Poklewski-Koziell,
    Minister of Russia, Zargundeh.

TREASURY GENERAL
OF THE
EMPIRE OF PERSIA.

TEHERAN, September 3, 1911.

Dear Mr. Minister:[1]

I am in receipt of your note of the 2d instant, stating that your Government, before giving a final answer to the points discussed in our friendly conversation some two weeks ago, would like to have certain information concerning the proposed Treasury Gendarmerie.

In reply, I take pleasure in laying before you all the data which I possess along these lines.

As to the numbers and composition of the Treasury Gendarmerie, and its functions: As the name implies, the main purpose of the proposed organization is to collect the taxes, both by direct intervention under the orders of the different representatives of the Treasurer-general, and by producing that feeling of public security and order without which, in this country at least, the collection of the internal taxes becomes impossible; the composition will be Persian, with the exception of a few European or American supervising officers; as to the number, I estimate that from 12,000 to 15,000 will eventually be necessary to perform the work properly throughout the Empire, though we will probably be unable to reach that strength for eighteen months or more.

As to whether there will be another gendarmerie, my own view is, very positively, that two gendarmerie forces would be both unnecessary and uneconomic in view of the existence of a regular army. This, however, is only my personal opinion. The mere presence, in most instances, of a well-organized and disciplined force will be sufficient to maintain public order; such attempts at local disturbances as might arise from time to time could well be repressed by a force having general police powers, unless the disorder became serious enough to demand the attention of the regular army.

With regard to your personal questions, I would say that, as I hope to see you at an early date, I will take that opportunity of giving you, in conversation, such information as I may have along these lines.

I have sought, dear Mr. Minister, to give you, with entire frankness, my views on this matter, and I trust that your Government will see by this statement that what is contemplated is but a necessary and proper organization for the accomplishment of the difficult task which I have undertaken. It seems unnecessary to add that, with the reorganization

---

[1] This letter was sent to replace the preceding letter of September 3, which was subsequently withdrawn.

of the finances and internal taxation system of Persia on a modern basis, nothing but benefit can accrue to all legitimate commercial interests, both foreign and domestic, which are connected with the Persian Empire.

With kindest regards, I remain, dear Mr. Minister,

Sincerely yours,

(Signed)   W. MORGAN SHUSTER,

Treasurer-general of Persia.

His Excellency
S. Poklewski-Koziell,
Minister of Russia, Zargundeh.

TREASURY GENERAL
OF THE
EMPIRE OF PERSIA.

TEHERAN, September 13, 1911.

His Excellency
S. Poklewski-Koziell,
Minister of Russia, Teheran.

My dear Mr. Minister:

I take pleasure in informing you that on the 15th ultimo I applied to Colonel H. R. Beddoes, the representative of Messrs. Seligman Bros. of London, for a loan of £4,000,000 sterling. I enclose herewith copy of my letter to him.

I now request the good offices of Your Excellency's Government and Your Excellency's great personal influence to the end that this loan may be successfully and satisfactorily negotiated.

I am, Mr. Minister, with great respect.

Sincerely yours,

(Signed)   W. MORGAN SHUSTER,

Treasurer-general of Persia.

TREASURY GENERAL
OF THE
EMPIRE OF PERSIA.

TEHERAN, September 13, 1911.

Dear Mr. Minister:

May I ask whether you have had any indication from your Government, which could be communicated to me, on the subject of our last conversation concerning Major Stokes. I would not trouble you on this score were it not for the fact that each day's delay is proving a very serious handicap to one of the most necessary features of our work.

With kindest regards, believe me, dear Mr. Minister,

Yours very sincerely,
(Signed)   W. MORGAN SHUSTER,
Treasurer-general of Persia.

His Excellency
S. Poklewski-Koziell,
Minister of Russia, Teheran.

LEGATION IMPERIALE DE RUSSIE,
TEHERAN.

September 16, 1911.

Dear Mr. Morgan Shuster:

I have not heard yet from my Government concerning Major Stokes, and am expecting a reply at any moment. The delay must be due to the absence of the Emperor from St. Petersburg.

I will not lose time in communicating with you, as soon as the telegram reaches me.

With kindest regards,

Yours sincerely,
(Signed)   S. POKLEWSKI-KOZIELL.

LEGATION IMPERIALE DE RUSSIE,
TEHERAN.

October 15, 1911.

Dear Mr. Shuster:[1]

I duly submitted to my Government the proposal you made at our last interview and I have now received their reply. It is to the effect that, as unfortunately it appears to be impossible to restrict Major Stokes' work to the South, my Government are compelled to adhere to their protest against the proposed appointment of the officer in question to organize a fiscal gendarmerie in Persia.

Believe me, dear Mr. Shuster,

Yours sincerely,
(Signed)   S. POKLEWSKI-KOZIELL.

---

[1] This was Russia's final refusal to withdraw her opposition to Major Stokes. Up to this time Mr. Shuster had been in negotiations with the British and Russian Legations to secure, on some terms not incompatible with Persia's recognition of the so-called "spheres of influence," his badly needed services.

Personal.

Dear Mr. Shuster:

Many thanks for your kind letter, which has deeply touched me.

I shall always keep the most pleasant recollection of our personal acquaintance * * *

With best wishes for your journey, I remain, dear Mr. Shuster,

Yours very sincerely,

(Signed) S. POKLEWSKI-KOZIELL.

FORM OF CONTRACT TENDERED MAJOR C. B. STOKES BY THE TREASURER-GENERAL OF PERSIA.

This Agreement, made this twenty-fourth day of July in the year nineteen hundred and eleven, by and between the Imperial Government of Persia, acting through its duly authorized agent, W. Morgan Shuster, Treasurer-general of Persia, and Major C. B. Stokes, a British subject, late of the Indian Army, resident in the City of Teheran, Persia, witnesseth that:

(1) Whereas the Imperial Government of Persia has by a law of the Medjlis voted on the 23d day of Jauza, 1329, authorized the Treasurer-general of Persia to establish a special corps of inspection, and to make contracts, with the approval of the Medjlis, for the financial aides who may form a part of said special corps of inspection, and whereas the Medjlis has by subsequent laws authorized among others, a contract to be made by the Treasurer-General with an European now residing in Persia, for the purpose of serving as financial aide to the Treasurer-general in charge of the organization of the Treasury Gendarmerie, said contract to be made on the same general terms as the contracts already made with certain other financial aides to the Treasurer-general, now therefore it is hereby stipulated and agreed:

(2) The Imperial Government of Persia does hereby appoint, designate and engage the said Major C. B. Stokes to be and serve as financial aide to the Treasurer-general, in special charge of the organization and formation of the Treasury Gendarmerie, for the full term of three years from the date of this contract.

(3) The Imperial Government of Persia hereby agrees to pay to the said Major C. B. Stokes, as full salary and compensation for his services as said financial aide, the sum of Five thousand (5,000.00) Dollars, U. S. Currency, or its equivalent in pounds sterling, per annum, in twelve monthly installments, at the end of each month.

(4) The said Major C. B. Stokes does hereby accept the appointment,

designation and engagement to serve as said financial aide to the Treasurer-general, with the general powers and duties, and at a salary and compensation and under the general terms and conditions hereinbefore and hereinafter set forth, and in consideration of the same does hereby agree faithfully and well to perform his duties during the continuance of this contract.

(5) The said Major C. B. Stokes hereby agrees to obey, in the performance of his duties, the instructions and rules of the Treasurer-general of Persia.

(6) In case the said Major C. B. Stokes shall neglect or fail to perform his duties or to obey the instructions or rules aforesaid, the Imperial Government of Persia, on the recommendation of the Treasurer-general, shall have the right to terminate this agreement on the payment of a sum equivalent to six months' compensation.

(7) In case the said Major C. B. Stokes shall resign of his own accord before the termination of the period prescribed in this contract, he shall be paid only for the period of actual service rendered.

(8) During the existence of this contract, the said Major C. B. Stokes hereby agrees not to interfere with the religious or political affairs of the Persian Empire, except in so far as the proper performance of his lawful duties might be in any manner so construed.

(9) The said Major C. B. Stokes hereby agrees, during the continuance of this agreement, to use his best efforts and • endeavors for the upbuilding of the finances and revenues of the Imperial Government of Persia and, in general, within the sphere of his proper activities, to work for the welfare, happiness, prosperity and progress of the people of Persia and for the honor and prestige of the lawfully constituted government of said Empire.

E.

"ONE BRITISH VIEW OF THE ANGLO-RUSSIAN CONVENTION OF 1907."

SPEECH DELIVERED BY MR. H. F. B. LYNCH, CHAIRMAN OF THE PERSIA COMMITTEE, AT A PUBLIC DINNER GIVEN UNDER THE AUSPICES OF THE COMMITTEE, IN HONOR OF W. MORGAN SHUSTER, AT THE SAVOY HOTEL, LONDON, ON MONDAY, 29TH JANUARY, 1912.

THE CHAIRMAN (Mr. H. F. B. Lynch): Ladies and Gentlemen, I have now to propose to you the toast of "The guest of the evening, Mr. Morgan Shuster." In welcoming Mr. Shuster and in inviting this distinguished company to meet him, the Persia Committee have been pursuing

20

a course strictly in accordance with their past action. From the very first we have supported Mr. Morgan Shuster in the extremely difficult and delicate task which was committed to his charge. When we realized that difficulties were being placed in the way of the execution of that task — I think it was towards the close of last summer's session — we approached the Foreign Secretary and pointed out the nature of those difficulties, and we asked that steps should be taken to have them, as far as possible, removed. On the 7th of November last, at a fully attended meeting held at the House of Commons, we passed unanimously a resolution which was sent in to the Secretary of State. I should like to read you that resolution, because it expresses the point of view which we of the Persia Committee have consistently taken up:— . . . " In view of the great importance to the interests of this country that the finances of Persia should be placed on a sound basis and that Persia may thereby be enabled to proceed with the reforms necessary for the proper administration of that country, including the security of her communications,

" And whereas Mr. Morgan Shuster, as Treasurer-general of Persia, has shown himself a capable and energetic administrator,

" This meeting of Members of Parliament and others invites the serious attention of His Majesty's Government to the difficulties placed by the Russian Government in the way of Mr. Shuster's efforts to reorganize Persian finance, and offers His Majesty's Government their support in any action His Majesty's Government may see fit to take, as signatories of the Anglo-Russian Convention, to support Mr. Shuster."

That was the resolution, and I am sorry to say that it only received a somewhat curt acknowledgment. That was in November. Those, of course, who follow events in Persia know that the despatch of that Resolution was followed pretty promptly by the issue of an ultimatum by the Russian Government to that of Persia, and then by the issue of a second ultimatum, which demanded the dismissal of Mr. Shuster. I still do not know the precise grounds upon which the Russian Government demanded his dismissal. I think a good deal of light ought to be thrown in Parliament upon that interesting point. But what, after all, concerns us most nearly is the attitude which was taken up towards Mr. Morgan Shuster by our own Government. (Hear, hear.) Sir Edward Grey, in the recent debate on Persia in the House of Commons, which took place as recently as the 14th of December last, stated to us pretty fully the nature of that attitude. I should just like to read you his words. He said: " The first demand of the Russian Government is that Mr. Shuster, the Financial Adviser to the Persian Government, should be withdrawn. We have said that we cannot object to that demand, and I will explain to the House why. A short time ago, to take only a most recent incident, I received news by telegram to say that Mr. Shuster had appointed three British officials in Persia as Treasury officials in important places. I quite admit Mr. Shuster's ability and his good intentions, but you cannot have the spirit or the intention of the Anglo-Russian Agreement upset by the action of any individual, however well intentioned. What advice I could give to avoid this I gave at the earliest possible moment; that advice having failed I, of course, have been absolutely powerless to support Mr. Shuster's action. Had I supported him " — I call your attention to these words — " Had I supported him, I should have been supporting him in the appointment of British officials in the Russian sphere of Persia, and I should at any rate have been breaking the spirit of the Anglo-Russian Agreement."

Now, Ladies and Gentlemen, we are not here to deliver an attack upon our Foreign Secretary. Many of us have a warm personal regard for him, and I am sure that anything which I, or any other speaker, may say will be couched in language which at all events we shall have calculated not to have any such effect.

I should like in the first place to dwell upon the satisfactory part of this pronouncement, because it contains a satisfactory part. Our Foreign Secretary tells us, in the name of His Majesty's Government, that he quite admits Mr. Shuster's ability and his good intentions. Therefore, you see there is no question either as to Mr. Shuster's capacity or character. The only question that we have to judge to-night — and which will have to be judged by larger audiences outside these walls — is this: whether or not Mr. Shuster has broken the spirit — there is no question of his having broken the letter — of the Anglo-Russian Agreement.

Now I scarcely know the exact date upon which our Foreign Secretary adopted this view of his, that Mr. Shuster had violated the spirit of the Agreement. Unless I be wrong — in that case he will correct me — Mr. Shuster, when he commenced to reorganize the administration of the Persian Treasury, approached our Foreign Office through our Minister at Teheran, and asked them whether they would have any objection to his appointing Major Stokes to reorganize the Treasury gendarmerie. Major Stokes, of course, is a British subject, and he was to take up his duties in Northern Persia. Now it is a matter of common knowledge that the reply which was handed to Mr. Shuster was to the effect that our Foreign Office saw no objection whatever to the appointment. When, therefore, did the change come over the attitude of our Foreign Secretary and what were the causes which brought it about? When and why did he come to his later conclusion that British nationality is a bar to appointments in the Persian Civil Service in Northern Persia? There again is another question upon which we require light. But if I ask myself: " Did Mr. Shuster violate the spirit of the Anglo-Russian Convention in making these appointments in Northern Persia?" then, as a careful student of that convention and of the declaration of policy issued in connection with it by His Majesty's Government, I answer without hesitation that there is nothing whatever in the spirit of that Agreement which would support a contention of that kind (cheers). We have had, quite a few days ago, a very interesting pronouncement as to the spirit of this Agreement by no less an authority than His Majesty's Ambassador at St. Petersburg, Sir George Buchanan, who in the course of an eloquent speech, delivered on the occasion of the British visit to Russia, spoke as follows: He said "I cherish the hope that the Anglo-Russian entente will take root in the hearts of the two peoples. It is not by diplomatic acts that true ententes are made between nations; it is by feelings of friendship, sympathy and mutual confidence that peoples are attracted towards each other. Let our entente repose on this basis and nothing can shake it." I think we can all subscribe to those words of our Ambassador (hear, hear) and take them as an authoritative and a perfectly just exposition of the spirit which ought to animate the execution of the Anglo-Russian Agreement. So we have to ask ourselves: — when Mr. Shuster appointed these three Englishmen, was he violating the spirit of the Agreement, as defined by His Majesty's Ambassador and as explained by His Majesty's Ministers when defending the Convention before Parliament — a spirit namely of mutual confidence between Great Britain and Russia giving place to the old spirit of rivalry and suspicion?

What did Mr. Shuster actually do? He appointed three Englishmen to subordinate positions in the Persian Treasury Service in three cities of Persia: Tabriz, Isfahan and Shiraz. Now Tabriz is sixty miles from the nearest Russian frontier and is the emporium of the great British trade with the north of Persia. Isfahan is hundreds of miles from any Russian frontier, and it is the terminus of two of the greatest of the British trade routes from the Gulf; Shiraz is within the area of what we may call the Gulf region. How could Mr. Shuster have known, when he was making those appointments of Englishmen in cities of that description, in subordinate posts, that he was violating the spirit of the Anglo-Russian Convention (cheers)? Ladies and Gentlemen, just let us consider the matter a little more closely. The Russian sphere, as drawn in the Anglo-Russian Agreement, is a sphere drawn for commercial purposes. It has nothing whatever to do with appointments to their Civil Service made by the Persian Government. Nothing whatever. Think what it would mean if we were to subscribe to the doctrine that no British subject can be appointed by the Persian Government within the Russian sphere! Why, it would mean that throughout a territory with an area greater than that of France, containing the capital and all the principal cities of Persia — throughout that immense area the fact that a man might happen to be a British subject would constitute an effectual bar to his employment in the Persian Service. (Shame!) Ladies and Gentlemen, suppose that any of you were to go out to Persia and were to desire to take up an appointment in the Persian Civil Service. Suppose they were to tell you: " House full, no applications received," and you were to demur to that, and they were to say: " Well, we are very sorry, we should like to have your services, but there are reasons against it." Then, if you inquired further, they might say to you: " Well, we refer you to the Russian Legation." (Laughter.) And, if you went to the Russian Legation, what would be the reply that you would receive? You would be told, I have no doubt in a very pleasant way, that the reason why you could not be appointed was that the Governments of Great Britain and Russia had signed a Convention; that this Convention was intended to inaugurate an era of reciprocal confidence and trust between those two great Powers, and that for that very reason you, a British subject, would never be allowed to enter the Persian Service anywhere nearer to the Russian frontier than a distance equal to the length and breadth of France (loud laughter) and that you would have to hand over your prospects of employment to the Russian, to the German, to the Italian, to the Belgian, to the Swede — they all would be welcome, but in the new halcyon era of Anglo-Russian confidence every Englishman would be shut out. (Cheers and laughter.)

Now I want to carry your minds from that point to another. I want to ask you to consider what were the circumstances which brought Mr. Shuster to Persia. I was very closely connected with those circumstances, and, therefore, you may excuse me if I tell you very briefly what exactly it was that brought Mr. Shuster there. At the commencement of the year 1909 the Persian people, seeing that their monarchy, a dynasty of Turcoman rulers, was falling upon evil days, seeing that their country was being sold, as they put it, to foreigners, owing to the large amount of foreign loans that were being raised — the Persian people determined to put an end to this state of things. They had before them the example of the West, and their aim was to infuse new life into their political institutions. They organized two expeditions, one from the North, the other from the South; and in July, 1909, was consummated in Persia an almost bloodless revolution, the result of which was that the reigning monarch, Mohammed Ali, was forced to take refuge in the Russian Legation, and a Constitutional régime was established — or rather, I ought to say, restored, because it had had a very short life before.

But the new Government found itself in this predicament. Here was a people which had existed for centuries under an absolute despotism — a despotism which had crushed out all the elements of vitality in the nation, which had prevented all young Persians from traveling to Europe, which, whenever a man showed signs of integrity, capacity or independence, put him on the shelf, or proscribed him. Here was a country which had long lain under the heel of the despot — and, where the heel of the despot has once trodden, the seeds of national life are slow to sprout and still more slow to bear fruit. It was out of ground of that kind that the Persian Government had to call forth a new race of administrators and law-givers. They recognized that they could not do that at once, and they said to themselves, and I think rightly: Let us go to the West, let us take from the West our first lessons in civil order and administration. Let us find there men to recognize our great administrative departments, and to train up a new generation of Persian Officials. Ladies and Gentlemen, in pursuing that course, Persia was merely copying the example of Japan; and is there any one here who would be inclined to throw a stone at the Japanese people because they called into their councils foreign administrators — administrators from the West — to inculcate some of the lessons of Western civilization?

Well, their first necessity was the reform of their financial system. They turned for help in this department, in the first instance, I think, to France. M. Pichon was then Foreign Minister. M. Pichon was quite willing to send them a Financial Mission; but obstacles were raised by Russian diplomacy in Paris, and these overtures came to nothing. Italy was also approached, with a view to despatching a mission to reorganize the Gendarmerie. Here, again, the Persian overtures were brought to nothing. Persian statesmen then bethought themselves that, perhaps, the same impediments might not be operative in the United States of America. They applied to the President of a Free Republic, and he sent them Mr. Morgan Shuster (cheers). That accounts for Mr. Shuster's presence in Persia.

Let me say one word as to the nature of his work. It has been said that Mr. Shuster endeavored to upset the Anglo-Russian Agreement. Now I think that is the exact contrary of the fact. I had the bad fortune to be kept all last summer in London — you know it was a very hot summer, and I had to be in attendance all August and September in London, where I was in constant communication by telegraph with Mr. Shuster in connection with railway operations in Persia. All through those negotiations it was Mr. Shuster's aim to reconcile the railway policy of the Persian Government with the provisions of the Anglo-Russian Agreement. He went further, and he was prepared to use his great influence over the Medjlis in order to induce them to accept — as regards British and Russian participation in railway construction — those commercial spheres which were delimited by the Convention. Mr. Shuster proved himself an excellent friend to the Convention, in so far as its objects were public and avowed.

Then what was the real reason for his dismissal? It can be expressed in a sentence — not one of my own coining, but extracted from a letter which 1 received some time ago from a countryman, resident in Persia, who is not a sympathizer with the Nationalist or Democratic Party. It was penned immediately after Mr. Shuster's dismissal, and it runs: — " Mr. Shuster's mission was doomed at its inception, seeing that a prosperous Persia would have brought about a weakened Russian control."

In conclusion, Ladies and Gentlemen, what are our objects in giving this dinner? First of all, what are not our objects? I need scarcely tell you that we of the Persia Committee are not in any way animated by feelings of hostility towards the Russian people. Most of us, I imagine, are great admirers of the Russian people. If we could summon to this table the great spirits of Russian thought and of Russian literature — the Tolstoys, the Tourgénieffs and the rest — why, they would all be on our side! (Cheers.) At this very moment the Liberal Press of Russia are writing articles on Persian affairs, which, if you were to translate them, might almost have been taken from the columns of the *Daily News* or the *Manchester Guardian*. The representatives of Labor in the Russian Duma — speaking for the coming force in politics not only in Russia, but all over the world — have gone so far as to refuse to participate in the reception of the British visitors, on the ground that Great Britain is joining with their own Government in stamping out an ancient people like the Persians.

It is sometimes said that we of the Persia Committee are bent on destroying the Anglo-Russian Agreement. That is a deliberate and it is a wicked falsehood. We are not out for the destruction of the Agreement; but we are out for its loyal fulfilment. (Cheers.) Hostility to Russia, destruction of the Agreement — those are not our objects: How, then, can they be defined? First, we have come here to receive at first hand from Mr. Morgan Shuster an account from the inside, culled from his own experience and insight, of the situation in Persia. He will be able to state how far in his opinion the Persian people are capable of effecting their own regeneration, provided that they be given elbow-room and breathing-space by their two powerful neighbors. Our second object is, perhaps, a more personal one. It is to give expression to our appreciation of the high purpose which distinguished Mr. Shuster's work in Persia, and to our sympathy with him in the untoward circumstances which brought that work to a premature close. We are also hoping, by this demonstration of our appreciation and of our sympathy with Mr. Shuster, to dispel any doubts which may be felt by our kinsmen across the Atlantic as to the sentiments of the British nation towards this distinguished citizen of the United States. It is with these objects in mind that I ask you to raise your glasses and to drink to the health of Mr. Morgan Shuster. (Cheers.)

F.

Two Articles Republished from *The Nation*.

I. "THE LOST INDEPENDENCE OF PERSIA."

Two weeks ago there seemed to be for one brief moment a ray of hope in the Persian situation. Persia lay, indeed, under the menace of a Russian invasion. But there came from Lord Curzon a plea for a change in British policy, as weighty as it was unexpected. The Persians threw themselves upon our mercy, and, whether from calculation or from sympathy, the good offices of our diplomacy were placed at their disposal. If our Foreign Office had been capable of firmness in its dealings with a slippery and unscrupulous partner, and if there had existed in the minds of Russian statesmen the smallest intention of obliging a friendly and singularly complacent associate, the invasion must at once have been checked, and Persia, at the cost of some humiliation, must at least have kept her territory intact. We fear that these hopes are ended. The Russians have proved themselves implacable and disobliging. They have turned a deaf ear alike to the apologies of Persia and the mediation of Great Britain. Their armies continue to advance on Teheran, and their diplomacy at length avows a claim which destroys forever the pretense that Persia is a sovereign state. This would not in itself be decisive. But, on Monday, Sir Edward Grey defined his own attitude. In a speech rather fuller and rather franker than any he has yet delivered, there is not a sentence which can be interpreted even as a faint depreciation of Russian action, not a word to limit her drastic intervention, not a hint of resentment at the rejection by Russia of the counsels of moderation which apparently he gave, not a phrase which could assist the Persians in saving something from the wreck of their national fortunes. The case is even worse than this. Sir Edward Grey has not merely gone out of his way to make a wholly gratuitous defense of the action which Russia is now taking; he has explicitly sanctioned and adopted the stealthy extension of the Anglo-Russian compact which underlies the whole of the Russian aggression. So far as the wording of that treaty goes, it provides for the division of Persia into economic spheres, within which each power binds itself not to compete with the other for concessions. We have never thought that arrangement compatible with the integrity and independence of Persia, and we have always argued that it would be stretched, and must be stretched, into a political partition. At length, the avowal has been made, and made apparently without any consciousness that the terms of the compact have been left behind. The word "political" has been subtly introduced by Sir Edward Grey to describe the character of the particular interests which each power reserves to itself in its own sphere. When once that word is used, the independence of Persia is gone, and its partition virtually accomplished.

It may be advisable to set forth very briefly the grounds of the quarrel between Mr. Shuster and the Russian Government, which is the pretext for this intervention. The quarrel dates almost from his arrival in the country, and it has passed through many phases. It began with an attempt by Russia to veto his demand that, as Financial Controller, the customs payments should pass through his hands. The next phase was a steady, detailed effort to prevent him from increasing Persian revenues from direct taxation, by shielding of Russian protégés, the Persian grandees who had hitherto evaded their taxes. Then came the Russian veto on the appointment of Englishmen versed in the Persian language, and trusted by the Persian people, to posts under the Treasury in Northern Persia. We are not sure that Mr. Shuster was altogether wise to press these appointments in the absence of any backing either from Mr. Taft or from Sir Edward Grey. But, as a matter of right, he did well. Here was a test case as to the meaning of the agreement. If Persia is still an independent state, she may appoint whom she pleases to supervise the collection of her taxes. If Britain and Russia are bound only to respect each other's monopoly in economic concessions in their respective spheres, then clearly the nationality of a tax collector is not a matter affected by their bargain. But if it is political predominance which they claim north and south of two arbitrary lines, then clearly the sending of an English official into the Russian sphere may be regarded, as both parties to the Treaty do regard it, as a breach of its spirit, if not of its letter.

This episode served finally to define the political character of the partition. Next came the Shuau's-Saltana incident, over which Sir Edward Grey passed lightly. Not even the *Times* has attempted a defense of Russian action here. If a Persian Government may not send Persian gendarmes to serve a warrant on a Persian subject who is its debtor, it has ceased to be the sovereign of its own territory. This incident led to the Russian invasion, but the pretext for the continuance of the Russian march after the Persian Government, under British advice, had tendered an apology, and for the presentation of new Russian demands, whose acceptance Sir Edward Grey will, we suppose, again counsel, is that Mr. Shuster meanwhile had circulated a translation of the *Times* letter, in which he defended himself against Russian criticisms, and made with deadly effect some countercharges against Russian agents for the assistance they had given to the ex-Shah. It seems to be doubtful whether Mr. Shuster was personally responsible for circulating this document. But if a little country may be invaded by a great power because a foreign official in its service has ventured to write a reasoned and temperate letter to the *Times*, in reply to editorial attacks of semi-official British and Russian newspapers, we must revise all our conceptions of international intercourse. If a German official had written to the *Times* to deny McKenna's charges of accelerated shipbuilding, should we have been entitled to treat his letter as a *casus belli?* It is a case of the wolf and the lamb, so flagrant and so cynical, that one is hardly tempted to analyze it further.

The plain fact is that Russia from the first has determined to thwart Mr. Shuster, because he displayed an American energy and fearlessness, which would soon have made Persia solvent and well governed. He was not the man to succumb without a struggle, and in the end the Russian sword has got the better of Mr. Shuster's pen. The episode ends in the formal presentation at a bayonet's point of a Russian demand, which Sir Edward Grey justified in his speech on Tuesday, for the recognition of a Russian right to put her veto on the employment of foreigners in Persia. With that claim, the powers have formally torn up their guarantees of Persian independence. The usual loan to pay the usual indemnity for the Russian invasion will be the next step, and, with the installation of a foreign official supervisor subservient to Russia, her dictatorship in Teheran will be finally established. The next question will, of course, be how far we are prepared to allow Southern Persia to be governed from Teheran after that city has become a center of Russian policy. In the end, the logic of partition must be followed, and some separate political organization provided for the South. A British sphere can hardly be administered from a city wholly dominated by Russian Cossacks, Russian diplomatists, Russian financiers, and foreign inspectors subject to a Russian veto. Our own procedure has been less drastic, less brutal, less hasty than that of our partner. But, because we have acquiesced in what she has done, we shall sooner or later be forced to imitate it. The lapse of a few years will almost inevitably see us as openly in occupation of the South as Russia is of the North, and the nightmare which has haunted generations of Anglo-Indian soldiers will at length have been realized with our own consent. Russian and British armies will confront each other across a vague land frontier and we shall have become in the military sense a Continental Power, with Russia and Turkey and their vast conscript armies for our uneasy neighbors.

Had it been possible to argue this Persian question on its merits, the history of recent years would have followed a totally different course. With or without an agreement, we should have held Russia to a policy of abstention in Persian affairs. We have, from first to last, violated our natural instincts of chivalry, our liberal principles of respect for nationality, and every sane calculation based on our Eastern interests.

Disastrous and foolish though we believe this policy to be, we do not call it unintelligible. It is a consequence, and one of the worst consequences, of Sir Edward Grey's European policy. One simple and elementary principle has governed it from the first — his dread lest this or the other power might be drawn into what he has called the " orbit " of German diplomacy. Year in, year out, we have been paying, chiefly in other people's goods, for the satisfaction of keeping certain Powers from coming to any intimate understanding with Germany. The French side of the account is represented by the Moroccan transaction and its sequels. To Russia we have given a free hand over the greater part of Persia. It was a large price to pay for anything. But what has been gained, even on the low plane of such diplomatic huckstering? Russia was the more or less reliable ally of France when the chapter opened. To-day no one even suggests that she would have intervened with arms, had war resulted from the Agadir incident. For that we are far from blaming her. But the fact is that we have failed to keep her even where she originally was within the Franco-British " orbit." She came to terms with Germany at Potsdam, and neither a free hand in Persia nor even the rain of British gold which falls upon all her investments and enterprises avails to buy her loyalty. The reason is simple. We cannot assist her in the military difficulties to which our policy may at any moment expose her. Our failure to make good our violent words in the Bosnian crisis settled that forever. We are playing a continental rôle without continental resources, and from great ambition based on unsuitable means there must issue in the end either the humiliation of a surrender or the disaster of a defeat. When we are driven to pay so high a price as Persia to secure the bare neutrality of Russia, it is evident that our star is not in the ascendant.— From *The Nation* (London), December 2, 1911.

II. " THE PERSIAN SUPPLIANT."

In the days when the predatory instincts of mankind were qualified by a tradition of chivalry, the suppliant enjoyed certain rights which it was the pride of the strong to respect. A wretch who embraced the knees of a Homeric chieftain became from that moment a *protégé*, whose life and cause he was bound by honor to defend. A fugitive who flings himself on the mercy of an Albanian clan may count upon it to espouse his interests as though they were its own. These are the pretty manners of savages; modern diplomacy has evolved its own code of honor and decency. Two weeks ago Persia, menaced by a Russian invasion, performed the conventional rites, made herself a suppliant at our doors, and embraced the stony knees of Downing Street. We accepted the flattering but responsible position. We gave her sage, though by no means heroic, advice. We recommended her to conform to Russian demands, which even our diplomatists cannot have thought equitable, and we bade her go in sackcloth and ashes to apologize for the offense of being so obviously in the right. The advice was followed, and the Persians in their simplicity supposed that our influence would then be used to stay the Russian advance. If pity did not move us, one might have supposed that pride would have prompted us to aid them. They had followed our unpalatable counsels, they had made what we considered an adequate reparation to Russia. It seemed to follow that our prestige, if not our honor, required us to protect them from further exactions and aggressions. The event has taught them that one should not rashly assume that a modern Foreign Secretary will act with the spirit of a Homeric chief or an Albanian brigand. We have done nothing to protect them, but, on the other hand, we cannot be accused of mere inaction or indifference. We have, it appears, approved of the further exactions of our Russian partner. He has presented three demands — the dismissal of Mr. Shuster, the acceptance by Persia of an Anglo-Russian veto on all denominations of foreign experts, and the payment of an indemnity to compensate Russia for her trouble in pressing these demands by an armed invasion. Of these claims, the first two have been presented with our acquiescence, and apparently with our approval, and the second of them establishes for us a privilege which we shall share with Russia. Our magnanimity is triumphantly vindicated by the reserves which we have expressed against the Russian demand for money. We have suffered the suppliant to be torn from our knees; we have joined in violating his rights. We save our honor by averting our eyes while his pockets are rifled at the conclusion of the process.

Public opinion has not authorized the Government which acts in its name to follow a policy at once so mean and weak as this. Sir Edward Grey cannot be wholly indifferent to the wishes of his countrymen, and his policy may yet be reversed. It is worth while to show that the instinctive disgust which every normally constituted Englishman feels at this climax of a disastrous course is based on reasonable grounds. It is hardly necessary to how that the Anglo-Russian demands involve a violation of Persian sovereignty. To require the dismissal of Mr. Shuster because he dared to defend himself in the *Times* against the scurrilous personal attacks of the Russian press, is an act which any self-respecting nation would treat as an attempt at coercion and interference to which in the last resort war would be the only possible reply. But this is not the most fundamental of the three demands. A nation may be coerced by invasion or the threat of invasion into an isolated compliance with the will of the stronger power, and yet retain its independence, subject only to the risk of a repetition of the aggression. But the second demand renders the interference normal and continuous. Persia is so unluckily situated that she must employ foreigners to reorganize her armed forces and her finances. She cannot hope in any other way to achieve rapid and effective reform, and on no other terms could she secure the loans which she requires in foreign money markets. Mr. Shuster's integrity and strength of will was an asset which entirely satisfied the bankers. So long as Persia was allowed to go to neutral and disinterested powers for such assistance, her independence remained intact. The new condition, imposed as much by Sir Edward Grey as by Russia, will henceforth enable them to force upon her foreign experts who will be their agents. It matters little whether they confine their choice to men of British and Russian birth; their object manifestly is to secure nominees who will be the tools of their policy. They will stand behind these men, and Persia must unavoidably be bound to do their bidding. We rule in Egypt by no other means. Our agents give " advice " — they hold in the civil departments no executive authority — but it is advice which the Egyptian Government is expected to accept. At the least, this condition is a gross infringement of Persian sovereignty; it will probably amount in practice to a dual control not less drastic than our single control in Egypt.

So far have we traveled since 1907. We cannot refrain from citing the despatch in which our Minister explained to the apprehensive Persian Government the meaning of the Anglo-Russian Convention. The object of the despatch was to assure the Persians that the Convention would lead neither to intervention nor partition. Sir Edward Grey and Mons. Isvolvsky, it declared, were in " perfect accord," that " neither of the two Powers will interfere in Persian affairs, unless some injury is inflicted on the property or persons of their subjects." No principle could be plainer than this, yet from first to last no suggestion has been made that this occasion for intervention has arisen. We need not consider whether Mr. Shuster was well advised in choosing British subordinates, or in attempting to levy taxes on Persian grandees, or in writing to the *Times*. Nothing which he has done has touched the person or property of a Russian subject. Nor can it be urged that we are not our brother's keeper. We have, in fact, approved the Russian intervention. But, if we had merely tolerated it, we should still have violated our own interpretation of the obligations which we assumed in the Convention. The despatch concluded by assuring Persia that the two Powers desired to " ensure her independence forever," and it went on:

> " Not only do they not seek a pretext for intervention, but their aim in these friendly negotiations is not to permit one

another to intervene in Persia on the pretext of safeguarding their own interests."

If this sentence meant anything at all, it was intended to suggest to the Persians that the Anglo-Russian partnership was actually a league for the protection of Persia, in which each partner would check the other if he were tempted unduly to intervene. We are breaking our word to-day, and breaking it with a wanton completeness. Russia intervenes against her own pledge, and not only do we permit her to do so; we actually endorse their action. We promised that Persia should be "forever delivered from the fear of foreign intervention," and that she should "enjoy complete freedom to manage her affairs in her own way." Four years later, we insist that we shall nominate the foreigners who are to manage those affairs in our way. The ascendancy which Sir Edward Grey has retained over public opinion in this country during his anxious and ill-starred years of office rested, we believe, rather on his character than on his talents. No one has said of him that he was subtle, or adroit, or expert, or possessed of encyclopedic knowledge. But on his stability, his caution, and above all upon his honor, the nation builded. The final betrayal of Persia would not be the expression of such a character.

The act is not yet completed, and we refuse to recognize that it is inevitable. The brief and embarrassed replies of the Foreign Office to questions reveal that it is ill at ease, and Lord Morley's reply to Lord Curzon suggests at least a change of tone, which is even echoed in the *Times*. Let us hope that it is groping to find a way of escape. Some of the consequences, if the act should be consummated, are generally understood. It means, in moral and intellectual damage, perhaps the worst blow which our prestige could suffer in the East. For no one thinks that we have been wilfully base. We appear as the weak partner who dares not check a powerful and unscrupulous associate. It means in fresh commitments a burden at which the advocates of conscription must secretly rejoice, for it draws the real boundary of India across the sandy wastes of Central Persia, with Russian Cossacks confronting our Indian Cavalry upon a vague and indefensible frontier. It contains the possibilities of acute disputes with Russia, to which our present pusillanimity make a sorry preface. One-third of Persia is neutral territory, and within it is the greater part of the Gulf coast-line. When Russia dominates Teheran, who is to control this no-man's land? But of all the consequences latent in this situation, perhaps the gravest is the likelihood that Germany will demand the usual compensation. Russia has bought a free hand for herself at Potsdam. But we have not yet paid the usual toll. This remote Asiatic question may become, at any moment, a European problem, and if that should happen, we may find that Turkey, the neighbor of Persia and Egypt, will be deeply interested in the resulting " conversations." The Persians, indeed, are impotent to resent our share in strangling their national existence at its birth, and it will not be from motives of chivalry that another Power will embarrass us. But empires are commonly expected to submit to blackmail for an outrage on nationality. It is into some such embroilment as this that our complaisance to Russia may drag us. From this train of disasters Sir Edward Grey can yet escape. He can enter the most emphatic protest against the Russian ultimatum. He can demand the withdrawal from Persian soil by a fixed date, not merely of the new forces, but also of the garrisons permanently settled at Tabriz and other centers. He can declare that the invasion is a breach of the whole spirit of the convention. The mere intimation by private diplomatic channels of an intention to take this course would probably suffice. But, if it did not, it is time to ask for some return from France for the gift we made to her of a North African Empire. Russia could not survive a coldness which would close to her at once the Paris Bourse and the London money market. The means of dealing with this anxious situation are at Sir Edward Grey's disposal, if only he will bring himself to be half as rough with a disloyal partner as he was with an open, honest rival. A leading article in the *Times*, backed by another in the *Temps*, would probably avail to check the pace of the Russian advance. We can use such expedients to enslave the Moors. Let us use them to free the Persians.— From *The Nation* (London), December 9, 1911.

INDEX

415

THE END